The Inner Journey
Myth, Psyche, and Spirit

Series Editor: Ravi Ravindra
Associate Series Editor: Priscilla Murray

Titles in *The Inner Journey* series:
Views from the Buddhist Tradition
Views from the Christian Tradition
Views from the Gurdjieff Work
Views from the Hindu Tradition
Views from the Islamic Tradition
Views from the Jewish Tradition
Myth, Psyche, and Spirit
Views from Native Traditions

The Inner Journey
Myth, Psyche, and Spirit

Edited by Martha Heyneman

PARABOLA Anthology Series

MORNING LIGHT
PRESS

MORNING
○ IGHT
P R E S S

Published by Morning Light Press 2008

Editor: Martha Heyneman
Series Editor: Ravi Ravindra
Associate Series Editor: Priscilla Murray

Cover Image: Redon, Odilon (1840-1916)
Image Copyright © The Metropolitan Museum of Art/ Art Resource, NY.

Morning Light Press
323 North First, Suite 203
Sandpoint, ID 83864
morninglightpress.com

Printed on acid-free paper in Canada.

Philosophy
SAN: 255-3252

Library of Congress Cataloging-in-Publication Data

Myth, Psyche, and Spirit / edited by Martha Heyneman.
p. cm. -- (The Inner Journey)
Includes bibliographical references and index.
ISBN 1-59675-023-5 (978-1-59675-023-4 : alk. paper)
1. Myth. 2. Mythology. I. Heyneman, Martha, 1927-
BL312.M983 2008
201'.3--dc22
        2008006222

*To the path makers
and the pilgrims on the path*

General Introduction to
The Inner Journey: A Parabola Anthology Series

When *Parabola: Myth, Tradition, and the Search for Meaning* was launched in 1976, the founder, D. M. Dooling, wrote in her first editorial:

> *Parabola* has a conviction: that human existence is significant, that life essentially makes sense in spite of our confusions, that man is not here on earth by accident but for a purpose, and that whatever that purpose may be it demands from him the discovery of his own meaning, his own totality and identity. A human being is born to set out on this quest. … Every true teaching, every genuine tradition, has sought to train its disciples to act this part, to become in fact followers of the great quest for one's self.

For over thirty years, *Parabola* has honored the great wisdom traditions of every culture, turning to their past and present masters and practitioners for guidance in this quest. Recognizing that the aim of each tradition is the transformation of human life through practice supported by knowledge and understanding, *Parabola* on behalf of its readers has turned again and again to Buddhist and Christian monks, Sufi and Jewish teachers, Hindu scholars, and Native American and other indigenous peoples, evoking from each of them illumination and insight.

Over the years *Parabola*, in each of its issues, devoted to a central theme of the human condition as it is and as it might be, has gathered remarkable material. "The Call," "Awakening," "Food," "Initiation," "Dreams and Seeing," "Liberation," "The Mask," "Attention": in these and in scores of other issues, a facet of the essential search is explored, always with the aim of casting light on the way.

The purpose of the *Parabola Anthology Series* is to gather the material published in *Parabola* during its first thirty years in order to focus this light and to reflect the inner dimensions of each of these traditions. While every religious tradition has both external and inner aspects, the aim of each is the transformation of the whole being. The insights and understandings that ring true and carry the vibration of an inner meaning can provide guidance and support for our quest, but a mere mechanical repetition of forms which were once charged with great energy can take us away from the heart of the teaching. Every tradition must change and evolve; it has to be reinterpreted and reunderstood by successive generations in order to maintain its relevance and application.

Search carries a connotation of journey; we set out with the hope for new insight and experience. The aim of the spiritual or inner journey is transformation, to become more responsible and more compassionate as understanding and being grow. This demands an active undertaking, and insights from those who have traveled the path can provide a call, bring inspiration, and serve as a reminder of the need to search.

For this series, selections have been made from the material published in *Parabola* relating to each of the major traditions and teachings. Subtle truths are expressed in myths, poetry, stories, parables, and above all in the lives, actions, and expressions of those people who have been immersed in the teaching, have wrestled with it and have been informed and transformed by it. Some of these insights have been elicited through interviews with current practitioners of various teachings. Each of the great traditions is very large, and within each tradition there are distinct schools of thought, as well as many practices, rituals, and ceremonies. None of the volumes in the present series claims to be exhaustive of the whole tradition or to give a complete account of it.

In addition to the material that has been selected from the library of *Parabola* issues, the editor of each volume in the series provides an introduction to the teaching, a reminder of the heart of the tradition in the section, "The Call of the Tradition," as well as a list of books suggested for further study and reflection. It is the hope of the publishers and editors that this new series will surprise, challenge, and support those new to *Parabola* as well as its many readers.

—*Ravi Ravindra*

CONTENTS

THE CALL OF MYTH

*The signs and symbols of the Quest of Life which have so often survived
in oral tradition, long after they have been rationalized or romanticized
by literary artists, are our best clue to what must have been the primordial
form of the one spiritual language of which, as Alfred Jeremias says ... "the
dialects are recognizable in the divers existing cultures."[1]*

—Ananda K. Coomaraswamy

*Behind the myth are concealed the greatest realities,
the original phenomena of the spiritual life. ...
Christianity is entirely mythological, as indeed all religion is.[2]*

—Ananda K. Coomaraswamy

*It is from Unknowing that all the myths, and, one may say, all religions
issue forth and reveal themselves. Not invented but, as it were, summoned.[3]*

—P. L. Travers

Myths and fairy tales are not moral treatises, but supports of contemplation.[4]

—Ananda K. Coomaraswamy

*The ancient mythical perception of a rhythm in human history corresponding
to successive World Ages issued from a concern for future generations rather
than a desire to dazzle the ignorant with feats of mechanistic astrology. Such
myths exist to alert us to "future-presents," those rare, millennial times when
humankind is called upon to undertake a particular kind of creative action—
to fashion a new world from the remains of one that is dying. ... Myth is the
ark which carries this perception, the knowledge of what it takes to remain
human, set loose upon the vast sea of time.[5]*

—William Sullivan

Not only were the Navajos careful to tell the stories only in winter, but they believed the stories must be told, else their children would grow up in a meaningless world.[6]

—Barre Toelken

The mystical side of all the great religious traditions teaches that both the universe and the psyche of man are measured against the same cosmic model. The universe and the psyche are the same and only differ in scale. From this, it follows that spiritual order within oneself corresponds to the harmony of the universe. This means that the maintenance of inner order is man's necessary duty because such work helps maintain order in the universe.[7]

—Richard Temple

As our psycho-physical organism is a microcosmic replica of the universe, Meru is represented by the spinal cord in our nervous system; and just as the various centers (chakra, in Sanskrit) of consciousness are supported by and connected with the spinal cord (meru-danda), from which they branch out like many-petalled lotus-blossoms, in the same way Mount Meru forms the axis of the various planes of supramundane worlds.[8]

—Lama Anagarika Govinda

We cannot hope to find wholeness by repressing the shadow sides of ourselves, or by the most heroic efforts of the ego to climb up, to achieve goodness. … We do not see the mountain again until, having passed through the fog and murk of the darkness of Hell. Dante, climbing on the body of Satan himself, emerges with Virgil into another kind of darkness and approaches the threshold of the great mountain under the stars.[9]

—Helen M. Luke

Myths are not stories of remote happenings in the past; they are dramas that are living themselves out repeatedly in our own personal lives and in what we see around us here and now.[10]

—Edward F. Edinger

When Francis Harwood, anthropologist, asked a Sioux elder why people tell stories, he answered, "In order to become human beings." She asked, "Aren't we human beings already?" He smiled. "Not everyone makes it."[11]

—Laura Simms

When spiritual practice is grounded in the low, earthy religion of the soul's ordinariness, then it can soar as high as it wants without loss of humanity. The great cathedrals and temples of the world teach this reconciliation of soul and spirit with their towering steeples, their stained-glass windows and sculptured friezes teeming with stories and images, their community-gathering naves and welcoming portals, and their mysterious, death-inspired, secret-laden crypts. We could learn from these holy buildings how to make a many-tiered life that gives full honor to body, soul, and spirit.[12]

—Thomas Moore

The Inner Journey: Introduction

And the earth was without form, and void; and darkness was upon the face of the deep. And the Spirit of God moved upon the face of the waters ...

This is the way the inner journey begins, as well as the world. The psyche is in darkness, tossed by every wind that blows, and more than half under water. The Spirit is moving, but there is no stillness in her to receive it. Pulled in all directions, from within and without, she cannot feel it. There is only darkness and noise.

And a voice calling.

She is like a woman in the dark marketplace, who goes with every man who strokes her hair, but he is never the One.

Before sunrise, she is still sleeping. In a dream, perhaps, she hears the voice. Slowly the sky turns from black to grey. On earth there is still no color. The birds are silent.

One by one they awaken and call, until they become a throbbing chorus, a choir of angels announcing the Advent. Hope arises like steam from the grass. Color returns to the garden: green grass, flowers, yellow and red and the color of blood. Warmth penetrates the chill.

Here comes the Sun.

I am lost in the wilderness of myth—numberless stories tangled together like thick underbrush, impenetrable. I have a fly's eyes: something very simple is reflected in a thousand mirrors.

I go with every book that comes out. Surely this interpreter will have the answer, will show me the way through the wilderness of myth. Someone moves toward me out of the crowd and, unnoticed by me, throws all the books in the swimming pool.

Be still and wait. Listen.

Heaven and earth. Spirit and psyche. Prince and sleeping Princess. Active and passive aspects of the psyche, masculine and feminine values. The same relationship on many levels.

And from beyond the clashing rocks of the opposites, in the instant between two jarring collisions, this call.

Begin again. Listen to the body—the inner sensation of these postures and movements—not to the gabbling head.

The body standing erect, feet on the floor, in the field of gravity, stronger pull below, sensation of heaviness. Higher up, less dense, sensation of the upward pull of something else. Echo, from one of the drowned books, of something Sri Anirvan said:

> *All spiritual experiences are sensations in the body. They are simply a graded series of sensations, beginning with the solidity of a clod of earth and passing gradually, in full consciousness, through liquidness and the emanation of heat to that of a total vibration before reaching the Void. The road to be traveled is long.*[1]

Muscles arrange themselves to keep the body upright.

The sense of a central axis: I. Natural orientation in space: symmetry of left and right, asymmetry of front and back, asymmetry again of above and below—six directions, three axes, intersecting at the heart, the zero point, the center.

The sense of the breath, moving between above and below, an axis of air, in ancient languages a synonym for spirit: inspiration, aspiration, expiration. Breathing in, breathing out.

We begin to move, *Go—not knowing where; bring—not knowing what; the path is long, the way unknown; the hero knows not how to arrive there by himself alone; he has to seek the guidance and help of Higher Forces.*

Now we can find our way.

Chapter One offers a selection of examples of different approaches to myth by P. L. Travers, an author of children's books and lifelong lover of myths and fairy tales; Mircea Eliade, a world-renowned scholar of the history of religions; Laura Simms, a master storyteller; Edward Edinger, a Jungian psychiatrist; and, lastly, the author who can be of most help to us in our exploration of myths and fairy tales as guides on the inner journey, because he was himself a pilgrim on this path: Ananda K. Coomaraswamy. Having been born of an English mother and Ceylonese father, Coomaraswamy united East and West in his very flesh, and by virtue of his sensitive intelligence and command of the languages and mythologies of cultures from all over the world, was able to present such a bewildering number of examples of the universal occurrence of the same motif that the mosaic our flies' eyes see resolves itself into a single image.

When it comes to myth, P. L. Travers (another pilgrim) said: "Thinking is linking."[2] This is not the same as automatic association, but amounts to discernment of the same inner form hidden in a bewildering array of different national costumes. Coomaraswamy seemed to see all the links at once. In "The Crack between Two Worlds," the excerpt included in Chapter One from his essay "Symplegades,"[3] he begins with a quotation from Walt Whitman and moves through occurrences of the motif in American Indian myth, the *Rig Veda*, Hermes Trismegistus, Boehme, Rumi, the Upanishads, Greek myth, the Old and New Testaments, and *Tales and Traditions of the Eskimo*—all this in three *Parabola* pages and thirteen footnotes. In the original essay the footnotes often occupy more than half of any given page, and the most striking examples and quotations are frequently buried in those footnotes. In their abundance, the "links" he has at his fingertips overflow the main body of the text.

This abundance of links creates an excitement of growing conviction that some unified understanding of the universe and the place and purpose of human beings within it once embraced the whole earth. Most exciting are those moments when some outer event or inner experience begins to evoke the dawning recognition of the action of one of those universal configurations upon one's own life and inner journey. Something in the morning paper awakens the question, "What does this remind me of?" and sets off the irresistible pursuit of this clue until the event becomes transparent in its structure—its "mythematical formula"—recognized in an underlying myth. When Patty Hearst was abducted into the underworld by the Symbionese Liberation Army, Mrs. Travers got a faraway look and murmured, " … and her mother sought her sorrowing." Here was the myth of Demeter and Persephone being acted out in the daily paper. These are "signs of the times."

As Norman O. Brown[4] once remarked in a class on archetypes, "When the myth is no longer enacted on the ritual dancing ground, it acts itself out on the stage of history." Or, as Coomaraswamy put it, "Myths are not distorted records of historical events … events are demonstrations of the myths."[5]

In Chapter Two, "The Cosmic Model," you may begin to discern a link between the process of establishing order, inner and outer, in a culture and the establishment of erect posture and spatial orientation traced out in the first few paragraphs above. The body is a born cosmos, a gift, a temple, a template for us in our inner journey from chaos into cosmos. Active attention to inner sensation can bring analogous order to the inner world of a human being, who stands erect between earth and heaven, charged with the task of finding his way toward a wholeness encompassing many opposites: masculine and feminine natures; immortal spirit and mortal body; the timeless and time. A brief excerpt from René Guénon's *Symbolism of the Cross* stands at the center of this chapter, presenting the symbol at its most abstract. Joseph Campbell's beautiful essay on the hieratic city state comes next, this time the cosmic symbol at its most concrete, incarnate in brick or stone.

And at the end of an age, the worm of time, the ambiguous god Loki, who took part in the creation of Asgard, home of the gods, now helps bring it down, because, although the spirit is immortal, the body is not, nor is the soul until, like Psyche, she is married to Eros and can transmit that immortal influence to the body itself through loving attention.

So "time enters in from the outer halls of heaven," as William Morris said,[6] unerring as always in his insight into myth. The great cosmic model revolves. The universe expands from a center which is everywhere, circumference nowhere. The cycles of time revolve on scales within scales: minutes within hours, hours within days and nights, days and nights within years. … And on every scale the same sequence of stages.

In Chapter Three, William Sullivan reminds us of the view that finds the source of myth in the stars—the ancient view, which, as Giorgio de Santillana and Hertha von Dechend put it in *Hamlet's Mill* (1969), rearose before their astonished eyes "from the depths of prehistory with its bells still ringing." The ancient view of the stars was geocentric. The stars were of interest because what was happening in the heavens influenced what took place on earth. We suppose that both of those propositions were discredited once and for all at the time of the Copernican Revolution, but a little reflection shows that the Copernican Revolution itself is by now provincial. The sun is the center of gravity of the solar system, and the center of our galaxy is a black hole. The universe itself has no known center. If we take the origin of the expansion of the universe as a center, then, like God, the center is everywhere, circumference nowhere. Since there is no center, no motionless point of reference, all motion is relative.

As for the idea that the heavens influence life on earth, that was lost with the idea of the primacy of consciousness. Seyyed Hossein Nasr deals with this problem in "Ours Is Not a Dead Universe" (Chapter Four). In what he calls "the prevalent scientistic paradigm" (not "scientific" because it is composed of unquestioned notions that drifted down to us nonscientists, whereas many of the greatest scientists themselves have been mystics), primacy is in materiality rather than consciousness. "Even if you say," Nasr writes, "'My body is made of stardust, and I share the dust of the stars,' this is a nice poetic utterance, but it does not mean anything in the prevalent scientistic paradigm. Stardust is dead matter in a dead universe. ... In the Hindu view ... everything manifests a level of consciousness. A stone's being is a form of stony consciousness; the same holds true up the line, all the way to the level of human beings and beyond"—and certainly all the way to the stars.

That is the way I saw them when I was a child. When I looked at the stars, the stars were looking back. Later, my education taught me to be embarrassed by such ignorance.

And the great globe of the fixed stars revolved around me every night. That's the way I saw that too. I was soon taught better. My eyes still see it that way, though my brain has become disconnected from my eyes. I "know" better now.

Even when I set aside the obstacles created by my education, I still have trouble getting my head and body turned around to visualize and sense the sky from the geocentric point of view. Similarly, I don't dare believe again, for fear of ridicule, that the stars are conscious beings. But if I stop talking to myself and look in inner silence, I do begin to feel again a silent presence. …

To realize that we might be surrounded by great, silent, conscious presences is almost frightening. And fear of ridicule also prevents me from acknowledging that the position of the planets might have an effect on our lives. It smacks of the daily horoscope. The genuine knowledge upon which such predictions were once based and might have had some value was lost long ago, probably even before the Copernican Revolution. Ancient astrology was based on meticulous nightly observation of the movements of the planets in relation to the fixed stars, the positions of the solstitial and equinoctial points on the horizon at sunrise, etc., over thousands of years, and their careful recording in the language of myths. These dates were of vital importance because they were predictive of events on earth. The recovery of this vast body of lost knowledge has only recently begun.

The dimensions of mythic time are in the cycles of the heavens of different tempos and durations, of the marking of the moment when two or more cycles begin again together; or rarer moments when several cycles begin together; or all begin again together in a "Jubilee Year" like 1300, where Dante places his *Divine Comedy*, and the Church was issuing pardons to all who journeyed to Rome. In its seasonal feasts and fasts, weekly, yearly, and at longer intervals, marking the conjunction of certain planets, the Church has retained vestiges of the ancient view (which had probably belonged to the Old Religion, the religion of the Goddess), but dressed in suitable Christian clothing, as it dressed the barebreasted Hawaiian women in Victorian nightgowns.

This is the cyclic aspect of mythic time, and is reflected in ancient attempts to echo the harmony of the heavens in the spatial structures and calendars of cities and kingdoms on earth.

The other, omnipresent dimension of mythic time is stillness, the still point of the turning cycles, the present moment—Now—the strait gate through which the bird darts between the clashing rocks to the timeless realm beyond. In "Crossing into the Invisible" Laura Simms evokes the experience of this stillness in the course of telling and listening to stories.

Chapter Four is devoted to pleas for return to that long-lost awareness of the consciousness and sensitivity of everything that breathes
which Nasr describes, and to the faculty in human beings that could
perceive it. As P. L. Travers says in her book *About the Sleeping Beauty*,
"No amount of rationalizing will bring us to the heart of the fairy tale.
To enter it one must be prepared to let the rational reason go. The stories
have to be loved for themselves before they will release their secrets. ..."[7]
The unfeeling elder brothers who can't be bothered to free the snared
rabbit who calls to them for help as they pass on their way to find the
Water of Life for their dying father (and so inherit his throne and his
wealth) will never find the treasure. It is the third brother, the youngest,
the dummy according to external standards, who has a compassionate
heart, unconcerned with who is or is not looking, who frees the rabbit,
shares his lunch with the grotesque but hungry little man, clears the
brush from the clogged brook so that it can flow again. He is the one
who can penetrate to the secret of the fairy tale, who will ask the question that heals the Fisher King and "attain the Grail."

In "Come into Animal Presence" Denise Levertov communicates
directly the kind of sensitive, affectionate attention to "everything that
breathes" that has long been scorned as a "feminine value"—at least since
the time of the Renaissance and the scientific revolution, when prophetic
Shakespeare allowed Cordelia, the youngest Princess—the one who in
every story is threatened but is always rescued in the end—to be, not
rescued, but brutally hung. "Is there any cause in nature that makes these
hard hearts?" (*King Lear*).

With the turning of the heavens, feminine values alternate with masculine ones, feminine Goddess with masculine God, mercy with rigor.
When one or the other reaches its extreme, the pendulum begins to
swing the other way.

"The first high period of the kingdoms and the power and the glory
of the Goddess was that of the dawn of civilization in the valleys of the
Tigris–Euphrates and Nile," Joseph Campbell tells us.[8] It was she who
brought the world order to her people. The hymns to her in her ascen-
dency ("Inanna: Queen of Heaven and Earth") included in Chapter Five
portray a world of beauty and the joys of the body: bathing, feasting,

tender sexuality. She is both morning and evening star, radiant, kind, cruel only to the evil-doer.

In the story of Gilgamesh, one of the earliest known literary works, we have a remarkable record of one of the moments of transition from matriarchy to patriarchy. In "The First Tree" our hero is happy to serve the young goddess and to make for her from the first tree a shining throne and bed. She in turn fashions for him a drum from the roots of the tree and, from the branches, a drumstick.

Whereupon he strikes the drum, wakes the people of Uruk and orders them to follow his command! It is the old story.

Later in his own story (in an episode not included in the excerpt in Chapter Six), he reviles and humiliates her. Gilgamesh is an adolescent hero. He must indeed "leave home and seek his fortune," but the vehemence of his rejection of the Goddess (called Inanna in Sumer and Ishtar in Babylon) betrays his lingering dependence. He and Enkidu frolicking in the forest, slaying her favorite animals in naughty defiance, are like the "wolf cubs" of ancient Rome (palely echoed in the Boy Scouts of America) engaged in this form of initiation into manhood.

Beowulf (although his slaying of the underwater monsters, Grendel and Grendel's mother, may disguise the same throwing off of dependence on the mother), in his nobility and manly stoicism, strikes one as no adolescent, any more than do the young soldiers fighting in more recent wars and returning to the battlefield for no motive beyond fierce loyalty to their comrades. Beowulf risks his life again and again, not in service to any god or king, nor in hope of any reward. The story shows signs that Christianity has reached Britain in the form of words, but its power to evoke operative faith and hope shows no signs of having penetrated. Beowulf goes to other kingdoms to slay the monsters harassing their people because it is something that has to be done and he is the only one who can do it. He is an existential hero. No woman appears in the story (unless Grendel's mother qualifies). It is a man's world.

In the *Odyssey*, on the other hand, Odysseus, with the help of the goddess Athena, is trying to get home to his faithful wife and his son—to his own kingdom. This motive, and the kind of obstacles he encounters and overcomes on the way, lent itself so well that in the

Middle Ages the *Odyssey* provided abundant metaphors for the Christian's homeward journey—and for ours too: for any journey energized by the universal "cosmic homesickness"—the "Nostalgia for Paradise" that Eliade addressed in Chapter Two. This is an extended example of how myth works: the same structure underlies innumerable stories that at first glance appear different; and similarly, an individual episode in one of these stories may act as a powerful metaphor for some spiritual practice that will communicate directly "how," where the abstract description remains vague. When Odysseus knows his ship will soon be sailing close to the rocks of the Sirens, whose irresistible singing lures sailors to their deaths, he orders his men to bind him to the mast, the vertical axis, and at the same time stuff their ears with wax, so that they will not hear, while he himself, keeping his own ears open, can. The physical situation itself, and Odysseus's agonized pleadings to his men to release him, once they enter the field of the Sirens' power, communicate to the body and emotions what the actual experience of the spiritual effort to remember oneself—to cleave to the vertical—in the midst of life (at least in the early stages of the Way) is like, as no abstract diagram or set of instructions could.

In "Beyond Rapture" (Chapter Six), Tim Miller proposes that what the Sirens offer is not, as is usually supposed, superhuman sensual rapture, but wisdom. A book can be as alluring as a flamenco guitar.

In "A Tale of Wonders," Sir Gawain so charmingly resists the lovely siren, his host's wife, who approaches his bed each night, that she is not offended. He resists until the third night, that is, when, having withstood sexual temptation, he succumbs to the fear of death—a far greater disgrace for a knight—and then neglects to include that moment of weakness in his daily morning confession to his host. Gawain is "the best knight in England," so devoted to King Arthur that he would gladly die in his service. But he is still, one might say, "outer-directed," which configuration of inner forces leaves one open to concern for appearances, subject to cover-ups. However noble may be this devotion to kingdom or country—or spiritual master, or the accepted morality of the group—it is not yet conscience. Only motivation from within, even under the threat of ostracism by the group and loss of the leader's approval, can bring integrity and unity of being. A genuine master will test this integrity in his pupils again and again in indirect and even outrageous ways. There are many examples of this in the literature—and even more in the oral tradition—surrounding G. I. Gurdjieff.

Chapter Seven is concerned with the nature of this transformed quest: the Quest for the Holy Grail. P. L. Travers, in "Le Chevalier Perdu" (Chapter Seven) brings a story about "the third degree of knighthood": after taking up the challenge of the quest each of us is offered at the beginning of life, and after having lived the life of action—"doughty deeds, the righting of wrongs, the fellowship of knightly men,"—the knight comes to "the end of the world," where there is only one road to take: the road "Inwards. Into the heart of yourself."

The motive force comes from within—this longing—and the obstacles are also within: self-doubt; fear of beginning and imagination about what might happen if one steps out of one's habitual role ("The Monster of Grim Prospects"); the undefined nature of the goal ("In Search of Hidden Wonders"); conflicting longings ("Sir Launcelot's Dream"); conformity to one's conditioning when the appropriate action can only spring from one's essential nature ("Quest and Questioning in the Waste Land").

"Sleeping Beauty" is included in this chapter because in this version P. L. Travers gives us a taste of the quality and effect of the presence of the Grail. When, after a hundred years, the destined Prince has passed unhindered through the hedge of thorns, walked, bewildered, through the courtyards full of sleeping animals and the rooms full of sleeping people, has climbed to the top of the winding stair, come to the smallest, inmost room and opened the door, there lies his destined bride in her magical sleep. At that moment, time stops: "He knew himself to be at the centre of the world and that, in him, all men stood there, gazing at their hearts' desire—or perhaps their inmost selves."

In "Quest and Questioning in the Waste Land," James Karman tells how the poet T. S. Eliot recognized, in the ruined soil and disillusioned soul of Europe after the first World War, the wasteland that appears in the myth of Parsifal. After several more wars and our continuing abuse of the earth may have pushed it beyond its capacity to recover, the situation has only intensified. In the myth, relief of the intolerable situation awaits the advent of a knight who will ask the healing question.

On his first visit, Parsifal is introduced to the Fisher King, who lies suffering from an unhealing wound but cannot die, and witnesses the whole mysterious procession of maidens carrying the Grail.

But his mentor, a retired knight of King Arthur's Round Table, has taught him that a good knight does not ask too many questions. So he obeys his conditioning, struggles with his natural curiosity and compassion and does not ask. In the morning the castle and all its inhabitants have disappeared, the land is left waste, and Parsifal, baffled and desolate.

He gets a second chance. On his second visit he defies convention and obeys his innocent curiosity and compassion. The questions he asks the king are the scandalous ones a child would ask: "What's the matter with you?" ("What aileth thee?) and, referring to the whole inscrutable pageant, "What does it mean?" After he has asked, the king is healed, the springs and rivers flow again, and everything bursts into bloom.

The failure to ask "What aileth thee?" suggests the lack of feeling for other living things that has been one disastrous side effect of "the scientistic paradigm" that Seyyed Hossein Nasr brings forward in Chapter Four.

And the failure to ask "What does it mean?" lies at the very inception of the development of the scientific method, which does not ask, and was never intended to ask, "the teleological question": the question of the meaning and purpose of life.

This is the question that impelled G. I. Gurdjieff to set out on his search in the late nineteenth century, at the peak of the influence of scientific materialism, and marks the turn toward the inward journey in the West. Those who pursue it are like the early Christians meeting in the catacombs under brutal Rome—honeybees building in the carcass of the lion.

In Chapter Eight ("Psyche's Tasks") we come to the question of what is up to the psyche in the human quest for wholeness of being: the marriage of psyche and spirit. No one can dictate to the spirit: "The wind bloweth where it listeth." All we can do is "create conditions" in ourselves that make it possible for spirit to enter when it wishes. This requires a balancing of many opposites: left and right, feminine and masculine, mercy and rigor—the intersection of all the axes in that zero point at the center: "a condition of complete simplicity, costing not less than everything." As Thomas Moore points out, the flight of spirit away from the soul is as one-sided as the neglect of both for the sake of excessive indulgence in the appetites of body and ego.

What is up to Psyche? First she must invite the spirit. Her call is the beat of her silk drum. "What shall Cordelia speak? Love and be silent."

She must, like the Merchant's youngest daughter, cultivate her longing and set it like a scarlet flower on her windowsill, stay awake, watch, wait.

And if, like Finn the Keen Falcon, spirit should happen by and enter, suddenly be there in her room, taking human form when his feet touch the floor, her wicked stepsisters will overhear them whispering together. The next morning, when she is sleeping again, her sisters (coarser aspects of herself) will fasten needles and knives around the window frame so that when he returns he will be so sorely wounded that he will not enter again.

Then come all the tasks of atonement that her prospective mother-in-law (mother of Eros, Aphrodite, Goddess of Love) requires of her and Harriet Eisman enumerates in "That Other Loveliness." The last task, paradoxically, is one she must fail in order to succeed. Eros must come and wake her from the magical sleep hidden in Persephone's box of beauty, because the last gap between psyche and spirit must be filled by spirit, by an energy descending from above.

This is the marriage of heaven and earth, the task of human beings in the whole economy of the universe.

"The Marriage of Heaven and Earth" is the subject of the last chapter. The quiet "Tale of Baucis and Philemon" portrays the conditions we need to arrive at in ourselves so that the gods will want to visit us, to come and go and sanctify ourselves and our houses: simplicity, hospitality, harmony.

Nothing fancy.

Notes:

1. Lizelle Reymond and Sri Anirvan, *To Live Within* (Sandpoint, ID: Morning Light Press. 2007), p. 160.

2. Travers, *About the Sleeping Beauty*, p. 50.

3. Coomaraswamy, *Selected Papers, Vol. I*, p. 521-543.

4. Author of *Life Against Death* (Middletown, CT: Wesleyan University Press, 1985); and *Love's Body* (New York: Random House, 1966).

5. Coomaraswamy, *op. cit.*, p. 368.

6. Heyneman, *The Breathing Cathedral*, p. 188.

7. Travers, *op. cit.*, p. 62.

8. "Joseph Campbell on the Great Goddess," *Parabola* V:4, p. 80.

CHAPTER ONE

•

WHAT IS MYTH?

Myth is the secret opening through which the inexhaustible energies of the cosmos pour into human cultural manifestation.[1]

—Joseph Campbell

All the most important aspects of thought come from that which is thinking through us. And this process is the myth, one of the most profound things of life; it is creation itself, which becomes accessible and, in part, energizes and gives, of its own accord, a sense of direction to the human creature.[2]

—Sir Laurens van der Post

Parabola
Volume: 1.1
The Hero

The World of the Hero

P. L. Travers

I will preface what I am going to say with a few lines from e. e. cummings:

> *"May my mind walk about freely and supple*
> *And even if it's Sunday may I be wrong,*
> *For whenever men are right they are no longer young."*

This gives you leave to doubt me and to take what I say simply as hint and indication and not at all as assertion. It is meant as a whisper at the inner ear and designed to touch that part of you which is not accessible to the things that are spoken of in newspapers.

But before we begin to search for the hero, I think we should take a look at the element he moves in, the world where he functions—folklore, fairy-tale, allegory, legend, parable, even nursery rhyme; for all these are as it were the principalities that together comprise the homeland of myth, the country which in the old Russian stories is called East of the Sun and West of the Moon, and for which there is no known map.

But first I think it important to clarify what I mean by that word myth. We have so betrayed and brutalized language that we have forgotten that in itself it is, in a way, mythical, in the sense that it is sacred, in its essence, a gift at some immemorial time mysteriously bestowed.

Even the behaviorists are beginning to question their own theory that language is a simple human function that has evolved, over millenniums, from the grunting of bears and apes. We have lost our respect for this given treasure and now care so little to foster its growth that we have all become like Humpty-Dumpty: "When I use a word," he says in Alice in Wonderland, "it means exactly what I mean it to mean." This is all very well, perhaps, for somebody who is living down a rabbit hole, but not for us, if we are truly to understand each other and try to communicate ideas; we have to admit that words exist in their own right, that they have antecedents, long family trees and are not just foundlings left on a doorstep for anybody to pick up and do with as they will. If I were a hero the maiden I would set out to rescue would be language.

The word myth, for example, is largely accepted and used as something synonymous with lie. "It's a myth," we say, meaning something that is not to be believed, a tarradiddle, a tall story, an impossibility. Even the Oxford Dictionary describes it as a "fictional account". I would rather have said "unverifiable", but even that would not have been exact. For whether we know it or not, or wish or not, we all—like the hero—live in myth, or rather the context of myth, as the egg yolk lives in its albumen; and if we set about it, we can verify and confirm the fact in ourselves.

If we begin to look for the origin of myths, we hear first perhaps the answer of such Victorians as Frazer of *The Golden Bough* and Andrew Lang: that they are the relics of an ancient barbaric world, the avocations, even the aberrations, of savages. But when one thinks of Gilgamesh, of the Chinese structures that underlie that oldest of known books, the I Ching, of the Hindu myths, the African and those of the American Indians, one can only say: "What barbarians are these!" and pray to be turned forthwith into a savage.

Malinowsky, nearer the mark, called them the re-arising of primordial reality in narrative form. And Nietzsche, who in everything he did and wrote was deeply involved in the mythical process, said that myth was not merely the bearer of ideas and concepts but that it was also a way of thinking, a glass that mirrors to us the universe and ourselves. One of our own contemporaries, Robert Graves, has written that "they are all grave records of ancient religious customs, events or ritual, and reliable enough as history once their language is understood." And William Blake said: "The Authors"—and he spelled the word with a capital A—"the

Authors are in Eternity." And in eternity is where we have to leave them, I think, if we are looking for inventors. We shall never know what species of man it was that first unfolded from his own subjective understanding this Orphic and objective art. And as to the meaning of the myths, the more one studies them the more one sees that this heritage from archaic man—the rituals and concepts that guided his conscious life—miraculously survives and is ever present in the subterranean layers of ourselves. It can be tapped as one taps the waters under the earth; it can be questioned as once our forefathers questioned the oracles, seeking an answer to what, in essence, is perhaps not so different from our own question. We go to the myths not so much for what they mean as for our own meaning. Who am I? Why am I here? How can I live in accordance with reality?

Now, this problem of meaning can literally overwhelm us, particularly nowadays when there are no rituals, no rites of passage, as the ancients called them, to help us to make the transition from one stage of life to the next. One moment we're children and a moment later, as it seems, we're adolescents and then grown-ups, facing alone our own existence and all the dubiousness of things. And yet, perhaps not so alone as we imagine. The myths have something to say here; not an absolute, not one sole word, no blanket phrase—although every religion, every tradition, to say nothing of every anthropologist, every archeologist, and of course, every psychoanalyst lays claim to the myths as his special province, his own particular possession, "We know," they say, in the kind voice that makes one reach immediately for one's hat. "We know and we will interpret. The myth means this, the myth means that; it means of course, *our* meaning."

Well, to be honest, so it may; but that is not the end of it. One of the characteristics of this ancient art is that it won't go into any particular pocket, it won't be coerced or owned. The myths never have a single meaning, once and for all and finished. They have something greater; they have meaning itself. If you hang a crystal sphere in the window it will give off light from all parts of itself. That is how the myths are; they have meaning for me, for you, and for everyone else. A true symbol has always this multisidedness. It has something to say to all who approach it.

One could say, I think, that the myths never were and always are and therefore they are indestructible. Whenever there are men, there are myths; and no matter where on the globe they arise, these myths have a startling likeness to one another. At some particular moment, always unknown—for they are not subject to the carbon test and can't be dated; and they may appear at different periods among different peoples—the selfsame themes seem to emerge, as though something in the psyche of a race had ripened and produced a fruit that corresponded, not in its form but in its substance, with the fruit of all other races. The fact that the same stories arise in India, the Middle East, Europe, the Americas, as well as in China and Japan is an intimation that their proper soil and seeding-place is not in any geographical location but in man himself. This alone could insure, if we believed it, (I'm speaking ideally and myth-ologically, of course) that no one on the planet need be a stranger to any other. Indeed, there is a Hindu myth that illustrates this. The high god Indra, it is said, once made a net to enclose the world, and at each knot or intersection, he fastened a little bell. If you think of a seine fishing net, with a bell in every knot of the string, you can see what this would mean. Nothing could move, not a man, not the wind, not a thought in the mind, without setting one bell ringing; and that one bell would set all the others going. It is a wonderfully graphic way of telling people who could not read, who received things through the ear rather than the eye, that everything is inevitably connected with everything else.

But if the myths always are, who is it that enacts them? Who sustains them? Who keeps them alive? You have only to read *The New York Times* to see the myths crowding into it with their splendid and terrible deeds. The daily disclosures in the papers show the material on which the mythmaking process inherent in man is always at work, however unconsciously—not only among poets and mystics, Boehme, Bunyan, Blake and the rest, but also, and chiefly, in the folk; and by folk I mean you and me and anyone walking in the street. Take as an instance the story of Galileo. Galileo is not a myth; he is in all the history books, where you will read the undoubted fact that at a time when it was believed that the sun moved round the earth, Galileo dared to assert that the very opposite was true, that the earth moved round the sun. Under pressure, however, and on pain of death, he was forced to deny his truth. Thus he was able to save his life; but as he turned away from recanting he muttered firmly into his beard: "*Eppur si muove*"—"Nevertheless, it moves." The story is known to everyone. Galileo is famous for the "*Eppur si muove*"; but the recantation of his recantation has nowhere been recorded. How could it have been? The only people near enough to hear it were his inquisitors, and had they heard it, his fat would have been in the fire. He never said "*Eppur si muove*"—except, of course, in his accurate heart. But in its unconscious shaping of the hero, the folk required that it be said, the story required that it be said; the truth had somehow to be told that Galileo was not a liar. So, mythologically, Galileo was required to say it. It is a truth but it is not a fact.

Then there is the case of Lady Godiva. Everybody knows the story: how in order to get from her skinflint husband a gift of land for the poor of Coventry, she offered to ride through the streets naked, having first taken the precaution of ordering the people into their houses and all the shutters closed. The whole of Coventry obeyed except for one man by the name of Tom who peeped at her through the crack of a door and had his eye shriveled up for his pains. It is from him that we get the phrase "a peeping Tom". But the fact of the matter is that Tom did not enter the story until it was two hundred years old. Gradually and mythologically, the folk must have come to realize that nakedness without an eye to observe it has no meaning whatever—like Bishop Berkeley's cow that didn't exist until somebody beheld it—and that an order without somebody to disobey it is somehow incomplete. A story can't live with a heroine only, it needs a villain to bring her to life. So, of course, the matter was at last put right and Peeping Tom now belongs to the myth. He also is true but he is not a fact.

So you see how the mythmaking mind works, balancing, clarifying, adjusting, making events somehow correspond to the inner necessity of things. It is in this tension, the uncompromising insistence on both ends of the stick—black and white, good and evil, positive and negative, active and passive—that gives the myths their ambivalent power. In our Aristotelian, Apollonian world, where we constantly applaud the good, uphold law and order and stand on the side of what is right (while keeping the atom bomb in our pocket), the bloodiness of the myths, their vengefulness and brutality, their Dionysian recklessness—and, on the other hand, their splendor—are difficult to accept. They are too large for us, too mighty. Perhaps that is why we give them to children who, with their strong stomachs and their minds as yet untainted with knowledge, are more likely to understand them. To understand: for years I pondered on that word and tried to define its effect on myself. At last I came to the conclusion that what it means is the opposite of what it says; to understand is to stand under. Later I discovered that this was, in very fact, its meaning in the Middle English. So, in order to understand, I come to something with my unknowing—my nakedness, if you like: I stand under it and let it teach me, rain down its truth upon me. That is, I think, what children do; they let it make room in them for a sense of justice, for the Wicked Fairy as well as the Sleeping Beauty, for dragons as well as princes.

This grasping of the whole stick is an essential feature of the hero. So what or rather who is the hero? We're all familiar with the paladins of myth: Theseus slaying the Minotaur and finding his way through the labyrinth by means of a single linen thread; Aeneas finding the way to the underworld with the help of a little golden twig; Daniel outfacing his pride of lions; Jonah measuring the dark in the belly of the whale. But what is the common denominator among these—and indeed, all other heroes? Could it be (and it's a question, not an assertion) that first and foremost the hero is one who is willing to set out, take the first step, shoulder something? Perhaps the hero is one who puts his foot upon a path not knowing what he may expect from life but in some way feeling in his bones that life expects something from him. I think, too that no hero would ever protest that he didn't ask to be born. If he isn't sure that he did ask, at least he is ready to behave as if he had, as if, having been given life, he is ready to answer for his life. And so he has to leave home, or safety, or his own conditioned way of thinking and feeling, and put himself, naked, at the service of whatever necessity arises; a dragon to be slain, a Gorgon beheaded, fire brought down from Heaven. All the tasks are different, but if you closely examine the myths you will see that fundamentally the quest is always the same. Looked at from the point of view of the story, the hero's work is to rescue a beleaguered maiden from an unspeakable fate, to gather up some hoarded treasure after slaying a seven-headed serpent, or to fetch a cup of the Water of Life from the well at the world's end; all of these asking no less than all. But what do they mean essentially? Perhaps the myths are telling us that these endeavors are not so much voyages of discovery as of rediscovery; that the hero is seeking not for something new but for something old, a treasure that was lost and has to be found, his own self, his identity.

And by finding this, by achieving this, he takes part in the one task, the essential mythical requirement: the reinstatement of the fallen world. It is a long and perilous journey back from the nadir to the zenith, from lying amid the husks and the swine to eating the fatted calf.

Now, the hero is not a god, nor even a saint, though many saints have been heroes. He has a human heart and therefore a dimension of vulnerability and the possibility of failing. The idea that there is a flaw in creation is fundamental to all myths. But only by studying them does one realize that it is *only* by the flaws, only by its imperfections (because they summon up the perfections) that creation can proceed. It is the same with the hero. Each one is a fallible man. Achilles has his inordinate pride; but where would his battle fervor be without that very pride? Lancelot, perhaps the most cherished hero in all myth, envied by men, loved by women, set out to find the Holy Grail while at the same time betraying his friend and king with the wife of his king and friend. He never saw the Holy Grail; it passed him by, by a hair's breadth, but by his heroic faithfulness to his own unfaith he not only sustained his place at the Round Table but was its brightest ornament. And his son, Galahad (or his own unsullied part, perhaps) was the one who found the Grail. Ulysses, whom one might call Lancelot's runner-up in popularity, succumbed to temptation in every known port in the world until he dropped anchor in his own haven of Ithica; he succumbed, yes, but unlike his men, whom he left behind in various stages of beastlihood, he was alive to what he was doing, he kept an eye upon himself—the cunning man, the crafty one—and came home as a hero. David, spying Bathsheba from the housetops, arranged to have her husband Uriah the Hittite set in the forefront of the battle so that he might marry her himself; and we are surprised (but the myth is not) that the outcome of this distasteful deed was Solomon the Wise. Generations later the lineal descendant of David's tree will say to the man who loved him and betrayed him thrice: "Thou art Peter, and on this rock shall I build my church." This rock, this matrix of gross earth and crystal, is the essential hero stuff. For it is through his human failings and his human triumphs that the hero serves his purpose, which is to make himself a channel for the gods to come down to men. In the process of discovering his own identity, he becomes for us mythologically, the mediating or reconciling element and indeed the pattern. And, also mythologically, in an antique way, we comfort and sustain ourselves with what in us corresponds to the hero.

But is this enough? Perhaps if we could really listen to what the myths are telling us we would hear what I heard myself saying not so long ago: "Everybody has to be the hero of one story: his own." I said it lightly; or rather something said it in me, for we know more than we know we know, more than we understand. And if it is true, what an awesome undertaking! All those dragons—give them whatever name you like; those journeys to our own dark underworld, all those imprisoned princesses to be rescued. One would shrink from such an obligation if the alternative was not also so awesome. Not to be the hero of one's own story—could one agree to that? Could I fail to be some sort of Demeter, searching the world for my child, myself, my lost Persephone? It is not a question to be answered but responded to, stood under, as it were, with a kind of fear and trembling. Because, to attempt it, I have to be in the same situation as the hero in the Russian story called *Go I know not whither, Bring back I know not what*. It is with this unknowing that I have set out to find the homeland of myth, that homeland so well described in *Rumpelstiltzkin* where it is called "the country where the fox and the hare say goodnight to each other." This phrase embodies all we need to know. For in effect, this is the country, the conditions where the opposites are reconciled, the place where one goes beyond them. Goodnight, fox, goodnight, hare! I wonder where we can find it, where in ourselves we can look for it?

And yet, it is not always there, and are we ever really out of this East of the Sun, West of the Moon land of myth? Can we escape from it, even if we wish? If you feel that in what I have said about myth (whose garment I have hardly touched), I have drawn too long a bow, you must remember that the long bow itself comes out of a myth, the myth of Philoctetes. And if, as I said at the beginning, you wish to take anything I have said with a grain of salt, do so, always remembering that salt also is an essential mythological ingredient.

Parabola
Volume: 13.2
Repetition and
Renewal

THE ETERNAL RETURN

Mircea Eliade

Parabola has condensed the following essay from Mircea Eliade's The Myth of the Eternal Return, *in the hope of presenting a kind of distillation of some of the book's principal ideas which throw so much light on our present theme. We have necessarily omitted many of the author's insights and a wealth of examples and documentation; we hope that our readers will turn, or return, to read or reread the entire book, which Eliade himself considered his "most significant." It was published in French by Gallinard in 1949, and by the Princeton University Press for the Bollingen Foundation, in Willard Trask's translation, in 1954. It has also appeared under the title* Cosmos and History *in a paperback edition published by Harper Torchbooks, New York, 1959.)*

In Pre-modern or "traditional" societies, the symbol, the myth, the rite, express, on different planes and through the means proper to them, a complex system of coherent affirmations about the ultimate reality of things, a system that can be regarded as constituting a metaphysics. It is, however, essential to understand the deep meaning of all these symbols, myths, and rites, in order to succeed in translating them into our habitual language. If one goes to the trouble of penetrating the authentic meaning of an archaic myth or symbol, one cannot but observe that this meaning shows a recognition of a certain situation in the cosmos and that, consequently, it implies a metaphysical position. It is useless to search archaic languages for the terms so laboriously created by the great philosophical traditions: there is every likelihood that such words as "being," "nonbeing," "real," "unreal," "becoming," "illusory," are not to be found in the language of the Australians or of the ancient Mesopotamians. But if the word is lacking, the *thing* is present; only it is "said"—that is, revealed in a coherent fashion—through symbols and myths.

If we observe the general behavior of archaic man, we are struck by the following fact: neither the objects of the external world nor human acts, properly speaking, have any autonomous intrinsic value. Objects or acts acquire a value, and in so doing become real, because they participate, after one fashion or another, in a reality that transcends them. Among countless stones, one stone becomes sacred—and hence instantly becomes saturated with being—because it constitutes a hierophany, or possesses *mana*, or again because it commemorates a mythical act, and so on. The object appears as the receptacle of an exterior force that differentiates it from its milieu and gives it meaning and value. This force may reside in the substance of the object or in its form; a rock reveals itself to be sacred because its very existence is a hierophany: incompressible, invulnerable, it is that which man is not. It resists time; its reality is coupled with perenniality. Take the commonest of stones; it will be raised to the rank of "precious," that is, impregnated with a magical or religious power, by virtue of its symbolic shape or its origin: thunderstone, held to have fallen from the sky; pearl, because it comes from the depths of the sea. Other stones will be sacred because they are the dwelling place of the souls of ancestors (India, Indonesia), or because they were once the scene of a theophany (as the *bethel* that served Jacob for a bed), or because a sacrifice or an oath has consecrated them.[1]

Now let us turn to human acts—those, of course, which do not arise from pure automatism. Their meaning, their value, are not connected with their crude physical datum but with their property of reproducing a primordial act, of repeating a mythical example. Nutrition is not a simple physiological operation; it renews a communion. Marriage and the collective orgy echo mythical prototypes; they are repeated because they were consecrated in the beginning ("in those days," *in illo tempore, ab origine*) by gods, ancestors, or heroes.

In the particulars of his conscious behavior, the "primitive," the archaic man, acknowledges no act which has not been previously posited and lived by someone else, some other being who was not a man. What he does has been done before. His life is the ceaseless repetition of gestures initiated by others.

This conscious repetition of given paradigmatic gestures reveals an original ontology. The crude product of nature, the object fashioned by the industry of man, acquire their reality, their identity, only to the extent of their participation in a transcendent reality. The gesture acquires meaning, reality, solely to the extent to which it repeats a primordial act.

The world that surrounds us, then, the world in which the presence and the work of man are felt—the mountains that he climbs, populated and cultivated regions, navigable rivers, cities, sanctuaries—all these have an extraterrestrial archetype,[2] be it conceived as a plan, as a form, or purely and simply as a "double" existing on a higher cosmic level. But everything in the world that surrounds us does not have a prototype of this kind. For example, desert regions inhabited by monsters, uncultivated lands, unknown seas on which no navigator has dared to venture, do not share with the city of Babylon, or the Egyptian nome, the privilege of a differentiated prototype. They correspond to a mythical model, but of another nature: all these wild, uncultivated regions and the like are assimilated to chaos; they still participate in the undifferentiated, formless modality of a pre–Creation. This is why, when possession is taken of a territory—that is, when its exploitation begins—rites are performed that symbolically repeat the act of Creation: the uncultivated zone is first "cosmicized," then inhabited. The world which surrounds us, civilized by the hand of man, is accorded no validity beyond that which is due to the extraterrestrial prototype that served as its model. Man constructs according to an archetype. Not only do his city or his temple have celestial models; the same is true of the entire region that he inhabits, with the rivers that water it, the fields that give him his food, etc. The map of Babylon shows the city at the center of a vast circular territory bordered by a river, precisely as the Sumerians envisioned Paradise. This participation by urban cultures in an archetypal model is what gives them their reality and their validity.

Settlement in a new, unknown, uncultivated country is equivalent to an act of Creation. When the Scandinavian colonists took possession of Iceland, *Landnáma*, and began to cultivate it, they regarded this act neither as an original undertaking nor as human and profane work. Their enterprise was for them only the repetition of a primordial act: the transformation of chaos into cosmos by the divine act of Creation. By cultivating the desert soil, they in fact repeated the act of the gods, who organized chaos by giving it forms and norms.[3]

Better still, a territorial conquest does not become real until after— more precisely, through—the ritual of taking possession, which is only a copy of the primordial act of the Creation of the World. In Vedic India the erection of an altar dedicated to Agni constituted legal taking possession of a territory.[4] One settles (*avasyatī*) when he builds the *gārhapatya*, and whoever are builders of fire-altars are 'settled' (*avasitāh*), says the *Śatapatha Brāhmana* (VII, 1, 1, 1-4). But the erection of an altar dedicated to Agni is merely the microscosmic imitation of the Creation. Furthermore, any sacrifice is, in turn, the repetition of the act of Creation, as Indian texts explicitly state.[5]

It was in the name of Jesus Christ that the Spanish and Portuguese conquistadores took possession of the islands and continents that they had discovered and conquered. The setting up of the Cross was equivalent to a justification and to the consecration of the new country, to a "new birth," thus repeating baptism (act of Creation). In their turn the English navigators took possession of conquered countries in the name of the king of England, new Cosmocrator.

The importance of the Vedic, Scandinavian, or Roman ceremonials will appear more clearly when we devote a separate examination to the meaning of the repetition of the Creation, the pre-eminently divine act. For the moment, let us keep one fact in view: every territory occupied for the purpose of being inhabited or utilized as *Lebensraum* is first of all transformed from chaos into cosmos; that is, through the effect of ritual it is given a "form" which makes it become real. Evidently, for the archaic mentality, reality manifests itself as force, effectiveness, and duration. Hence the outstanding reality is the sacred; for only the sacred *is* in an absolute fashion, acts effectively, creates things and makes them endure. The innumerable gestures of consecration—of tracts and territories, of objects, of men, etc.—reveal the primitive's obsession with the real, his thirst for being.

Every ritual has a divine model, an archetype; this fact is well enough known for us to confine ourselves to recalling a few examples. "We must do what the gods did in the beginning" (*Śatapatha Brāhmana*, VII, 2, 1, 4). "Thus the gods did; thus men do" (*Taittirīya Brāhmana*, I, 5, 9, 4). This Indian adage summarizes all the theory underlying rituals in all countries. We find the theory among so-called primitive peoples no less than we do in developed cultures. The aborigines of southeastern Australia, for example, practice circumcision with a stone knife because it is thus that their ancestors taught them to do; the Amazulu Negroes do likewise because Unkulunkulu (civilizing hero) decreed *in illo tempore* "Let men circumcise, that they may not be boys."[6] It may be mentioned in passing that, among primitives, not only do rituals have their mythical model but any human act whatever acquires effectiveness to the extent to which it exactly *repeats* an act performed at the beginning of time by a god, a hero, or an ancestor.

However, as we said, such a "theory" does not justify ritual only in primitive cultures. In the Egypt of the later centuries, for example, the power of rite and word possessed by the priests was due to imitation of the primordial gesture of the god Thoth, who had created the world by the force of his word. Iranian tradition knows that religious festivals were instituted by Ormazd to commemorate the stages of the cosmic Creation, which continued for a year. At the end of each period—representing, respectively, the creation of the sky, the waters, the earth, plants, animals, and man—Ormazd rested for five days, thus instituting the principal Mazdean festivals (cf. *Bundahišn*, I, A 18ff.). Man only repeats the act of the Creation; his religious calendar commemorates, in the space of a year, all the cosmogonic phases which took place *ab origine*. In fact, the sacred year ceaselessly repeats the Creation: man is contemporary with the cosmogony and with the anthropogony because ritual projects him into the mythical epoch of the beginning. A bacchant, through his orgiastic rites, imitates the drama of the suffering Dionysos; an Orphic, through his initiation ceremonial, repeats the original gestures of Orpheus.

The Judaeo–Christian Sabbath is also an *imitatio dei*. The Sabbath rest reproduces the primordial gesture of the Lord, for it was on the seventh day of the Creation that God " ... rested ... from all his work which he had made" (Genesis 2:2). The message of the Saviour is first of all an example which demands imitation. After washing his disciples' feet, Jesus said to them: "For I have given you an example, that ye should do as I have done to you" (John 13:15).

Marriage rites too have a divine model, and human marriage reproduces the hierogamy, more especially the union of heaven and earth. "I am Heaven," says the husband, "thou art Earth" (*dyaur aham, prìvitī tvam;* Brhadāranyaka Upanisad, VI, 4, 20). Even in Vedic times, husband and bride are assimilated to heaven and earth (Atharva-Veda, XIV, 2, 71) while in another hymn (Atharva-Veda, XIV, 1) each nuptial gesture is justified by a prototype in mythical times: "Wherewith Agni grasped the right hand of this earth, therefore grasp I thy hand ... Let god Savitar grasp thy hand ... Tvashtar disposed the garment for beauty, by direction of Brhaspati, of the poets; therewith let Savitar and Bhaga envelop this woman, like Sūrya, with progeny (48, 49, 52)."[7]

What must be emphasized is the cosmogonic structure of these matrimonial rites: it is not merely a question of imitating an exemplary model, the hierogamy between heaven and earth; the principal consideration is the result of that hierogamy, i.e., the cosmic Creation. This is why, in Polynesia, when a sterile woman wants to be fecundated, she imitates the exemplary gesture of the Primordial Mother, who *in illo tempore*, was laid on the ground by the great god, Io. And the cosmogonic myth is recited on the same occasion. The cosmic myth serves as the exemplary model not only in the case of marriages but also in the case of any other ceremony whose end is the restoration of integral wholeness; this is why the myth of the Creation of the World is recited in connection with cures, fecundity, childbirth, agricultural activities, and so on. The cosmogony first of all represents Creation.

Demeter lay with Iasion on the newly sown ground, at the beginning of spring (*Odyssey*, V, 125). The meaning of this union is clear: it contributes to promoting the fertility of the soil, the prodigious surge of the forces of telluric creation.

The entire Paleo-Oriental symbolism of marriage can be explained through celestial models. The Sumerians celebrated the union of the elements on the day of the New Year; throughout the ancient East, the same day receives its luster not only from the myth of the hierogamy but also from the rites of the king's union with the goddess.[8] It is on New Year's day that Ishtar lies with Tammuz, and the king reproduces this mythical hierogamy by consummating ritual union with the goddess (i.e., with the hierodule who represents her on earth) in a secret chamber of the temple, where the nuptial bed of the goddess stands. The divine union assures terrestrial fecundity; when Ninlil lies with Enlil, rain begins to fall.[9] The same fecundity is assured by the ceremonial union of the king, that of couples on earth, etc. The world is regenerated each time the hierogamy is imitated, i.e., each time matrimonial union is accomplished. The German *Hochzeit* (wedding) is derived from *Hochgezit*, New Year festival. Marriage regenerates the "year" and consequently confers fecundity, wealth, and happiness.

Each of the examples cited reveals the same "primitive" ontological conception: an object or an act becomes real only insofar as it imitates or repeats an archetype. Thus, reality is acquired solely through repetition or participation; everything which lacks an exemplary model is "meaningless," i.e., it lacks reality. No less important is the second conclusion to be drawn from analyzing the facts cited in the foregoing pages—that is, the abolition of time through the imitation of archetypes and the repetition of paradigmatic gestures. A sacrifice, for example, not only exactly reproduces the initial sacrifice revealed by a god *ab origine*, at the beginning of time, it also takes place at the same primordial mythical moment; in other words, every sacrifice repeats the initial sacrifice and coincides with it. All sacrifices are performed at the same mythical instant of the beginning; through the paradox of rite, profane time and duration are suspended. And the same holds true for all repetitions, i.e., all imitations of archetypes; through such imitation, man is projected into the mythical epoch in which the archetypes were first revealed. Thus we perceive a second aspect of primitive ontology: insofar as an act (or an object) acquires a certain reality through the repetition of certain paradigmatic gestures, and acquires it through that alone, there is an implicit abolition of profane time, of duration, of "history"; and he who reproduces the exemplary gesture thus finds himself transported into the mythical epoch in which its revelation took place.

The abolition of profane time and the individual's projection into mythical time do not occur, of course, except at essential periods—those, that is, when the individual is truly himself: on the occasion of rituals or of important acts (alimentation, generation, ceremonies, hunting, fishing, war, work). The rest of his life is passed in profane time, which is without meaning: in the state of "becoming." Brahmanic texts clearly bring out the heterogeneity of these two times, the sacred and the profane, of the modality of the gods, which is coupled with immortality, and the modality of man, which is coupled with death. Insofar as he repeats the archetypal sacrifice, the sacrificer, in full ceremonial action, abandons the profane world of mortals and introduces himself into the divine world of the immortals. He himself, indeed, declares this, in the following terms: "I have attained Heaven, the gods; I am become immortal!" (*Taittirīya Samhitā*, 1, 7, 9). Just as profane space is abolished by the symbolism of the Center, which projects any temple, palace, or building into the same central point of mythical space, so any meaningful act performed by archaic man, any real act, i.e., any repetition of an archetypal gesture, suspends duration, abolishes profane time, and participates in mythical time.

This suspension of profane time answers to a profound need on the part of primitive man, as we shall have occasion to observe when we examine a series of parallel conceptions relating to the regeneration of time and the symbolism of the New Year. We shall then understand the significance of this need, and we shall see that the man of archaic cultures tolerates "history" with difficulty and attempts periodically to abolish it.

The beginning of the year varied from country to country as well as in different periods, calendar reforms being constantly introduced to make the ritual meaning of festivals fit the seasons with which it was supposed to correspond.

However, neither the instability and latitude in the beginning of the New Year (March–April, July 19—as in ancient Egypt—September, October, December–January, etc.)—nor the different lengths attributed to the year by different peoples, were able to lessen the importance attached, in all countries, to the end of a period of time and the beginning of a new period. The essential thing is that there is everywhere a conception of the end and the beginning of a temporal period, based on the observation of biocosmic rhythms and forming part of a larger system—the system of periodic purifications (cf. purges, fasting, confession of sins, etc.) and of the periodic regeneration of life. This need for a periodic regeneration seems to us of considerable significance in itself. Yet the examples that we shall presently adduce will show us something even more important, namely, that a periodic regeneration of time presupposes, in more or less explicit form—and especially in the historical civilizations—a new Creation, that is, a repetition of the cosmogonic act. And this conception of a periodic creation, i.e., of the cyclical regeneration of time, poses the problem of the abolition of "history." In broad outline, the ceremony of expelling demons, diseases, and sins can be reduced to the following elements: fasting, ablutions, and purifications; extinguishing the fire and ritually rekindling it in a second part of the ceremonial; expulsion of demons by means of noises, cries, blows (indoors), followed by their pursuit through the village with uproar and hullabaloo; this expulsion can be practiced under the form of the ritual sending away of an animal (type "scapegoat") or of a man (type Mamurius Veturius), regarded as the material vehicle through which the faults of the entire community are transported beyond the limits of the territory it inhabits (the scapegoat was driven "into the desert" by the Hebrews and the Babylonians). There are often ceremonial combats between two groups of actors, or collective orgies, or processions of masked men (representing the souls of the ancestors, the gods, and so forth). In many places the belief still survives that, at the time of these manifestations, the souls of the dead approach the houses of the living, who respectfully go out to meet them and lavish honors upon them for several days, after which they are led to the boundary of the village in procession or are driven from it. It is at the same period that the ceremonies of the initiation of young men are performed.

Naturally, we seldom find all these elements together in explicit conjunction; in certain societies the ceremonies of extinguishing and rekindling the fire predominate; in others, it is the material expulsion (by noise and violent gestures) of demons and diseases; in yet others, the expulsion of the scapegoat in human or animal form. But the meaning of the whole ceremony, like that of each of its constituent elements, is sufficiently clear: on the occasion of the division of time into independent units, "years," we witness not only the effectual cessation of a certain temporal interval and the beginning of another, but also the abolition of the past year and of past time. And this is the meaning of ritual purifications: a combustion, an annulling of the sins and faults of the individual and of those of the community as a whole—not a mere "purifying." Regeneration, as its name indicates, is a new birth. The examples cited clearly show that this annual expulsion of sins, diseases, and demons is basically an attempt to restore—if only momentarily—mythical and primordial time, "pure" time, the time of the "instant" of the Creation. Every New Year is a resumption of time from the beginning, that is, a repetition of the cosmogony. The ritual combats between two groups of actors, the presence of the dead, the Saturnalia, and the orgies are so many elements which denote that at the end of the year and in the expectation of the New Year there is a repetition of the mythical moment of the passage from chaos to cosmos.

The creation of the world is reproduced every year. Allah is he who effects the creation, hence he repeats it (Qur'an, X,4f.). This eternal repetition of the cosmogonic act, by transforming every New Year into the inauguration of an era, permits the return of the dead to life, and maintains the hope of the faithful in the resurrection of the body. The beliefs, held almost everywhere, according to which the dead return to their families (and often return as "living dead") at the New Year season (during the twelve days between Christmas and Epiphany) signify the hope that the abolition of time is possible at this mythical moment, in which the world is destroyed and re-created. The dead can come back now, for all barriers between the dead and the living are broken (is not primordial chaos reactualized?), and they will come back because at this paradoxical instant time will be suspended, hence they can again be contemporaries of the living. Moreover, since a new Creation is then in preparation, they can hope for a return to life that will be enduring and concrete.

That, for a primitive, the regeneration of time is continually effected —that is, *within* the interval of the "year" too—is proven by the antiquity and universality of certain beliefs in respect to the moon. The phases of the moon—appearance, increase, wane, disappearance, followed by reappearance after three nights of darkness—have played an immense part in the elaboration of cyclical concepts.

In the "lunar perspective," the death of the individual and the *periodic* death of humanity are necessary, even as the three days of darkness preceding the "rebirth" of the moon are necessary. The death of the individual and the death of humanity are alike necessary for their regeneration. Any form whatever, by the mere fact that it exists as such and endures, necessarily loses vigor and becomes worn; to recover vigor, it must be reabsorbed into the formless if only for an instant; it must be restored to the primordial unity from which it issued; in other words, it must return to "chaos" (on the cosmic plane), to "orgy" (on the social plane), to "darkness" (for seed), to "water" (baptism on the human plane, Atlantis on the plane of history, and so on).

We may note that what predominates in all these cosmic-mythological lunar conceptions is the cyclical recurrence of what has been before—in a word, eternal return. Here we again find the motif of the repetition of an archetypal gesture, projected upon all planes—cosmic, biological, historical, human. But we also discover the cyclical structure of time, which is regenerated at each new "birth" on whatever plane. This eternal return reveals an ontology uncontaminated by time and becoming. Just as the Greeks, in their myth of eternal return, sought to satisfy their metaphysical thirst for the "ontic" and the static (for, from the point of view of the infinite, the becoming of things that perpetually revert to the same state is, as a result, implicitly annulled and it can even be affirmed that "the world stands still"),[10] even so the primitive, by conferring a cyclic direction upon time, annuls its irreversibility. Everything begins over again at its commencement every instant. The past is but a prefiguration of the future. No event is irreversible and no transformation is final. In a certain sense, it is even possible to say that nothing new happens in the world, for everything is but the repetition of the same primordial archetypes; this repetition, by actualizing the mythical moment when the archetypal gesture was revealed, constantly maintains the world in the same auroral instant of the beginnings. Time but makes possible the appearance and existence of things. It has no final influence upon their existence, since it is itself constantly regenerated.

Hegel affirmed that in nature things repeat themselves for ever and that there is "nothing new under the sun." All that we have so far demonstrated confirms the existence of a similar conception in the man of archaic societies: for him things repeat themselves for ever and nothing new happens under the sun. But this repetition has a meaning, as we have seen: it alone confers a reality upon events; events repeat themselves because they imitate an archetype–the exemplary event. Furthermore, through this repetition, time is suspended, or at least its virulence is diminished. But Hegel's observation is significant for another reason: Hegel endeavors to establish a philosophy of history in which the historical event, although irreversible and autonomous, can nevertheless be placed in a dialectic which remains open. For Hegel, history is "free" and always "new," it does not repeat itself; nevertheless, it conforms to the plans of providence; hence it has a model (ideal, but none the less a model) in the dialectic of spirit itself. To this history which does not repeat itself, Hegel opposes nature, in which things are reproduced *ad infinitum*. But we have seen that, during a very considerable period, humanity opposed history by all possible means. May we conclude from all this that, during this period, humanity was still within nature, had not yet detached itself from nature? "Only the animal is truly innocent," Hegel wrote at the beginning of his *Lectures on the Philosophy of History*. The primitives did not always feel themselves innocent, but they tried to return to the state of innocence by periodically confessing their faults. Can we see, in this tendency toward purification, a nostalgia for the lost paradise of animality? Or, in the primitive's desire to have no "memory," not to record time, and to content himself with tolerating it simply as a dimension of his existence, but without "interiorizing" it, without transforming it into consciousness, should we rather see his thirst for the "ontic," his will to be, to *be* after the fashion of the archetypal beings whose gestures he constantly repeats?

The problem is of the first importance, and we certainly cannot hope to discuss it in a few lines. But we have reason to believe that among the primitives the nostalgia for the lost paradise excludes any desire to restore the "paradise of animality." Everything that we know about the mythical memories of "paradise" confronts us, on the contrary, with the image of an ideal humanity enjoying a beatitude and spiritual plenitude forever unrealizable in the present state of "fallen man." In fact, the myths of many peoples allude to a very distant epoch when men knew neither death nor toil nor suffering and had a bountiful supply of food merely for the taking. *In illo tempore*, the gods descended to earth and mingled with men; for their part, men could easily mount to heaven. As the result of a ritual fault, communications between heaven and earth were interrupted and the gods withdrew to the highest heavens. Since then, men must work for their food and are no longer immortal.

Hence it is more probable that the desire felt by the man of traditional societies to refuse history, and to confine himself to an indefinite repetition of archetypes, testifies to his thirst for the real and his terror of "losing" himself by letting himself be overwhelmed by the meaninglessness of profane existence.

It matters little if the formulas and images through which the primitive expresses "reality" seem childish and even absurd to us. It is the profound meaning of primitive behavior that is revelatory; this behavior is governed by belief in an absolute reality opposed to the profane world of "unrealities"; in the last analysis, the latter does not constitute a "world," properly speaking; it is the "unreal" *par excellence*, the uncreated, the nonexistent: the void.

Hence we are justified in speaking of an archaic ontology, and it is only by taking this ontology into consideration that we can succeed in understanding—and hence in not scornfully dismissing—even the most extravagant behavior on the part of the primitive world; in fact, this behavior corresponds to a desperate effort not to lose contact with *being*.

Notes:

1. Cf. our *Patterns in Comparative Religion* (English trans., London and New York, 1958), pp. 216 ff.

2. I use the term "archetype," just as Eugenio d'Ors does, as a synonym for "exemplary model" or "paradigm," that is, in the last analysis, in the Augustinian sense. But in our day the word has been rehabilitated by Professor C. G. Jung, who has given it a new meaning; and it is certainly desirable that the term "archetype" should no longer be used in its pre-Jungian sense unless the fact is distinctly stated.

3. Cf. van Hamel, cited by Gerardus van der Leeuw, *L'Homme primitif et la religion*, (French trans., Paris, 1940), p. 110.

4. Ananda K. Coomaraswamy, *The Rig Veda as Land-náma-bók* (London, 1935), p. 16, etc.

5. For example, *Śatapatha Brāhmana* XIV, 1, 2, 26, etc.

6. A. W. Howitt, *The Native Tribes of South-East Australia* (London, 1904), pp. 645 ff.; Henry Callaway, *The Religious System of the Amazulu* (London, 1869), p. 58.

7. W. D. Whitney and C. R. Lanman (trans.), *Atharva-Veda* (Harvard Oriental Series, VIII, Cambridge, Mass., 1905), pp. 750-751.

8. Cf. S. H. Hooke, ed., *Myth and Ritual* (London, 1935), pp. 9, 19, 34 ff.

9. Réné Labat, *Le Caractère religieux de la royauté assyro-babylonienne* (Paris, 1939), pp. 247 ff.; cf. the traces of a similar mythico-ritual complex in Israel: Raphael Patai, *Man and Temple* (London, 1947) pp. 90 ff.

10. See Henri-Charles Puech's fine exposition "Gnosis and Time," in *Men and Time* (New York and London, 1957), especially pp. 40-41.

Edited from Mircea Eliade. *The Myth of the Eternal Return: Or, Cosmos and History.* © 1954 Bollingen. Reprinted by permission of Princeton University Press.

Parabola
Volume: 23.3
Fear

Through the Story's Terror

Laura Simms

Tsvetaeva tells us, a fairytale that doesn't frighten is not a fairytale. It is terror that transports us to the place where Dostoyevsky was transported when he was condemned to death, this most precious place, the most alive, where you tell yourself you are going to receive the axe's blow, and where you discover, by the axe's light, what Kafka made Moses say: "How beautiful the world is even in its ugliness." It's at this moment, as Blanchot would say, that "we see the light."

—Helene Cixous, *Three Steps on the Ladder of Writing*

Fear is the uncompromising companion of the hero and heroine in story—as well as in life. She shakes loose the walls of our fixed ideas and conceptions, waking us up trembling and alert, in order to experience the reality of our inner world and the invisible realm of spirit and ancestors which lay locked behind thick chains of conventional logic. Fear is not to be avoided, repressed, or conquered. For from the very depths of fear itself arises fearlessness, awareness, and wisdom. The acknowledgment and experience of fear is the door that opens us to heightened presence and perception through which we learn to live in the world as it is.

The experience of fear is physical. It is neither imaginary nor conceptual, but is known directly through the body. Thus, one of the ways in which traditional peoples have prepared their children to live in the world, "to learn and survive," has been through the live telling of myth, legend, fairytale, and true story. The experience of events is known through an actual psychic enactment: the fear is confronted and endured in the imagined story as a kind of practice process or ritual. When Frances Harwood, anthropologist, asked a Sioux elder why people tell stories, he answered, "In order to become human beings." She asked, "Aren't we all human beings already?" He smiled. "Not everyone makes it."

The most powerful stories (those that are told with knowledge and experience informing the storyteller) are capable of engendering a visceral, imaginative, psychological, and intuitive response during the telling. Of all the stories that pierce to the heart of fear, the fairytales succeed best, second only to the retelling of long-unspoken personal narratives born of crisis or bliss. The direct involvement in becoming the story makes it an experience, one that occurs at the moment of the telling. A story is not an explanation. It is lived between teller and listener; it resonates far beyond the content. The text alone, separated from the enlivening experience, can be analyzed, but the result is different. It is not a transformative event. In other words, genuine story manifests when it is heard in the moment, when the listener is drawn out of self-consciousness—the thinking mind held entranced by the ongoing logic of the narrative—and becomes everything in the story. The meaning and the power of the story do not reside in the content alone; rather, they unfold in the dynamic processes of listening/creating.

The storytelling is potent because it is physical experience. The whole person is engaged in the making of meaning and story. Mind, body, and heart are synchronized and activated. The embodied listener is alert, with senses heightened, and naturally creates image and meaning from association, feeling, memory, dream, and a ceaseless source of archetypal symbol within. It is this holistic activity of listening, not the conceptual content of the text or plot alone, where true learning takes place. During the event, the inherent and natural wisdom of ear, eye, and heart are given voice.

In the Turkish fairytale of "The Three Golden Apples," the youngest prince, the most fearful of three sons, is the one who kills the monster that has caused massive hunger in the world. When the monster is dead, the audience cheers, relieved, breathing heavily, having overcome the monster and their own fear that they could not slay it. Then, just as the prince is about to return home, he is betrayed by his brothers and has to confront an even more challenging situation.

> *An old man advised him, "I know the only way back home. You must walk onto this meadow and close your eyes. You will hear three three-legged horses running. Jump on one, keeping your eyes closed. If it is the white one, you will return. If it is the red, you will remain here. If it is the black one, you will descend to another world beneath this one.*

The trembling prince leaps, eyes closed, onto the black horse. He descends to a desolate world ruled by a flesh-eating dragon which is ultimately responsible for the drought which produced the original monster.

This kind of storytelling, story, and listening, is akin to traditional rites of passage which create the ground for something to happen; for the practitioner to pass through a threshold of fear, in order to know the self and to face the awesome sacredness of life. The feeling of communion, relaxation, enchantment, and refreshment that is felt during and after a storytelling is proof that this has occurred. Something has opened, widened inside the listener, that makes visible the invisible world of image. "I didn't see you when you told the story," remarks a fourth-grade girl. I asked, "What did you see?" "My story," she answers.

It is like dreaming wide awake. Although the narrative plot carries the logical mind along, entranced with curiosity to know what will happen next, the images and meaning of story sink downward, plunging the listener deeper and deeper—drawing upward the richest source of intuitive knowing, memory, compassion, and wisdom. It is a gossamer, yet vivid, multilayered shadow play which cannot be reconstructed by the logical mind. It is dreaming. It is awake. It is alert.

Louis Bird, an Omuskego Cree elder said about telling stories:

How do you train your young ones or your next generation so they survive? To have skills you need a lot of education first. You need to see and act and experience everything but you must learn before you acquire skills to survive. The lessons are hard in the beginning. The lessons as story are told as soon as they can understand. They are geared as they grow. They change. There are different ways of telling them as the person grows older. They are flexible. They work because they also make the mind of the person flexible, able to live that kind of life. These stories help you live.

Life is dangerous without skills. The inner person has to be prepared to sustain the unpredictability of weather and mind, the intensity of experiencing sorrow and joy, acknowledging fear, change, and the truth of death. Without passing through the pulsating threshold of fear, the hero or heroine would remain ever stuck at the beginning of the story, enclosed in a fortress of systems and rigid beliefs.

In the Native American Modoc myth of Kokolimalayas (the Bone Man), an orphaned boy, Nulwee, is told that he must kill the monster that murdered his parents, destroyed his village, and caused the earth to be barren. His grandmother tells him the story. He is terrified. "How can I kill that monster?" The listener, hearing the story, asks the same thing. The boy's preparation is long and surprising. He is warned against waking the monster, but disobeys. He wakes the monster, watching him grow bone by bone back to life. He feeds the Bone Man, providing it with strength and size. Only then does he confess to his grandmother what he has inadvertently done. She then prepares him for the next stage of his initiation, more fearful than the first. He must learn to use the bow and arrow skillfully to save his life, and to think clearly on his feet while knowing absolute fear.

"Grandma," stutters the boy dressed for battle, "I am afraid."

She answers, while pushing him out the door to what might be his death, "A good warrior is always afraid."

In this way, the boy is educated to overcome his fear, not by escaping it, but by the total immersion in it while conscious. It is as if hidden in the darkest recesses of our fear itself lies the sustaining awareness of fearlessness. We, the listener, tremble for the boy Nulwee, because we have seen the monster, and we tremble for ourselves who will now confront him again.

The secret of the power of story is the essential realization that what happens to the character in the story is not important. What is of value is what happens to us who listen. In truth, the character does not exist except in our own invention of him or her. We have manifested all the characters, even the landscape, from within, just as a disciple embodies the energy of a deity and landscape within themselves during practice and prayer; or the masked sacred dancer calls for the spirits of the gods and demons and brings them to our world to be seen, felt, feared, and loved.

Of course, the listener is tricked, just as the boy is tricked. The necessary activity is to awaken the monster in the story and in ourselves. Logically, none of us would do it. In the fairytale, the heroine is warned, "Don't open that door" or "You can use any key but the tiny silver one. Don't use that key." Or as the grandmother cautions, "Sing the old holy songs and not your childish songs." Frightened into forgetfulness, Nul-wee sings those childish songs, bringing the skeleton back to life. Fear numbs the logical mind, awakening the dreaming mind to carry out what needs to be done.

The listener hears the warning and undergoes the consequences simultaneously. It is we who invest the monster with being, dress him into reality, and raise him up bone by bone. We feed him while the grandmother we have conjured waits in the distance, and the ghosts of invoked ancestors watch. We even summon the barren land and silent sky, pregnant with possibility and ready to be renourished.

Such profuse and brilliant creativity sleeps within, on the other side. It is fear that crumbles the thick walls of familiar convention and habitual patterns of ignorance. And it is fear that opens us to what treasures lie in wait within. In fairytales it is so often the youngest, least developed of the characters who is able to break through convention and acknowledge fear with humility and compassion. The trembling hero of "The Golden Apples" faces more and more fearful obstacles until he gives up hope. He destroys the final and most grotesque monster without hesitation in order to save twelve eagle babies in an uncanny place, two worlds beneath our own. In gratitude, the eagle mother attempts to save him and carry him home on her back. Midway, she loses strength and they begin to plummet toward death. The hero has no more fear of death. It has been transformed into compassion, which arises simply as a selfless act:

> *The prince felt pity for the eagle mother and her children. He took out a tiny knife and cut flesh from his own leg to feed her. When she tasted human flesh, she did not swallow, but she was nourished by his kindness and carried him back to this world.*

Her flight, like the shaman's flight, carries us back home. With her magic she healed him and then flew back to her children.

And so the young warrior Nulwee, instructed by his grandmother, confronts the monster for the last time knowing full well that at risk are not only his own life but also those of his grandmother, the people of the future, and the earth.

> *The boy's heart beat swiftly. His entire body shook, but he pressed his feet to the earth and faced the monster. His arrow pierced the monster and the Bone Man's heart flew from him. Nulwee caught it in his basket and began to run. The monster stumbled after him, but without a heart, the Bone Man had no strength and fell to the ground.*

In the fairytale, the hero still has to outwit his evil brothers in order to win the princess and to tell his story from beginning to end. In the myth, Nulwee throws the monster's heart into the sky and it transforms into thunder, bringing the long-needed rain.

At the threshold of the new or unknown is fear. The knowledge of fear is not abstract; instead, it is central to our awakening. In the cremation ground in India, the Hindu pilgrim invokes the wrathful aspect of Shiva: "The world considers You inauspicious, O Destroyer of fear, who plays in the Smashan smeared with the ashes from funeral pyres, wearing a necklace of human skulls, with ghouls for comrades. But for those who remember You with devotion, O Bestower of Boons, You are supremely auspicious."

Ultimately, Fear is in service of compassion. We, who have become all the characters, feel the pain and selflessness of the prince who offers his own flesh. The feeling evoked by this fearless act arises forcefully because we have been opened and prepared by the deep listening. Furthermore, because we are everyone, not hero or heroine alone, within us the consequences of actions have been enacted and felt. Such unbiased awareness is the mother of true compassion.

The terrible demons, wrathful goddesses and gods, monsters and nightmares, are hideous to the naked eye. "How frightening she is," we remark on seeing the eight-headed Mahakalis depicted in temples, or the headless blood-drinking goddesses of India and Tibet, or the unbearable monsters in our own dreams. Robert Svoboda, writing about the cremation grounds rites, expounds,

> Most people, unfortunately, are so attached to their snares [the emotions which cloud the mind] that they shrink from her in fear … thinking, "She wants to kill me." She does want to kill you—the false you, the limited you, which is accrued over so many births—when She cuts off your head, your mind becomes firm, unwavering in its concentration, which enables you to succeed.

Recently, I was barred from telling ghost stories to children in a conservative school, because it would frighten them and because of the school's religious beliefs. The level of child and adult violence in this city was frightening. Later that afternoon, in another school, after an hour of stories, the children asked for more. "What shall I tell?" I asked. In unison they called out, "Something scary." And so I proceeded, slowly, deliciously, to bring ghosts and demons into view, in the visceral, vivid, yet safe world of story—knowing that if I did not, the demons would clamor for attention and rise up again and again in our world. In this world, we do not know what to do with them except to build more prisons in which to control and hide them, or to make more wars to conquer them. The fairytale offers us a daring solution within ourselves.

When the two deceptive brothers of the prince see him, they say, "Don't believe a word he says. He is a liar and a coward." However, when the prince tells his story those who hear him know it is the truth and the two brothers are placed in a dungeon. The prince marries the youngest princess, whom he brought back to this world, but the golden apples don't grow again.

Not until princess becomes queen and prince becomes king. Then, united, they visit the two brothers, who by now have understood the full consequences of their evil. They who feared fear and caused betrayal become the protectors of the kingdom and vow to serve the king and queen and all the people, even the animals.

And that winter the three golden apples grew on the tree. There was no hunger of heart or belly and everyone lived happily ever after. Those of you who have listened and made the golden apples grow in your minds, may you live as well.

Parabola
Volume: 1.1
The Hero

THE TRAGIC HERO

Edward F. Edinger

What is mythology, and why should we study it?

To begin with, it fixes in concrete, graspable forms the universal, archetypal realities which underlie psychic experience, and which determine that experience—especially whenever these determinant factors are unconscious. A knowledge of mythological images is an essential requirement if the ego is to have a conscious relation to the deeper layers of the psyche, for they provide forms and categories of understanding by which to grasp and consciously to realize the nature of the transpersonal powers. The ego that lacks these categories of understanding will be either confined to the shallow level of personalistic meanings, or it will be taken over by the archetypal energies and forced to live them out unconsciously. So, as I see it, the psychological answer to the question of "Why study mythology?" is that the psyche will otherwise be invisible and that only through acquaintance with the mythological images is the psyche made manifest in its origins, its structure, and its transformations.

Mythology, it seems, performs the same service for developing culture and consciousness as does Athena's mirror for Perseus facing Medusa. In fact, this image of Athena's mirror is a very apt symbol for human culture in general because what culture, and mythology in particular, does is break up the terrifying totality of being into graspable images. The function corresponds to what Shakespeare has to say about the nature of drama in *Hamlet*: "The purpose of the playing is to hold as 'twere the mirror up to nature, to show virtue her own feature, scorn her own image, and the very age and body of the time his form and pressure." Myths promote consciousness, providing the relevant connections with our own personal life can be made. One must always ask, "How does this relate to me?" It sometimes happens that finding one's own particular myth or the particular myth that's operating at a given time in given circumstances can be a very moving experience that carries with it a kind of shock of recognition, a sudden realization that that is I that's looking back at me from the collective mythological images.

Greek mythology is one of the two main roots of the Western psyche, the other being Judaeo-Christian mythology. And the Greek myths are therefore our "scriptures" just as much as the Bible is, and should be approached with equal seriousness. Because myths are not stories of remote happenings in the past; they are dramas that are living themselves out repeatedly in our own personal lives and in what we see around us here and now. To be aware of this adds a dimension to existence which is usually reserved for the poets. Moses is eternally bringing down the law from Sinai. Jesus is eternally being crucified and resurrected. Likewise, Hercules is eternally performing his labors; Perseus continues to confront Medusa; Theseus forever stalks the Minotaur; and all the other myths are always recurring everywhere about us and within us. It may even be that Plato discovered his concept of the eternal ideas from contemplating the Greek myths.

It is from this perspective, viewing myth from the vantage of psyche, that I want to treat the theme of the tragic hero.

Viewed psychologically, the mythological hero can be defined as a personification of the urge to individuation. He stands midway between the Self and the ego—less than Self but more than ego. The tragic hero is more human than the mythological hero. He has no supernatural powers. He is a limited human being caught like Laocoön in the coils of a transpersonal destiny. He represents the ego gripped by the process of individuation.

The figure of the tragic hero emerged from two outstanding and inter-related instruments of civilization created by the ancient Greeks— the sacred games and the ritual drama. It is indicative of their psychological similarity that we refer to both games and drama by the same word, play. These action-forms give human energies a second world in which to function. We are apt to forget the crucial role that games and athletic contests played in civilizing the aggressive energies of early man. Nietzsche had a profound understanding of this fact as indicated by the following passage:

> When a victor in a fight among the cities executes the entire male citizenry in accordance with the laws of war and sells all the women and children into slavery, we see in the sanction of such a law that the Greeks considered it an earnest necessity to let their hatred flow forth fully; in such moments crowded and swollen feeling relieved itself; the tiger leaped out, voluptuous cruelty in his terrible eyes. Why must the Greek sculptor give form again and again to war and combat in innumerable repetitions: distended human bodies, their sinews tense with hatred or with the arrogance of triumph; writhing bodies, wounded; dying bodies, expiring? Why did the whole Greek world exult over the combat scenes of the Iliad? I fear that we do not understand these in a sufficiently "Greek" manner; indeed, that we should shudder if we were ever to understand them "in Greek." [1]

It is these wild and primitive energies that are contained, channeled, and finally transformed by means of organized games and athletic contests. In the beginning, the games were always dedicated to a god, indicating that the athletes' efforts were being offered up to a transpersonal meaning. Indeed, a transpersonal meaning is achieved whenever we succeed in transforming primitive psychic energy by humanizing it.

At such times we are serving the grand enterprise of the evolution of consciousness. I think this is Plato's meaning when he speaks about the need for men to play, in that late work written in his old age, *The Laws*:

> God is the real goal of all beneficent serious endeavor. Man, as we said before, has been constructed as a toy for God, and this is, in fact, the finest thing about him. All of us then, men and women alike, must fall in with our role and spend life in making our play as perfect as possible. We should pass our lives in the playing of games—certain

*games that is, sacrifice, song, and dance—with the result of ability to
gain heaven's grace.*

In later thinking the athletic contest, the *agone*, became a paradigm
for spiritual development. St. Paul used it for that purpose.[2] Today we
can see it as a symbol of the individuation process.

Drama is another type of play which has the capacity to transform
primitive psychic energy. Originally the drama was the ritual acting-out
of a myth. While watching the drama, the spectators became identified
with the mythical happening being portrayed, allowing them to participate briefly in the archetypal level of reality. We know from psychotherapeutic experience that an encounter with the archetypal dimension
can have healing and transformative effects. Drama is certainly very
important psychologically and has many parallels to dreams. Aristotle
described the effect of watching tragedy as a catharsis in which one has
the opportunity to release the emotions of pity and fear. The idea is that,
just as a possessed person is calmed by the playing of frenzied music, so
sad and fearful people are relieved by seeing the emotions which grip
them acted out. Thus, the play functions as a mirror which provides an
image to objectify the inner affect. Modern psychology can add another
aspect to the significance of tragic drama. The tragic hero depicts the ego
undergoing individuation. Individuation is, in part, a tragic process. We
define it as the ego's progressive awareness of and relation to the Self.
But, as Jung has taught us, "the experience of the self is always a defeat
for the ego," and a defeat for the ego is experienced as tragedy.

Gilbert Murray has given us a valuable description of the origin and
basic features of the classic tragedy. It is his view that Greek tragedy
started as the ritual re-enactment of the death and rebirth of the year-
spirit (equated with Dionysus), and that this ritual re-enactment had
four chief features. First, there was an agone or contest in which the pro-
tagonist, the representative of the year-spirit, is in contest with darkness
or evil. Secondly, there is a *pathos* or passion in which the hero undergoes
suffering and defeat. Third is a *threnos* or lamentation for the defeated
hero. And fourthly, there is a *theophany*, a rebirth of life on another level
with a reversal of emotion from sorrow to joy. This sequence is basically
the same as the ritual drama of Osiris and of Christ, each of which has
the characteristic features of the death and rebirth of the year-spirit. In

later Greek tragedy the final phase, the theophany, almost disappears, perhaps remaining only as a hint. In psychological terms we can say that the sequence of steps which constitute the tragic process involves the overcoming of the ego, the defeat of the conscious will, in order for the Self, the final epiphany, to manifest.

The Shakespearean scholar, Bradley, speaks of the tragic hero in terms of a fatal flaw. This would correspond to what Jungian psychology knows as the problem of the inferior function. One side of the circle of the personality is always undeveloped and open to the depths. The so-called "fatal flaw" is thus a typical and characteristic feature of the individual psyche. Bradley also speaks of Shakespeare's tragic heroes as having "a fatal tendency to identify the whole being with one interest, object, passion, or habit of mind." This, likewise, is a well-known psychological phenomenon in which the ego identifies with the superior function; but that identification with its greatest strength then leads to its falling victim to its greatest weakness. Bradley has a description of tragedy that is relevant to our purpose. He writes:

> ... (In Shakespearean tragedy, man) may be wretched and may be awful, but he is not small. His lot may be heart-rending and mysterious, but it is not contemptible. The most confirmed of cynics ceases to be a cynic while he reads these plays. And with this greatness of the tragic hero (which is not always confined to him) is connected, secondly, what I venture to describe as the center of the tragic impression. This central feeling is the impression of waste. With Shakespeare, at any rate, the pity and fear which are stirred by the tragic story seem to unite with, and even to merge in, a profound sense of sadness and mystery, which is due to this impression of waste. "What a piece of work is man," we cry; "so much more beautiful and so much more terrible than we knew! Why should he be so if this beauty and greatness only tortures itself and throws itself away?" We seem to have before us a type of the mystery of the whole world, the tragic fact which extends far beyond the limits of tragedy. Everywhere, from the crushed rocks beneath our feet to the soul of man, we see power, intelligence, life and glory, which astound us and seem to call for our worship. And everywhere we see them perishing, devouring one another and destroying themselves, often with dreadful pain, as though they

came into being for no other end. Tragedy is the typical form of this mystery, because that greatness of soul which it exhibits oppressed, conflicting and destroyed, is the highest existence in our view. It forces the mystery upon us, and it makes us realize so vividly the worth of that which is wasted that we cannot possibly seek comfort in the reflection that all is vanity.

Bradley expresses beautifully how the fourth phase of the ritual drama of the year-spirit, the phase of theophany, which no longer appears in the tragic drama itself, is transferred to the experience of the spectator. In watching the tragedy, the spectator becomes aware of the transpersonal worth of man. The spectator becomes the ground, so to speak, on which the theophany is experienced.

This same sequence of four stages—the *agone* or contest, the *pathos* or defeat, the *threnos* or lamentation, and the *theophany*—is found in all important processes of psychological development and certainly in every psychotherapeutic process that goes at all deep. At times a given phase may repeat itself. For example, take the first phase, the agone or contest. As long as the agone ends in success, the process won't go any further. It is short-circuited, so to speak, and the happy victor leaves the scene little knowing that he has missed the main thing. But no one experiences success perpetually; sooner or later defeat does come, and that then leads to the possibility of the completion of the sequence.

Let us examine now the two Oedipus plays of Sophocles, *Oedipus the King* and *Oedipus at Colonus*, as an example of the tragic process. These plays are of particular significance to depth psychology because Oedipus was the first archetype to be discovered. Freud made the important observation that this archetype can give rise to a complex, the so-called Oedipus complex. Since then we have learned that any archetypal image can manifest itself as a personal complex in the individual psyche. Other tragic hero figures besides Oedipus can be at the root of complexes. I have personally seen an Orestes complex, an Iphigenia complex, a Hamlet complex and a Coriolanus complex.

Oedipus the King begins in the middle of the story and requires an introduction to bring the reader up to date. Because of an oracle that prophesied that Oedipus would kill his father and marry his mother, Oedipus was abandoned at birth and left for dead. However, unbeknown to his parents, a shepherd rescued him and took him to the king of Corinth, who adopted him and reared him in his own house. About fifteen years before the opening of the play, Oedipus had been told by the oracle at Delphi that he was destined to murder his father and marry his mother. Shocked by this prediction, he determined never to go back to Corinth whose king and queen he thought were his parents. His wanderings brought him eventually to the city of Thebes where his real father and mother were reigning. However, on the way he brawled with an old man in a carriage over the right of way, and in a fit of temper, killed him. Arriving at Thebes, he finds the city in an uproar because the king, Laius, has gone on a journey and never returned. Also a female monster, the Sphinx, has taken up a position on a rock outside Thebes and is strangling the inhabitants one by one because they are not able to answer her riddle. Oedipus answers it, and the Sphinx throws herself from the rock. The citizens in gratitude make Oedipus their king and he marries Jocasta, their widowed queen. But no one knows that Jocasta is Oedipus' real mother, and that the old man he killed on the road was Laius, his father. There follow fifteen years of apparent prosperity, but only apparent, because the gods are disgusted by the corruption that exists. Therefore Thebes is struck by a plague. The people, led by their priests and elders, flock around the great and successful Oedipus and ask him to save them. This is where the play begins.

At the start, Oedipus is in his prime. He signifies the successful, confident ego that thinks it has met life and its problems (represented by the Sphinx) successfully and has nothing more to fear. Concerning Oedipus' over-confidence, Jung writes:

> *The tragic consequences could easily have been avoided if only Oedipus had been sufficiently intimidated by the frightening appearance of the terrible or devouring mother whom the Sphinx personified. ... Little did he know that the riddle of the Sphinx can never be solved merely by the wit of man. ... A factor of such magnitude cannot be disposed of by solving a childish riddle. The riddle was, in fact, the trap which the Sphinx laid for the unwary wanderer. Over-estimating his intellect in a typically masculine way, Oedipus walked right into it.* [3]

The play begins with Oedipus in an illusory state of well-being which is broken into by the plague which has struck Thebes. He is told:

> *… look upon the city, see the storm*
> *that batters down this city's prow in waves of blood.*
> *The crops diseased, disease among the herds.*
> *The ineffectual womb rotting with its fruit.*
> *A fever-demon wastes the town*
> *and decimates with fire, stalking hated*
> *through the emptied house where Cadmus lived:*
> *while poverty-stricken night grows fat*
> *on groans and elegies in Hades Halls.*

Here we have the theme of the diseased or barren land as in the beginning of the Grail legend. The psychological counterpart to this condition is a state of depressed emptiness, a loss of energy, interest and life-meaning. This neurotic condition requires action and Oedipus, the ego, is asked to do something about it.

> *So, Oedipus, you most respected king,*
> *we plead with you to find for us a cure;*
> *some answer blown from God or—could it be?*
> *enlightenment from man…*
> *Mend the city, make her safe. …*
> *Be equal to your stature now.*
> *If king of men (as king you are),*
> *then be it of a kingdom manned and not a desert.*

Oedipus resolutely sets out to discover what is wrong. There is a distressing symptom that needs attention. This would correspond to the first indication of a psychological problem. The individual realizes he must act; so perhaps he will enter psychotherapy. In the play Oedipus sends Creon to consult the oracle at Delphi. The message that comes back is, "Banish the murderer of Laius." The unconscious has been consulted, perhaps by examining dreams, and the answer that comes is to bring the guilty one to justice. In other words, the shadow must be made conscious. Oedipus readily agrees to this procedure. Little does he know that he is the one. The evil is his own, but he still naively imagines himself innocent. Oedipus might well be told at this point, "Never send to know for whom the bell tolls; it tolls for thee."

Next, Teiresias the seer is called. The unconscious is consulted again on another level. Replies to his questions are gradually forced out of Teiresias by Oedipus. When the incriminating evidence first appears Oedipus accuses Teiresias and Creon of the crime. The first emerging awareness of the shadow leads to its projection. But that won't hold up, and Oedipus' origin gradually unfolds as he seeks it out. The shepherd is questioned and Oedipus learns that he is, in fact, Jocasta's child. Jocasta realizes the dreadful truth and disappears within. Finally and cataclysmically the insight bursts upon Oedipus that *he* is the one. Awareness of his identity and his guilt conjoined rushes in on him and he cries:

> *Lost! ah lost! At last it's blazing clear.*
> *Light of my eyes, good bye—my final gaze!*
> *My birth all sprung revealed from those it never should;*
> *myself entwined with those I never could;*
> *and I the killer of those I never would.*

He goes into the palace, sees Jocasta who has hanged herself, and blinds himself with the pins of Jocasta's brooches.

The symbol of blindness has an important role in the Oedipus plays. It has a paradoxical quality. At the moment that Oedipus sees himself as he really is, he blinds himself. Earlier Teiresias had said to him,

> *I'm blind you say. You mock at that! I say*
> *you see and still are blind—appallingly:*
> *Blind to your origins and to a union*
> *in your house. Yes, ask yourself, "where are you from?"*
> *You'd never guess what hate is dormant in your home*
> *or buried with your dear ones dead;*
> *or how a mother's and a father's curse*
> *will one day scourge you with its double thongs*
> *and whip you staggering from the land.*
> *It shall be night where now you boast of day.*

Oedipus had been blind all along, but when he sees his blindness he blinds himself. When he can see physically, he is blind psychologically; and as he comes to see psychologically, he becomes blind physically. Along with this paradoxical symbolism is the fact that Teiresias the seer is blind, indicating that sight of one kind is deleterious to sight of another kind—as though inner and outer sight work reciprocally.

Let us consider the nature of Oedipus' insight. What he discovered literally was that he had murdered his father and married his mother. These were probably the worst possible crimes of which ancient man could conceive. The paternal Logos principle and the maternal Eros principle have both been violated. Simultaneously, Oedipus discovers his identity and his guilt. He experiences for himself the teaching of traditional Christianity, that man is a miserable sinner. In psychological terms, Oedipus has been overwhelmed by a sudden realization of the shadow. The intensity of his reaction indicates that he has encountered not the personal shadow but the archetypal shadow. The abyss opens before him and he is utterly demoralized. There is a parallel to Oedipus' self-horror in John Bunyan's description of his own self-loathing.

> *But my original and inward pollution, that was my plague and my affliction. By reason of that, I was more loathsome in my own eyes than was a toad; and I thought I was in God's eyes too. Sin and corruption, I said, would as naturally bubble out of my heart as water would bubble out of a fountain. I could have changed heart with anybody. I thought none but the Devil himself could equal me for inward wickedness and pollution of mind. … I was both a burden and a terror to myself; nor did I ever so know, as now, what it was to be weary of my life, and yet afraid to die. How gladly would I have been anything but myself! Anything but a man! And in any condition but my own.* [4]

Oedipus the King ends with the total defeat of Oedipus. There is no theophany. This is reserved for *Oedipus at Colonus*, which is part two of *Oedipus* and is very similar to part two of *Faust*. As the second play opens, Oedipus has long been banished from Thebes and is wandering from place to place, guided by his daughter. The theme of the wanderer is characteristic of one stage of individuation. Cain was condemned to wander.

According to legend, Elijah and the Wandering Jew are both required to wander homelessly until the Messiah comes. In Gnostic thought the whole earthly life of man is considered to be a banishment from his heavenly home. One of the hexagrams of the *I Ching*, No. 56, is entitled "The Wanderer." Psychologically, the state of banishment and wandering is a necessary intermediate condition in the process of individuation. One cannot find a durable relation to the inner center, the Self, until he has been deprived of outer comfortable containments and identifications.

After long wanderings, Oedipus comes at last to a sacred spot close to Athens. He is now a sage and holy man, a precious sacred entity. His two sons, who are fighting one another for Thebes, both want his approval because an oracle has said that whoever gets his approval wins. The oracle has also announced that his tomb will bless the land it's on. Oedipus has become a sacred object, he is a living theophany. In this passage, he describes the holy power of his tomb.

> *Come, listen, son of Aegeus,*
> *I'll lay before you now a city's lasting treasure.*
> *There is a place where I must die,*
> *and I myself, unhelped, shall walk before you there.*
> *That place you must not tell to any human being:*
> *not where it lurks, nor where the region lies—*
> *if you would have a shield like a thousand shields,*
> *and a more perpetual pact than spears of allies.*
> *No chart of words shall mark that mystery.*
> *Alone you'll go: alone your memory*
> *shall frame it in that spot.*
> *For not to any persons here*
> *not even to my daughters so beloved*
> *am I allowed to utter it.*
> *You yourself must guard it always.*
> *And when your life is drawing to its close*
> *divulge it to your heir alone*
> *and he in turn to his, and so forever.*
> *This way you'll keep your city safe against the dragon seed,*
> *though many a state attack a peaceful home,*
> *though sure be the help from heaven (but exceeding slow)*

against earth's godless men and men gone mad.
No such fate for you, good son of Aegeus.
But all of this you know without my telling you.
And now to that spot—God signals me.

The life of Oedipus, as it is revealed in these two plays, parallels the alchemical process. Like the *prima materia* with which the alchemists began, Oedipus is subjected to fiery ordeals and sufferings until he is transformed into a sacred object that benefits all who touch him. Here is the theophany that redeems the suffering of the first play.

Taken together, the two Oedipus plays reveal explicitly the four stages of tragedy previously mentioned. The first, the agone or contest, is represented by Oedipus' encounter with the Sphinx, followed later by the struggle to discover the hidden knowledge that was causing the plague. The second stage, the pathos or passion, corresponds to the blinding insight and the ego-defeat which it caused. The threnos or lamentation is represented by the chorus which bemoans the downfall of the mighty Oedipus followed by Oedipus' prolonged wanderings. The fourth stage, the theophany, comes at the end of *Oedipus at Colonus* when his tomb becomes a sacred sanctuary and a perpetual blessing. These four stages portray quite precisely the steps in every major increase of consciousness. In each case a suffering, deflating ordeal for the ego must precede the epiphany of the Self. This is necessary because the ego starts out in a state of identification with the Self. It can only realize its separate and dependent condition by a tragic ordeal which enforces the separation. Sophocles describes this process in the final lines of *Antigone*.

Where wisdom is, there happiness will crown
a piety that nothing will corrode.
But high and mighty words and ways
are flogged to humbleness, till age,
beaten to its knees, at last is wise.

Notes:

1. Friedrich Nietzsche, "Homer's Contest," in *The Portable Nietzsche*, ed. by Walter Kaufman (New York: Viking, 1968), p. 33.

2. 1 Cor. 9: 24-27

3. C. G. Jung, *Symbols of Transformation, Collected Works* Vol 5. (Princeton: Princeton University Press, 1957), para. 264 and 265.

4. Quoted in William James, *Varieties of Religious Experience* (New York: New American Library, 1958), p. 155.

Parabola
Volume: 15.1
Time and Presence

THE CRACK BETWEEN TWO WORLDS

Ananda K. Coomaraswamy

"All waits undreamed of in that region, that inaccessible land"
—Walt Whitman

The subject of "Clashing Rocks" has been dealt with at considerable length [in mythological studies][1]; but although so fully treated, the subject is by no means exhausted, and remains of absorbing interest, especially if we are concerned at the same time with the universal distribution and with the significance of the motif.

Here, for the sake of brevity, we are considering only a single component of the complex pattern, that of the "Active Door." It has been quite generally recognized that these Wandering Rocks "presuppose the ancient popular belief in a doorway to the Otherworld formed by clashing mountain-walls."[2]

We can cite an American Indian myth in which, amongst the series of living obstacles that bar the way of the hero Nayanezgani there are not only "Crushing Rocks" which he stays apart, but also "Cutting Reeds" which "tried to catch him, waving and clashing together."

The Cutting Reeds are, of course, only one of the many forms of the Active Door, of which the passage is so dangerous.

As we shall presently come to see more clearly, the two leaves or jambs of the Active Door at the same time stand for the "pairs of opposites" or "contraries" of whatever sort, between which the Hero must pass in the Quest of Life, without hope or fear, haste, or delay, but rather with an equanimity superior to any alternative.

An unmistakable reference to the Clashing Rocks is to be found in *Rig Veda*, VI.49.3, where the "Rocks" are *times*, viz., day and night, described as "clashing together and parting." This is an important case, whether we consider day and night as *times* or as *light and darkness*. Its bearing will be realized if we recall that the Vedic Hero's greatest feat is performed at dawn; Indra has agreed that he will not slay Namuci "either by day or by night," and keeps his word to the letter by lifting his head at dawn, thus dividing heaven from earth and making the sun rise—dividing the light from the darkness, and day from night. It is no wonder, then, that the Mahavra's feat is so often described as having been performed "suddenly" and "once for all," for whatever is done when it is neither day nor night is done *ex tempore, sub specie aeternitatis* and forever.

Conversely, for those who are already in time and would be liberated, would *s'eternar*, day and night are, as it were, two impassible, revolving Seas or wandering Pillars, and one should not perform the Agnihotra (sacrifice of the burnt-offering) either by day or by night but only at dusk (after sunset and before dark), and at dawn (after dark and before sunrise).

> *Night and day are the sea that carries all away, and the two twilights are its fordable crossings; and as a man would cross over it by its fordable crossings, so he sacrifices at twilight ... Night and day, again, are the encircling arms of Death; and just as a man about to grasp you with both arms can be escaped through the opening between them, so he sacrifices at twilight ... this is the sign of the Way-of-the-Gods, which he takes hold of, and safely reaches Heaven.[3]*

In the same way for Philo, day and night, light and darkness, are archetypal contraries, divided in the beginning "lest they should be always clashing" by median boundaries, dawn and dusk, which are not sensible extents of time but "intelligible forms"; and though he does not say so, it is evident that if anyone would return from the chiaroscuro of this world to the "supercelestial" Light of lights he will only be able to do so—if he *is* able—by the way of these "forms" in which the day and night are *not* divided from one another.

Thus the Way "to break out of the universe"[4] into that other order of the Divine Darkness that Dionysus describes as "blinding by excess of light," and where the Darkness and the Light "stand not distant from one another, but together in one another,"[5] is the single track and "strait way" that penetrates the cardinal "point" on which the contraries turn; their unity is only to be reached by entering in there where they actually coincide. And that is, in the last analysis, not any where or when, but within you: "World's End is not to be found *by walking*, but it is within this very fathom-long body that the pilgrimage must be made."[6]

> *Our soul is, as it were, the day, and our body the night;*
> *We, in the middle, are the dawn between our day and night.*[7]

H. Rink[8] records from Greenland the myth of the Eskimo hero Giviok, whose way to the Otherworld, in which he finds his dead son living, is confronted by "two clashing icebergs," with only a narrow passage between them, alternately opened and closed. He cannot circumnavigate them because, when he tries to do so, *they always keep ahead of him*.[9] He therefore speeds between them, and has barely passed when they close together, bruising the stern-point of his *kayak*. As Professor A. B. Cook sees, this is "a mariner's version of the gateway to the Otherworld." In this northern setting, the floating islands are naturally thought of as icebergs.

It is a highly characteristic feature of the "Active Door" that whoever or whatever passes through it must do so with all speed and suddenly, and even so may be docked of its "tail"; which tail may be either the stern-point of a boat or one of two brothers; or, if there is a flock of birds (doves of Zeus or Eskimo geese), then the last of the line; or if the Hero wins through, his pursuer may be caught.

It remains only to consider the full doctrinal significance of the Symplegades.[10] What the formula states literally is that whoever would transfer from this to the Otherworld, or return, must do so through the undimensioned and timeless "interval" that divides related but contrary forces, between which, if one is to pass at all, it must be "instantly." The passage is, of course, that which is also called the "strait gate" and the "needle's eye." What are these contraries, of which the operation is "automatic"? We have already seen that the antitheses may be of fear and hope, or north and south, or night and day. These are but particular cases of the polarity that necessarily characterizes any "conditioned" world. A "world" without pairs of opposite—good and evil, pleasure and pain, love and hate, near and far, thick and thin, male and female, positive and negative—would be an "unconditioned" world, a world without accidents, change or becoming, logically inconceivable and of which experience would be impossible.

It is, then, precisely from these "pairs" that liberation must be won, from their conflict that we must escape, if we are to be freed from our mortality and to be as and when we will: if, in other words, we are to reach the Farther Shore and Otherworld "where every where and every when are focused," "for it is not in space, nor hath it poles."[11]

It is then deeply significant that in the Greenland saga, the Hero, on his way to the Otherworld in which he finds his "dead" son "living," cannot circumvent the paired bergs (which are the "lions in his path"), for they "always get ahead of him" however far he goes to either side. It is inevitably so, because the contraries are of indefinite extension, and even if we could suppose an equally indefinite journey to the point at which "extremes meet," this would be still a meeting place of both extremes, and there would be no way through to a beyond or a within except at their meeting point.

It is for the same reasons that the passage must be made so "suddenly": it is from the world of time (i.e., past and future) to an eternal Now; and between these two worlds, temporal and timeless, there can be no possible contact but in the "moment without duration" that for us divides the past from the future, but for the Immortals includes all times.

The "moment" has come at last to understand the poignant words of Nicolas of Cusa in the *De visione Dei* (Ch.IX, *fin.*): "The wall of the Paradise in which Thou, Lord, dwellest, is built of contradictories, nor is there any way to enter but for one who has overcome the highest Spirit of Reason who guards its gate," and to recall the promise, "To him that overcometh will I give to eat of the Tree of Life, which is in the midst of the Paradise of God."[12] In this doctrine and assurance are reaffirmed what has always been the dogmatic significance of the

Symplegades and of the Hero's Quest,—"I am the Door" and "No man cometh to the Father but by Me."[13]

Notes:

1. Here, in addition to A. B. Cook's article "Floating Islands" in Zeus III, ii, Appendix P., we can only cite from the vast literature of the whole subject such works as G. Dumézil, *Le festin d'immortalité*, Paris, 1924; J. Charpentier, *Die Suparnasaga*, Uppsala, 1920; S. Langdon, *Semitic Mythology*, Boston, 1931; J. L. Weston, *From Ritual to Romance*, Cambridge, 1920; R. S. Loomis, *Celtic Myth and Arthurian Romance*, New York, 1927; A. C. L. Brown, *The Origin of the Grail Legend*, Cambridge, 1943; E. L. Highbarger, *The Gates of Dreams*, Baltimore, 1940.

2. A. B. Cook. *op.cit.* See also, for other material on this subject, Coomaraswamy, "The Symbolism of the Dome," and "Svayamātrnnā, Janua Coeli."

3. Kausītaki Brāhmana II.9.

4. Hermes Trismegistus, *Lib.* XI.2.9, note 48.

5. Jacob Boehme, *Three Principles*, XIV.78.

6. Samyutta-Nikāya I. 62.

7. Rūmī, *Dīvān*, cited in Nicholson's "Additional Notes," p. 329.

8. *Tales and Traditions of the Eskimo* (London, 1875), pp. 157-161.

9. "For there is no approach by a side path here in the world"—Maitri Upanishad VI. 30.

10. The Symplegades, classical archetype of the Clashing Rocks, were two floating islands in the Euxine Sea, which came together crushing all between them; Jason and the Argonauts passed them successfully on their voyage to find the Golden Fleece, only grazing the Argo's stern.

11. Dante, *Paradiso*. XXIX.22 and XXII.67.

12. Revelation 2:7.

13. St. John X:9 and XIV:6.

Coomaraswamy, Ananda K.; *Coomaraswamy:Selected Papers.* © 1977 Princeton University Press, 2005 renewed PUP. Reprinted by permission of Princeton University Press.

CHAPTER TWO

•

THE COSMIC MODEL

The architectonic symbolism of the Center may be formulated as follows:

*1. The Sacred Mountain—where heaven and earth meet—is
situated at the center of the world.*
*2. Every temple or palace—and, by extension, every sacred city or royal
residence—is a Sacred Mountain, thus becoming a Center.*
*3. Being an axis mundi, the sacred city or temple is regarded as the meeting
point of heaven, earth, and hell.[1]*

—Mircea Eliade

*When the priest or shaman took his stand at the navel of the earth, his
upright body coincided with the axis of the universe. The North Star—the
only still point in all the turning heavens and hence the doorway
to timelessness—was the "north nail," the point where the upper
end of this axis mundi turned in its socket or passed through the
dome of the sky to the unconditioned realm beyond. In the daytime,
the sun at the zenith became the doorway in and out of time
(the Sundoor). On the scale of the body, this role was played by the
opening in the top of the skull through which the spirit was supposed to
enter the body at birth and depart at death.[2]*

—Martha Heyneman

*... the Sun is described as seven-rayed; of which seven, six represent the arms
of the three-dimensional cross of spiritual light ... by which the universe
is at once created and supported. Of the six rays, those which correspond to
the zenith and nadir correspond with our Axis of the Universe. The seventh
ray alone passes through the Sun ... and is represented accordingly ... by*

the point at which the arms of the three-dimensional cross intersect. ... It is by this "best ray" ... that the "heart" of every separated essence is directly connected with the Sun. ... when the separated essence can be thought of as returned to the center of its own being, ... this seventh ray will evidently coincide with the Axis of the Universe. In the case of the Buddha's "First Meditation," it is evidently just because he is for the time being completely reverted and thus analogically situated at the "navel of the earth," the nether pole of the Axis, that the Sun above him casts an unmoving shadow while the shadows of trees other than the one under which he is seated change their place. We need hardly say that the position of the Axis of the Universe is a universal and not a local position: the "navel of the earth" is "within you," else it were impossible to "build up Agni intellectually," as the Śatapatha Brāhmana expresses what is formulated in Christianity as the "bringing to birth of Christ in the soul." In the same way the center of every habitation is analogically the center, an hypostasized center, of the world, and immediately underlies the similarly hypostasized center of the sky at what is the other pole of the Axis at once of the edifice and of the universe it represents.

Every house is therefore the universe in a likeness ...[3]

—Ananda K. Coomaraswamy

"Further up and further in!" roared the Unicorn, and no one held back. They charged straight at the foot of the hill and then found themselves running up it almost as water from a broken wave runs up a rock out at the point of some bay. Though the slope was nearly as steep as the roof of a house and the grass was smooth as a bowling green, no one slipped. Only when they had reached the very top did they slow up; that was because they found themselves facing great golden gates.[4]

—C. S. Lewis

Parabola
Volume: 1.1
The Hero

Nostalgia for Paradise

Mircea Eliade

Certain myths and symbols have circulated throughout the world, spread by certain types of culture; this means that those myths and symbols are not, as such, spontaneous discoveries of archaic man, but creations of a well defined cultural complex, elaborated and carried on in certain human societies: such creations have been diffused very far from their original home and have been assimilated by peoples who would not otherwise have known them. *What is it that these myths and symbols answer to, that they should have had such a wide diffusion?*

The nostalgia for Paradise is universal, although its manifestations vary almost indefinitely. Are we condemned to be content with exhaustive analyses of particular manifestations and their differences? Have we no means of approach to the Image, the symbol, the archetype, in their own structures; in that "wholeness" which embraces all their "histories", without, however, confusing them? There are universally attested formulas for the "Center of the World", by which communication with Heaven is opened and the entire Universe is "saved". But the notion of "salvation" does no more than repeat and complete the notions of perpetual renovation and cosmic regeneration, of universal fecundity and of

•

sanctity, of absolute reality and, in the final reckoning, of immortality—all of which coexist in the symbolism of the Center.

In archaic and traditional societies, the surrounding world is conceived as a microcosm. At the limits of this closed world begins the domain of the unknown, of the formless. On this side there is ordered—because inhabited and organized—space; on the other, outside this familiar space, there is the unknown and dangerous region of the demons, the ghosts, the dead and of foreigners—in a word, chaos or death or night. Because they attack, and endanger the equilibrium and the very life of the city or the nation, enemies are assimilated to demonic powers, trying to reincorporate the microcosm into the state of chaos; that is, to suppress it. The destruction of an established order, the abolition of an archetypal image, was equivalent to a regression into chaos, into the pre-formal, undifferentiated states that preceded the cosmogony. Let us note that the same images are still invoked in our own days when people want to formulate the dangers that menace a certain type of civilization: there is much talk of "chaos", of "disorder", of the "dark ages" into which "our world" is subsiding. All these expressions, it is felt, signify the abolition of an order, of a Cosmos, of a structure, and the re-immersion in a state that is fluid, amorphous, in the end chaotic.

Every microcosm, every inhabited region, has what may be called a "Center"; that is to say, a place that is sacred above all. It is there, in that Center, that the sacred manifests itself in its totality, either in the form of elementary hierophanies—as it does among the "primitives" (in the totemic centers, for example, the caves where the *tchuringas* are buried, etc.)—or else in the more evolved form of the direct epiphanies of the gods, as in the traditional civilizations. But we must not envisage this symbolism of the Center with the geometrical implications that it has to a Western scientific mind. For each one of these microcosms there may be several "centers". All the Oriental civilizations—Mesopotamia, India, China, etc.—recognized an unlimited number of "Centers". Moreover, each one of these "Centers" was considered and even literally called the "Center of the World". The place in question being a "sacred space", consecrated by a hierophany, or ritually constructed, and not a profane, homogeneous geometrical space, the plurality of "Centers of the Earth" within a single inhabited region presented no difficulty. What we have here is a sacred, mythic geography, the only kind effectively *real*, as opposed to profane geography, the latter being "objective" and, as it were, abstract and non-essential—the theoretical construction of a space and a world that we do not live in, and therefore do not *know*.

In mythical geography, sacred space is the essentially *real* space, for in the archaic world the myth alone is real. It tells of manifestations of the only indubitable reality—the *sacred*. It is in such a space that one has direct contact with the sacred—whether this be materialized in certain objects (*tchuringas*, representatives of the divinity, etc.) or manifested in the hierocosmic symbols (the Pillar of the World, the Cosmic Tree, etc.). In cultures that have the conception of three cosmic regions—those of Heaven, Earth and Hell—the "center" constitutes the point of intersection of those regions. It is here that the breakthrough on to another plane is possible and, at the same time, communication between the three regions. We have reason to believe that this image of three cosmic levels is quite archaic; we meet with it, for instance, among the Semang pygmies of the Malay peninsula: at the center of their world there stands an enormous rock, Batu-Ribn, and beneath it is Hell. From Batu-Ribn a tree-trunk formerly reached up towards the sky. Hell, the center of the earth and the "door" of heaven are all to be found, then, upon the same axis, and it is along this axis that the passage from one cosmic region to another is effected. The Semang say that the trunk of a tree *formerly* connected the summit of the Cosmic Mountain, the Center of the World, with Heaven. This is an allusion to a mythic theme of extremely wide diffusion: formerly, communication with Heaven and relations with the divinity were easy and "natural"; until, in consequence of a ritual fault, these communications were broken off, and the gods withdrew to still higher heavens. Only medicine-men, shamans, priests and heroes, or the sovereign rulers, were now able to re-establish communication with Heaven, and that only in a temporary way and for their own use.

It is chiefly in the early Oriental civilizations that we meet with the archetypal image of the three cosmic regions connected in a "Center" along one axis. The name of the sanctuaries of Nippur, Lars and Sippara was *Dur-an-ki*, "link between Heaven and Earth." Babylon had a whole list of names, among others "House of the basis of Heaven and Earth" and "Link between Heaven and Earth." But there was also in Babylon the link between the Earth and the lower regions, for the town had been built upon *bāb-apsū*, the "Gate of *apsū*"; *apsū* meaning the waters of Chaos before the Creation. We find the same tradition among the Hebrews. The Rock of Jerusalem went deep down into the subterranean waters (*tehōm*). It is said in the Mishna that the Temple stood just over the tehom (the Hebrew equivalent for apsū), and just as, in Babylon, they had "the Gate of apsū", so in Jerusalem the Rock of the Temple covered the "mouth of the *tehōm.*" We encounter similar traditions in the Indo-European world. Among the Romans, for example, the *mundus* constitutes the meeting-point between the lower regions and the terrestrial world. The Italic temple was the zone of intersection between the higher (divine) world, the terrestrial world and the subterranean (infernal) world.

Every Oriental city was standing, in effect, at the center of the world. Babylon was *Bāb-ilāni*, a "gate of the Gods", for it was there that the gods came down to earth. The capital of the ideal Chinese sovereign was situated near to the miraculous Tree "shaped Wood" (*Kien-mou*) at the intersection of the three cosmic zones, Heaven, Earth and Hell. Examples could be multiplied without end. These cities, temples or palaces, regarded as Centers of the World are all only replicas, repeating *ad libitum* the same archaic image—the Cosmic Mountain, the World Tree or the central Pillar which sustains the planes of the Cosmos.

This symbol of a Mountain, a Tree or a Column situated at the Center of the World is extremely widely distributed. We may recall the Mount Meru of Indian tradition, Haraberezaiti of the Iranians, the Norse Himingbjör, "the Mount of the Lands" in the Mesopotamian traditions, Mount Tabor in Palestine (which may signify *tabbur*—that is, "navel" or *omphalos*), Mount Gerizim, again in Palestine, which is expressly named the "navel of the earth," and Golgotha which, for Christians, represented the center of the world, etc. Because the territory, the city, the temple or the royal palace thus stood at the "Center of the World"—that is, on the summit of the Cosmic Mountain—each was regarded as the highest place in the world, the only one which had not been submerged at the Deluge. "The land of Israel was not submerged by the Deluge," says a rabbinical text. And, according to Islamic tradition, the highest elevated place on earth is the Ka'aba, because "the Pole Star proves that ... it lies over against the center of Heaven." The Babylonian *ziqqurat* was, properly speaking, a cosmic mountain—that is, a symbolic image of the

Cosmos; its seven stages represented the seven planetary spheres; by ascending them, the priest attained to the summit of the Universe.

The summit of the Cosmic Mountain is not only the highest point on the Earth, it is the navel of the Earth, the point at which creation began. "The Holy One created the world like an embryo," affirms a rabbinical text. "As an embryo proceeds from the navel onward, so God began the creation of the world from its navel onward, and from thence it spread in different directions." "The world was created, beginning at Sion," says another text. The same symbolism occurs in Ancient India, in the *Rig Veda*; where the Universe is conceived as expanding outward from a central point.

The creation of man, a replica of the cosmogony, took place similarly from a central point, in the Center of the World. According to the Mesopotamian tradition, man was fashioned at the "navel of the earth," where there is also *Dur-an-ki*, the "link between Heaven and Earth." Ohrmazd created the primordial man Gajomard, at the center of the world. The Paradise in which Adam was created out of clay is, of course, situated at the Center of the Cosmos. Paradise was the "navel of the Earth" and, according to a Syrian tradition, was established "upon a Mountain higher than all the others." According to the Syrian book *The Cavern of Treasures*, Adam was created at the center of the earth, on the very same spot where, later on, the Cross of Jesus was to be erected. The same traditions have been preserved by Judaism. The Judaic apocalypse and the Midrash specify that Adam was fashioned in Jerusalem. And Adam, having been buried at the same spot where he was created—that is, at the center of the world, upon Golgotha—the blood of the Lord will redeem him also.

The most widely distributed variant of the symbolism of the Center is the Cosmic Tree, situated in the middle of the Universe, and upholding the three worlds as upon one axis. Vedic India, ancient China and the Germanic mythology, as well as the "primitive" religions, all held different versions of this Cosmic Tree, whose roots plunged down into Hell, and whose branches reached to Heaven. In the Central and North Asiatic mythologies its seven or nine branches symbolize the seven or nine celestial planes—that is, the seven planetary heavens. The majority of the sacred and ritual trees that we meet with in the history of religions are only replicas, imperfect copies of this exemplary archetype, the Cosmic Tree. Thus, all these sacred trees are thought of as situated in the Center of the World, and all the ritual trees or posts which are consecrated before or during any religious ceremony are, as it were, magically projected into the Center of the World. Let us content ourselves with a few examples.

In Vedic India, the sacrificial stake is made of a tree which is similar to the Universal Tree. While it is being felled, the priest of the sacrifice addresses these words to it: "With thy summit, do not rend the Heavens; with thy trunk, wound not the atmosphere ..." It is easy to see that what we have here is the Cosmic Tree itself. From the wood of this tree the sacrificial stake is fashioned, and this becomes a sort of cosmic pillar: "Lift thyself up, O Lord of the forest, unto the summit of the earth!" is the invocation of the Rig Veda (III, 8, 3). "With thy summit thou doest hold up the Heavens, with thy branches thou fillest the air, with thy foot thou steadiest the earth," proclaims the *Satapatha Brāhmana* (III, 7, 1, 4).

The installation and consecration of the sacrificial stake constitute a rite of the Center. Assimilated to the Cosmic Tree, the stake becomes in its turn the axis connecting the three cosmic regions. Communication between Heaven and Earth becomes possible by means of this pillar. He who makes the sacrifice does, indeed, go up to heaven, alone or with his wife, upon this post now ritually transformed into the World-Axis itself. While setting up the ladder, he says to his wife: "Come, let us go up to Heaven!" she answers: "Let us go up!" (*Sat. Br.* V, 2, i, 9), and they begin to mount the ladder. At the top, while touching the head of the post, the sacrificer cries out: "We have reached Heaven!". Or, while climbing up the steps of the stake, he stretches out his arms (as a bird spreads its wings!) and on reaching the top cries out: "I have attained to heaven, to the gods: I have become immortal" (*Taittirīya Samhitā*, 1, 7, 9). "In truth," continues the *Taittirīya Samhitā* (VI, 6, 4, 2), "the sacrificer makes himself a ladder and a bridge to reach the celestial world."

The bridge or ladder between Heaven and Earth were possible because they were set up in a Center of the World—like the ladder seen in a dream by Jacob, which reached from earth to the heavens. "And behold! the angels of God were ascending and descending on it." (Genesis XXVIII, 11-12). The Indian rite also alludes to the immortality that is attained in consequence of the ascent into Heaven. As we shall see presently, a number of other ritual approaches to a Center are equivalent to a conquest of immortality.

The assimilation of the ritual tree to the Cosmic Tree is still more apparent in Central and North Asiatic shamanism. The climbing of such a tree by the Tatar shaman symbolizes his ascension to heaven. In fact, seven or nine notches are cut in the tree and the shaman, while he is climbing up them, makes the pertinent declaration that he is going up to heaven: he describes to the onlookers all that he sees at each of the celestial levels which he passes through. At the sixth heaven he worships the moon, at the seventh, the sun. Finally, at the ninth, he prostrates himself before Bai Ulgan, the Supreme Being, and offers him the soul of the horse that has been sacrificed.

The shamanic tree is only a replica of the Tree of the World, which rises in the middle of the Universe and at whose summit is the supreme God, or the solarized god. The seven or nine notches on the shamanic tree symbolize the seven or nine branches of the cosmic Tree—that is, the seven or nine heavens. The shaman feels, moreover, that he is united with this Tree of the World through other mystical relationships. In his initiatory dreams, the future shaman is believed to approach the Cosmic Tree and to receive, from the hand of God himself, three branches of it, which are to serve as frames for his drums. We know the indispensable part that is played by the drum during the shamanic ceremonies; it is above all by the aid of their drums that shamans attain to the ecstatic state. And, when we think that *the drum is made of the very wood of the World Tree*, we can understand the symbolism and the religious value of the sounds of the shamanic drum—and why, when he beats it, the shaman feels himself transported in ecstasy near to the Tree of the World. Here we have a mystical journey to the "Center", and thence into the highest heaven. Thus, either by climbing up the seven or nine notches of the ceremonial birch-tree, or simply drumming, the shaman sets out on his journey to heaven, but he can only obtain that rupture of the cosmic planes which makes his ascension possible or enables him to fly ecstatically through the heavens, because he is thought to be already at the very Center of the world; for, as we have seen, it is only in such a Center that communication between Earth, Heaven and Hell is possible.

Among the Arctic and North American population, the centerpost of the cabin they live in is assimilated to the Cosmic Axis. And it is at the foot of this post that one deposits the offerings intended for the heavenly divinities, for it is only along this axis that offerings can mount up in to heaven. When the form of the dwelling is changed and the hut is replaced by the yurt (as, for example, among the nomadic stock-breeders of central Asia), the mythico-ritual function of the central pillar is performed through the opening left in the roof to let out the smoke. On sacrificial occasions, they bring a tree into the yurt, so that the top of it projects through this opening. This sacrificial tree with its seven branches symbolizes the seven celestial spheres. Thus, on the one hand, *the house is made to symbolize the Universe, and, on the other, is supposed to be situated in the Center of the World*, the smoke-hole opening upwards towards the Pole Star.

Let us look at the ritual of ascension that takes place in a "center". We saw that the Tatar or Siberian shaman climbs a tree, and that the Vedic sacrificer mounts a ladder: the two rites are directed to the same end, the ascension into Heaven. A good many of the myths speak of a tree, of a creeper, a cord, or a thread of spider-web or a ladder which connects Earth with Heaven, and by means of which certain privileged beings do, in effect, mount up to heaven. These myths have, of course, their ritual correlatives—as, for instance, the shamanic tree or the post in the Vedic sacrifice. The ceremonial staircase pays an equally important part, of which we will now give a few examples:

Polyaenus (*Stratagematon*, VII, 22) tells us of Kosingas, the priest-king of certain peoples of Thrace, who threatened to desert his subjects by going up a wooden ladder to the goddess Hera. The ascension to Heaven by ritually climbing up a ladder was probably part of an Orphic initiation; in any case, we find it again in the Mithraic initiation. In the mysteries of Mithra the ceremonial ladder (*climax*) had seven rungs, each being made of a different metal. According to Celsus (Origen, *Contra Celsum*, VI, 2.2), the first rung was made of lead, corresponding to the "heaven" of the planet Saturn; the second of tin (Venus) the third of bronze (Jupiter); the fourth of iron (Mercury); the fifth of "monetary alloy" (Mars); the sixth of silver (the Moon) and the seventh of gold (the Sun). The eighth rung, Celsus tells us, represented the sphere of the fixed stars. By going up this ceremonial ladder, the initiate was supposed to pass through the seven heavens, thus uplifting himself even to the Empyrean—just as one attained to the ultimate heaven by ascending the seven stages of the Babylonian *ziqqurat*, or as one traveled through the different cosmic regions by scaling the terraces of the Temple of Barabudur, which in itself constituted a Cosmic Mountain and an *imago mundi*.

We can easily understand that the stairway in the Mithraic initiation was an Axis of the World and was situated at the Center of the Universe: otherwise the rupture of the planes would not have been possible. "Initiation" means the symbolic death and resurrection of the neophyte or, in other contexts, the descent into Hell followed by ascension into Heaven. Death—whether initiatory or not—is the supreme case of a rupture of the planes. That is why it is symbolized by a climbing of steps, and why funerary rites often make use of ladders or stairways. The soul of the deceased ascends the pathways up a mountain, or climbs a tree or a creeper, right up into the heavens. We meet with something of this conception all over the world, from ancient Egypt to Australia. In Assyrian, the common expression for the verb "to die" is "to clutch the mountain". Similarly in Egyptian, *myny*, "to clutch", is a euphemism for "to die". In the Indian mythological tradition, Yama, the first man to die, climbed up the mountain and over "the high passes" in order to show "the path to many" as it is said in the Rig Veda (X, 14, 1). The road of the dead , in popular Ural-Altaic beliefs, leads up the mountains: Bolot, the Kara-Kirghiz hero and also Kesar, legendary king of the Mongols, enter into the world of the beyond by way of an initiatory ordeal, through a cave at the summit of the mountains: the descent of the shaman into Hell is also effected by way of a cavern. The Egyptians have preserved, in the their funerary texts, the expression *asket pet* (*asket* means "a step") to indicate that the ladder at the disposal of Rē is a real ladder, linking Earth to Heaven. "The ladder is set up that I may see the gods," says the *Book of the Dead*, and again, "the gods make him a ladder, so that, by making use of it, he may go up to Heaven." In many tombs of the periods of the archaic and the middle dynasties, amulets have been found engraved with a ladder (*maqet*) or a staircase. The custom of the funerary ladder has, moreover, survived until our days: several primitive Asian peoples—as, for instance, the Lolos, the Karens and others—set up ritual ladders upon tombs, to enable the deceased to ascend to heaven.

As we have just seen, the ladder can carry an extremely rich symbolism without ceasing to be perfectly coherent. *It gives plastic expression to the break through the planes necessitated by the passage from one mode of being to another*, by placing us at the cosmological point *where communication between Heaven, Earth and Hell becomes possible*. That is why the stairway and the ladder play so considerable a part in the rites and the myths of initiation, as well as in funerary rituals, not to mention the rites of royal or sacerdotal enthronement or those of marriage. But we also know that the symbolism of climbing-up and of stairs recurs often enough in psychoanalytic literature, an indication that it belongs to the archaic content of the human psyche and is not a "historical" creation, not an innovation dating from a certain historical moment (say, from ancient Egypt or Vedic India, etc.). The ideas of sanctification, of death, love and deliverance are all involved in the symbolism of stairs. Indeed, each of these modes of being represents a cessation of the profane human condition; that is, a breaking of the ontological plane. Through love and death, sanctity and metaphysical knowledge, man passes—as it is said in the Brihadāranyaka Upanishad, from the "unreal to the reality".

But it must not be forgotten that the staircase symbolizes these things because it is thought to be set up in a "center", because it makes communication possible between the different levels of being, and, finally, because it is a concrete formula for the mythical ladder, for the creeper or the spider-web, the Cosmic Tree or the Pillar of the Universe, that connects the three cosmic zones.

We have seen that it was not only temples that were thought to be situated at the "Center of the World", but that every holy place, every place that bore witness to an incursion of the sacred into profane space, was also regarded as a "center". These sacred spaces could also be constructed; but their construction was, in its way, a cosmogony—a creation of the world—which is only natural since, as we have seen, the world was created in the beginning from an embryo, or from a "center".

Let us note one thing which is of importance in our view: to the degree that the ancient holy places, temples or altars, lose their religious efficacy, people discover and apply other geomantic, architectural or iconographic formulas which, in the end, sometimes astonishingly enough, represent the same symbolism of the "Center". To give a single example: the construction of a *mandala*. The term itself means "a circle"; the translations from the Tibetan sometimes render it by "center" and sometimes by "that which surrounds". In fact a mandala represents a whole series of circles, concentric or otherwise, inscribed within a square;

and in this diagram, drawn on the ground by means of colored threads or colored rice powder, the various divinities of the Tantric pantheon are arranged in order. The mandala thus represents an *imago mundi* and at the same time a symbolic pantheon. The initiation of the neophyte consists, among other things, in his entering into the different zones and gaining access to the different levels of the mandala. This rite of penetration may be regarded as equivalent to the well-known rite of walking round a temple (*pradakshina*), or to the progressive elevation, terrace by terrace, up to the "pure lands" at the highest levels of the temple. On the other hand, the placing of the neophyte in a mandala may be likened to the initiation by entry into a labyrinth; certain mandalas have, moreover, a clearly labyrinthine character. The function of the mandala may be considered as at least twofold, and is that of the labyrinth. On the one hand, penetration into a mandala drawn on the ground is equivalent to an initiation ritual; and, on the other hand, the mandala "protects" the neophyte against every harmful force from without, and at the same time helps him to concentrate, to find his own "center".

Every human being tends, even unconsciously, toward the Center, and towards his own center, where he can find integral reality—sacredness. This desire, so deeply rooted in man, to find himself at the very heart of the real—at the Center of the World, the place of communication with Heaven—explains the ubiquitous use of "Centers of the World". We have seen above how the habitation of man was assimilated to the Universe, the hearth or the smoke-hole being homologized with the Center of the World; so that all houses—like all temples, palaces and cities—are situated at one and the same point, the Center of the Universe.

But is there not a certain contradiction here? A whole array of myths, symbols and rituals emphasizes with one accord *the difficulty of obtaining entry into a center*; while on the other hand another series of myths and rites lays it down that *this center is accessible*. For example, pilgrimage to the Holy Places is difficult; but any visit whatever to a church is a pilgrimage. The Cosmic Tree is, on the one hand, inaccessible; but on the other, it may be found in any yurt. The way which leads to the "Center" is sown with obstacles, and yet every city, every temple, every dwelling-place *is already* at the Center of the Universe. The sufferings and the "trials" undergone by Ulysses are fabulous; nevertheless *any return to hearth and home* whatever is equivalent to Ulysses' return to Ithaca.

All this seems to show that man *can live only in a sacred space*, in the "Center". We observe that one group of traditions attests the desire of man to find himself at the Center *without any effort*, whilst another group insists upon the *difficulty*, and consequently upon the *merit*, of being able to enter into it. We are not here concerned to trace the history of either of these traditions. The fact that the first-mentioned—the "easy" way which allows of the construction of a Center even in a man's own house—is found nearly everywhere, invites us to regard it as the more significant. It calls attention to something in the human condition that we have called the *nostalgia for Paradise*. By this we mean the desire to *find oneself always and without effort* in the Center of the World, at the heart of reality; and by a short cut and in a natural manner to transcend the human condition, and to recover the divine condition—as a Christian would say, the condition before the Fall.

There is an episode in the legend of Parsifal and the Fisher King, concerning the mysterious malady that paralyzed the old King who held the secret of the Grail. It was not he alone who suffered; everything around him was falling into ruins, crumbling away—the palace, the towers and the gardens. Animals no longer bred, the trees bore no more fruit, the springs were drying up. Many doctors had tried to cure the Fisher King, all without the least success. The knights were arriving there day and night, each of them asking first of all for news of the King's health. But one knight—poor, unknown and even slightly ridiculous—took the liberty of disregarding ceremony and politeness: his name was Parsifal. Paying no heed to courtly custom, he made straight for the King and, addressing him without any preamble, asked: "Where is the Grail?" In that very instant, everything is transformed: the King rises from his bed of suffering, the rivers and fountains flow once more, vegetation grows again, and the castle is miraculously restored. Those few words of Parsifal had been enough to regenerate the whole of Nature. But those few words propound the central question, the one question that can arouse not only the Fisher King but the whole Cosmos: where is the supreme reality, the sacred, the Center of Life and the source of immortality, where is the Holy Grail? No one had though, until then, of asking that central question—and the world was perishing because of that metaphysical and religious indifference, because of a lack of imagination and absence of desire for reality.

That brief episode of a great European myth reveals to us at least one neglected aspect of the symbolism of the Center: that there is not only an intimate interconnection between the universal life and the salvation of man; but that it is *enough only to raise the question of salvation*, to pose the central problem; that is, *the* problem—for the life of the cosmos to be forever renewed. For—as this mythological fragment seems to show—death is often only the result of our indifference to immortality.

Parabola
Volume: 2.3
Cosmology

The World-Tree Yggdrasil

Retold by Ann Danowitz

This version of The World-Tree Yggdrasil *is derived from the Norse* Eddas.

In the beginning, there was only the Yawning Gap. And in the north, the frozen Mist-World appeared: in the midst of it there was a well from which all the world rivers flowed. In the south, appeared the world of heat, fiery and burning. And when those frozen streams from the north pressed toward the south and met with the heat, they sent up a yeasty venom. And the venom cooled and hardened into ice; and the mist congealed to rime. And when the breath of southern heat melted the rime, it dripped. And from the yeasty drops, drip by drop, life was quickened, in the form of a great sleeping giant, Ymir.

And a sweat came over Ymir, and under his left hand there grew a male and female; one of his feet begat a son with the other. And thus the race of Rime Giants came to be. And also from the rime there came a cow, her name Audhumla. With the four streams of milk flowing from her udder, she nourished Ymir and the giants. She herself licked the blocks of ice, which were salty. And the first day she licked, hair appeared on the blocks; the second day, a man's head; and the third day she licked, the whole man appeared. His name was Buri, fair of feature, great and mighty.

And Buri begat Borr, who married the daughter of a giant, and Borr had three sons, the gods Odin, Vili, and Ve. These three young gods slew the giant Ymir and from his body they fashioned the earth.

Of his blood they made the sea and waters; of his flesh they made the land; mountains and crags of his bones, gravel and stones of his teeth and broken bones. They made Heaven of his skull and set it over the earth, and they put a dwarf under each corner to support it. Of Ymir's brain they made the clouds. Then they took fire and sparks from the south and scattered them: some to wander in the sky, others to stay always in one position. And so were made the sun, moon, and stars. And the earth was round, with the deep sea around it. The outer edge of the world they gave to the giants; and around the inner part they made a great citadel of Ymir's eyebrows. This they called Midgard, the world for men. But Midgard was silent, so the three gods took an ash tree and fashioned a man. They called him Aske. And they took an alder and made a woman called Embla. Odin gave them spirit and life; Vili gave them wit and feeling; and Ve gave them form, speech, hearing and sight, names and clothing. And high over the middle of the world, in Heaven, the gods made a city for themselves, Asgard. Odin sat there on high with his wife Frigg, ruling over the race of the gods, the Aesir. All-father is he, creator of gods and men, and of all that was fulfilled of his might.

And the mighty ash tree, Yggdrasil, sprang from Ymir's body. Passing through the very center of our world, it supports the whole universe. From crown to roots, it links and binds into one whole all of the nine worlds: Asgard, Vanaheim, Alfheim; Midgard, Jötunheim, Muspellheim; Svartalfheim, Niflheim, and the Water World. It has three great roots which strike through all worlds above Midgard and life-giving arms that spread through those below.

The first root reaches to Asgard, seat of the Aesir in Heaven. The second to Jötunheim, land of the Rime Giants, where formerly was the Yawning Gap. The third root stands over Niflheim, realm of cold and darkness, over the Fountain of Hvergelmer; this fountain feeds the serpent Nidhogg, who constantly gnaws the roots of the world tree with all his reptile brood.

Under the second root in Jötunheim stands the Fountain of Mimer. The name Mimer means knowing. He guards the wisdom of the well; he is the watcher, full of ancient lore. Every morning he drinks of its waters with the golden Gjallarhorn. Once, Odin came to beg a drink from the well of wisdom, for the giants, being older even than the gods, looked deeper into the darkness of the past. The Rime Giants had witnessed the birth of the gods, the beginning of the world; and they foresaw its downfall. For this knowledge Odin went to Mimer, for the knowledge concealed in his well. Under cover of darkness he went to Jötunheim, and penetrated the mysteries of the deep. But he had to leave his eye in payment for the draught he took from the fountain. In the morning, when the sun rose over Jötunheim, Mimer drank from his golden horn the clear mead which flowed over Odin's eye.

Under the first root, in Asgard, lies the holy Fountain Urdar. Here the gods sit in judgment, riding up every day on horseback over the rainbow bridge Bifrost. At Urdar Fountain dwell three goddesses, the three Fates Urd, Verdande, and Skuld, the past, present, and future. These guardians of the holy fountain are the Norns, and they determine the lifespan of every man. They spin the thread of his fate at birth, and mark out with it the sphere of action of his life. Their decrees are inviolable destiny; even the gods must bow before the laws of the Norns. Urd and Verande stretch a web of threads from east to west, from the dawn of life to its sunset. And Skuld tears it to pieces.

Each day, the Norns draw water from the spring at Urdar Fountain, and with the clay that lies around the well, they sprinkle the World-Tree Yggdrasil so that its branches may ever continue to be green and flourishing. This water is so holy that anything placed in it becomes as white as the film of an egg shell. Two pure white swans swim ever in the Urdar Fountain, the parents of all their race.

There are four stags which leap about the upper branches of Yggdrasil, the four winds Daain, Dvalin, Duneyr, and Durathor. And these four constantly feed upon the new growth of the tree. On its topmost bough sits an eagle who knows many things; and between his eyes sits the hawk, Vedfolner. And a little squirrel, named Ratatosk, constantly runs up and down the whole length of the tree, carrying stories, gossip and rumor, seeking to generate strife between the serpent Nidhogg and the eagle.

And Odin tethers his steed, Sleipner, to Yggsdrasil. "Yggr" means deep thinker; "drasil" horse or carrier. So Yggdrasil becomes at times the bearer of god. Odin hung once nine nights upon the tree, a sacrifice to himself, pierced by his own lance. And he won there for all the wisdom of the runes, and passed it on as a magic for gods and men.

And ever stands the World-Tree Yggdrasil, the best of trees, axis upon which the world turns. And it will tremble only to announce the coming of ragna rok, when the Sons of Muspell shall come a-harrying out of the South, and Bifrost, the Rainbow Bridge to Asgard, shall break, and even the gods must meet their fate.

Parabola
Volume: 18.3
Crossroads

SYMBOLISM OF THE CROSS

René Guénon

We refer to the cross as a symbol of the union of comple-
ments. For this purpose it suffices to envisage the cross
in the most usual manner, namely in its two-dimensional
form; to return from that to the three-dimensional
form, however, one need only remember that the single
horizontal line can be considered as the projection of the
entire horizontal plane upon the vertical plane in which
the figure is traced. In the present context the vertical
line is taken as representing the active principle, and the
horizontal line the passive one. These principles are also
respectively designated masculine and feminine, by analogy with the human order; if they are considered in their
widest sense, namely in relation to universal manifestation
in its totality, they are then the principles that the Hindu
doctrine calls *Purusha* and *Prakriti*.[1] It is not material
here to recapitulate or develop the considerations arising
out of the relationship between these two principles, but
merely to show that despite appearances there is a certain
connection between this significance of the cross and
what has been called its metaphysical significance.

In the first place, while reserving the right to return
to the point more explicitly later, we would say that this
connection follows from the relationship between the
vertical axis and the horizontal plane in the metaphysical
signification of the cross. It should be clearly appreciated

that terms such as active and passive, or their equivalents, have no meaning except in relation to each other, for complementarism is essentially a correlation between two terms. This being so, it is clear that a complementarism such as that of active and passive can be regarded at different levels, so that one and the same term may play an active or a passive role, according to what it is being placed in correlation with; but in every case it can always be said that in such a relationship the active term is, in its own order, the analogue of *Purusha* and the passive one that of *Prakriti*. Now, it will be seen later that the vertical axis, which connects together all the states of being by passing through their respective centers, is the locus of manifestation of what the Far-Eastern tradition calls the "Activity of Heaven"; and this is precisely the "actionless" activity of *Purusha*, which determines in *Prakriti* the productions that correspond to all the possibilities of manifestation. As for the horizontal plane, it will be seen that this forms a "plane of reflection," symbolically represented as "the surface of the waters," and it is well known that in all traditions the "Waters" are a symbol of *Prakriti* or "universal passivity" …[2]

The vertical and the horizontal can be taken as representing two complementary terms; but obviously the vertical and the horizontal cannot be said to oppose each other. What do clearly represent opposition, in the same figure, are the contrary directions of the two half-lines from the center which form the two halves of one and the same axis, whichever one it may be; opposition may thus be equally conceived in either the vertical direction or the horizontal …

At the center of the cross, all oppositions are reconciled and resolved; that is the point where the synthesis of all contrary terms is achieved, for really they are contrary only from the outward and particular viewpoints of knowledge in distinctive mode. This central point corresponds to what Moslem esotericism calls the "Divine station," namely "that which combines contrasts and antimonies" (*El-maqâmulilahi, huwa maqâm ijtimâ ed-diddaîn*);[3] in the Far-Eastern tradition, it is called the "Invariable Middle" (*Ching-Ying*), which is the place of perfect equilibrium, represented as the center of the "cosmic wheel,"[4] and is also, at the same time, the point where the "Activity of Heaven" is directly manifested.[5] This center directs all things by its "actionless activity" (*wei wu-wei*), which although unmanifested, or rather because it is unmanifested, is in reality the plentitude of activity, since it is the activity of the Principle whence all particular activities are derived; this has been expressed by Lao-tze as follows: "The Principle is always actionless, yet everything is done by It."[6]

Notes:

1. See *Man and his Becoming according to the Vedanta*, ch. 4.

2. *Ibid.*, ch. 5.

3. This "station" or degree of the being's effective realization, is attained by *El-fanâ*, i.e. by the "extinction" of the ego in the return to the "primordial state"; such "extinction," even as regards the literal meaning of the term denoting it, is not without analogy to the *Nirvâna* of the Buddhist doctrine. Beyond *El-fanâ*, there is still *Fanâ el-fanâi*, the "extinction of the extinction," which similarly corresponds to *Parinirvâna* (See *Man and his Becoming*, ch. 13). In a certain sense, the passage from one of these degrees to the other is related to the identification of the center of a state of the being with that of the total being.

4. See *Le Roi du Monde*, ch. 1 and 4, and *L'Esotérisme de Dante*, 3rd ed., p. 62.

5. Confucianism develops the idea of the "Invariable Middle" in the social order, whereas its purely metaphysical meaning is given by Taoism.

6. *Tao-te-Ching*, 37.

Excerpted from René Guénon, *Symbolism of the Cross*, Angus MacNab, tr. (London: Luzac & Company, 1958), pp. 27, 33, 34-35.

Parabola
Volume: 18.4
The City

THE HIERATIC CITY STATE

Joseph Campbell

Stage four in the development in the Near East of the
agriculturally based civilization from which all the high
cultures of the world have been derived took place about
3500 B.C. Half a millennium earlier, c. 4000 B.C. (the
date assigned in the Book of Genesis to the creation
of the world), a number of the neolithic villages had
begun to assume the size and function of market towns
and there had been, furthermore, an expansion of the
chalcolithic culture area southward into the mud flats
of riverine Mesopotamia. That was the period in which
the really great and still mysterious race of the Sumerians first appeared on the scene, to establish in the torrid
Tigris and Euphrates delta flats those sites that were to
become, by c. 3500 B.C., the kingly cities of Ur, Kish,
Lagash, Eridu, Sippar, Shuruppak, Nippur, and Erech.
The only natural resources in that land were mud and
reeds. Wood and stone had to be imported from the north.
But the mud was fertile, and the fertility was annually
refreshed. Furthermore, the mud could be fashioned into
sun-dried bricks that could be used for the construction
of temples—which now appear for the first time in the
history of the world, their form being of the ziggurat in
its earliest stage: a little height, artificially constructed,
supporting a chapel for the ritual of the world-generating
union of the earth goddess with a god of the sky. And if

we may judge from the evidence of the following centuries, the queen or princess of each city was in these earliest days identified with the goddess, and the king, her spouse, with the god.

During the course of the fourth millennium B.C. the temples in these riverine towns increased in size and importance, becoming the economic as well as the religious and political centers of the growing communities. And then, at a date that can now be almost precisely fixed at 3200 B.C. (the period of the archaeological stratum known as Uruk B), there appeared in this little Sumerian mud-garden—as though the flowers of its tiny cities were suddenly bursting into bloom—the whole cultural syndrome that has, ever since, constituted the ground base of the high civilizations of the world. This, the fourth and culminating stage of the development that I am here tracing, we may term that of the *hieratic city state*.

But let us pause, to repeat: We have named the proto-neolithic period of the Natufians, c. 9000 B.C., where the first signs of an incipient grain agriculture appear; the basal neolithic of the aceramic, ceramic, and early chalcolithic villages, c. 7500-4500 B.C., when the mother goddess of an already well-established peasantry makes her first dramatic appearance; then the high neolithic (middle and late chalcolithic) of the Halaf and Samarra painted wares, c. 4500 B.C., when the abstract concept of a geometrically organized aesthetic field first appears and the late neolithic market towns begin to elevate temple towers; and now, finally, we have come to an epochal date, c. 3200 B.C., when, suddenly, at precisely that geographical point where the rivers Tigris and Euphrates reach the Persian Gulf, the wonderful culture-flower comes to blossom of the *hieratic city state*.

The whole city now (not simply the temple area) is conceived as an imitation on earth of the celestial order—sociological middle cosmos, or mesocosm, between the macrocosm of the universe and the microcosm of the individual, making visible their essential form: with the king in the center (either as sun or as moon, according to the local cult) and an organization of the walled city, in the manner of a mandala, about the central sanctum of the palace and the ziggurat; and with a mathematically structured calendar, furthermore, to regulate the seasons of the city's life according to the passages of the sun and moon among the stars; as well as a highly developed system of ritual arts, including an art of rendering audible to human ears the harmony of the visible celestial spheres. It is at this moment that the art of writing first appears in the world, and that literately documented history begins. It is at this moment that the wheel appears. And we have also evidence that the two numerical systems that are still normally employed throughout the civilized world had just been developed, namely, the decimal and the sexagesimal: the former used for business accounts in the offices of the temple compounds, where the grain was stored that had been collected in taxes, and the latter used for the ritualistic measuring of space and time: three hundred and sixty degrees still represent the circumference of the circle—that is to say, the mandala of space; while three hundred and sixty days, plus five, mark the measurement of the mandala of time, the cycle of the year. And those five intercalated days—which represent the opening through which spiritual energy flows into the sphere of time from the pleroma of eternity, and which consequently, are days of feast and festival—correspond in the temporal mandala to that mystical point in the center of the spatial mandala which is the sanctuary of the temple, where the earthly and heavenly powers join. The four sides of the temple tower, oriented to the four points of the compass, come together at this fifth point, where the energy of the pleroma enters time—and so once again we have the number five added to three hundred and sixty to symbolize the mystery of the immanence of eternity in time.

This temple tower, of course, and the hieratically organized little city surrounding it, where everyone plays his role according to a celestially inspired divine plan, is the model of paradise that we find not only in the Hindu-Buddhist imagery of Mount Sumeru, the Greek Olympus, and the Aztec Temples of the Sun, but also in Dante's Earthly Paradise, for which Columbus went in search, and in the Biblical image of Eden, from which the medieval concept was developed, and which—according to the date that you will find in the marginal notes of your Bible—would have been created just about at the time of the founding of the first Sumerian towns: 4004 B.C.

It appears, in short, to have been demonstrated in a manner hardly to be doubted, that the idea of the hieratic city state, conceived as a mesocosm, or sociological imitation of the celestial order, first emerged as a paradigm in the little cities of Sumer, c. 3200 B.C., and was then disseminated westward and eastward, along the ways already blazed by the earlier Neolithic. The wonderful, life-organizing assemblage of ideas and principles—including those of writing, mathematics, and calendrical astronomy—reached the Nile and inspired the civilization of the First Dynasty of Egypt, c. 2800 B.C.; reached Crete, on one hand, and, on the other, the Indus Valley, c. 2600 B.C.; Shang China, c. 1500 B.C.; and finally Peru and Middle America—from China, by way of the Pacific?—possibly as early as c. 1000 B.C. We have, therefore, to recognize what now appears to be the demonstrated and documented fact that all of the high civilizations of the world are, finally, but so many variants and developments of a single marvelous monad of mythological inspiration—and that, whereas the history and prehistory of the human race covers some one million seven hundred and fifty thousand years, this monad was constellated and brought into a living form in the mud flats and among the reeds of Mesopotamia hardly more than five thousand years ago.

If we now should attempt to put into words the sense or meaning of this monad, the sense or character of the realization that appears to have precipitated with such force this image of man's destiny as an organ participating in the organism of the universe, we might say that the psychological requirement already noted for a coordinating principle, to bring the parts of a differentiated social body into an orderly relationship to each other and simultaneously to suggest the play through all of a higher, all-suffusing, all-informing principle or energy—this profoundly felt psychological as well as sociological requirement—must have been fulfilled with the recognition, some time in the fourth millennium B.C., of the orderly round dance of the five visible planets and the sun and moon through the constellations of the zodiac. And this celestial order was to become for all the civilizations and philosophers of the world the model of the revelation of destiny. In the words of Plato:

> *The motions akin to the divine part in us are the thoughts and*
> *revolutions of the universe; these, therefore, every man should follow,*
> *and correcting those circuits in the head that were deranged at birth,*
> *by learning to know the harmonies and revolutions of the world, he*
> *should bring the intelligent part, according to its pristine nature, into*

the likeness of that which intelligence discerns, and thereby win the fulfillment of the best in life set by the gods before mankind both for this present time and for the life to come.

The Egyptian term for this order was Ma'at; in India it is Dharma, and in China, Tao. And if we now should attempt to epitomize in a sentence the sense or meaning of all the myths and rituals that have sprung from this conception of a universal order, we might say that they are its structuring agents, functioning to bring the human order into accord with the celestial. "Thy will be done on earth, as it is in heaven." The myths and rites constellate a mesocosm—a mediating, middle cosmos, through which the microcosm of the individual is brought into relation to the macrocosm of the universe. And this mesocosm is the entire context of the body social, which is thus a kind of living poem, hymn, or icon, of mud and reeds, and of flesh and blood, and of dreams, fashioned into the art form of the hieratic city state. Life on earth is to mirror, as nearly perfectly as possible in human bodies, the almost hidden—yet now discovered—order of the pageant of the spheres. This pageant is what has shaped the mesocosm, the middle, sociological cosmos of the City; and the patterns of this mesocosm are what, then, have shaped the soul. Art and custom shape the soul: art lived—as ritual.

Parabola
Volume: 9.2
Theft

THE COSMIC BEE

Lawrence Russ

*For my thoughts are not your thoughts, neither are your ways
my ways, saith the Lord: For as the heavens are higher than the
earth, so are my ways higher than your ways, and my thoughts
than your thoughts. ... I form the light, and create darkness: I
make peace, and create evil: I the Lord do all these things.*
—Isaiah 55:8-9, 45:7

The contradictory and frightening aspects of the divine
have always been an enigma to human beings. In Norse
mythology, this enigma is embodied in the figure of Loki,
whose acts disrupt all seeming fixity and defy all apparent
divisions. He is like a Nordic Siva, dancing on skulls. The
world which he inhabits is one of danger and mystery,
where death is many-faced and ever-threatening. Even
the gods live in peril, their realm of Asgard surrounded
by menacing giants; Asgard itself is a place of deceptive
magic, shifting identities, and shadowy alliances. Odin,
chief of the gods, frequently goes about in disguise, and
practices sorcery to bring about misfortune and death.
The thunder god, Thor, who protects Asgard from the
frost-giants, consorts with giant maidens. Without questions, however, the most puzzling and unsettling figure in
Norse mythology is Loki.

Though always named as a god, Loki seems as strongly
bound to frost-giants and demons as to his fellow Aesir.

His mother and his mistress are giants. Although divine, he fathers monsters. Time and again, by his folly or scheming, Loki renders Asgard vulnerable to the plotting or assaults of its enemies. At the same time, he obtains for the gods many of their greatest treasures, such as Odin's spear, Gungnir, which never misses its mark; Thor's hammer, Mjollnir, which cannot be shattered; and Freyr's boar, Gullinbursti, who can outrun the swiftest horse, and whose golden bristles make the darkest night as light as day.

Loki's nature is as mixed as his loyalties. He changes shape and character from moment to moment. He is male, yet he not only assumes the shapes of females, but on one occasion gives birth. At times he resembles a shaman, at times a trickster. And while there is little question about Odin's majesty or Thor's strength, Loki's stature and the extent of his powers are more difficult to gauge. In some tales, he seems merely a childish prankster, a mischievous fool at Odin's court. Out for a spin in the goddess Frigg's falcon-coat, Loki can't resist flying into the giant Geirrod's castle to spy on the giant-folk. As Loki perches on the ramparts, Geirrod spots the strange "bird" and orders it seized. Loki is so delighted, though, by the sight of the clumsy henchman clambering up the wall that he tarries too long and is captured.

But in other tales, Loki acts with purposeful malevolence, and appears to have powers and resources rivaling those of any other god. No simple jester could sire children like Loki's: Hel, the demigod who holds sway over Niflheim, the underworld of the dead: Fenrir the Wolf, whose jaws can reach from the earth to the heavens; and the Midgard Serpent, whose coils encircle the globe. Loki's ultimate display of power will come at Ragnarök, the Twilight of the Gods, when he will command an army of Asgard's enemies—including the Wolf, the Serpents, Garm the giant hound, frost-giants and fire-demons, and hordes of dead men—in an apocalyptic assault on the gods' bright realm.

To add to the puzzle, the divine Loki is, quite prominently and unbecomingly, a thief. By subterfuge, he arranges the theft of Idun's golden apples, the source of the gods' immortality. He steals the dwarf Andvari's gold, giving rise to the strife which Wagner made the subject of his Ring trilogy. In a less literal way, Loki steals the life of the peaceful god Balder and the very existence of Asgard.

Theft implies that the stolen object belongs to a particular being or place, and that the offender has taken the object beyond the bounds within which it rightfully rests. To be a thief, therefore, is to violate proprieties and boundaries recognized by others. That is just what Loki does at every opportunity. He violates the boundaries between the godly and the monstrous when he turns into an aged giantess; between the divine and the bestial when he becomes a horse, a salmon, a flea. He is the most peripatetic of gods, traversing the borders between Asgard and Utgard (the outer realm of the frost-giants) for mischief, larceny, or murder. He violates propriety with foul-mouthed taunts and sexually deviant behavior, and by causing the murder of his brother and sister gods.

Loki's opposite is the sentinel god, Heimdall, whose duty, as guard of the rainbow bridge, Bifröst, is to maintain the boundary between the realms. If Heimdall's nature is defined by his task, Loki's seems similarly defined by his breaking and entering at Ragnarök, slaying Heimdall and thereby opening the reigning order to attack. Loki's transgressions bewilder and disturb even his fellow gods. In "Lokasenna" ("The Insolence of Loki"), he baits an assembly of gods with bitter gibes, accusing them of promiscuity and perversion, cowardice and dishonesty, feebleness and faithlessness, and even goes so far as to taunt them with the prospect of their doom, which he himself will bring about:

> *Now we see Jord's son before us, tough-talking Thor!*
> *But you won't be brave enough to battle*
> *the Wolf, and he'll eat Odin.*[1]

Although Loki often seems to be merely a clown or a fiend, in "Lokasenna" he claims that Odin and he are blood-brothers, and that Odin has sworn always to share his good fortune with him. Odin seems, by his silence, to assent; and indeed, in the guise of the giant-king Utgard-Loki, Loki appears as a figure akin to the All-Father. (Loki, under his usual name, appears in the same tale as Utgard-Loki; but students of the myth have felt that whether the giant-king is a remnant from older myths or a disguise of sorts, his deeds should be considered as part of Loki's history.)

In the central part of Utgard-Loki's story, Thor, Loki, and a young couple—Thjalfi ("who could run faster than anyone else") and Röskva—

gain entry to a stronghold of giants. There, the king of the land, Utgard-Loki, challenges the male visitors to engage in contests of skill. After Loki loses an eating contest and Thjalfi is embarrassed in successive foot-races, Thor suffers three apparent failures which are still more perplexing and humiliating. He first attempts a feat of drinking. But after three long draughts from a drinking-horn, he has barely lowered the level of the brew. Utgard-Loki ridicules him and urges him to try his hand at a feat the children of the kingdom perform: picking up the king's pet cat. When Thor can raise only one of its paws from the ground, Utgard-Loki is mockingly sympathetic. He invites Thor to display his wrestling prowess, but adds that since his men would consider it beneath their dignity to grapple with such a little fellow, Thor should try wrestling with Utgard-Loki's aged foster-mother, Elli. But the more Thor strains to throw her, the stronger Elli grows. At last she forces him down onto one knee, and Utgard-Loki stops the match. By that time it is late evening, and the giant-king and his court give Thor and his companions a feast, treating them royally for the rest of the night.

The dénouement comes when Utgard-Loki, after escorting his guests out of the stronghold, reveals the truth about their experience in his realm. The travelers have been deceived by his enchantments; Loki's voracious opponent was fire, and Thjalfi's fleet rival was Utgard-Loki's own thought. The king confesses that Thor's powers in truth had proven so great that the giants had been terrified: the bottom of the drinking-horn had been placed in the sea, whose level Thor had lowered visibly; the cat whose paw he'd lifted was the Midgard Serpent, whose length spans the earth; and Elli, the hag whom he had held off for so long, was none other than old age incarnate, who, as the king says, eventually trips up every man who lives long enough to meet her.

Utgard-Loki announces that he will use his spells to make certain that Thor never enters the giants' stronghold again. With that, he vanishes; and when Thor, enraged, whirls around to raze the giant's domain, he sees nothing but "spacious and beautiful plains." The strange peace of that closing phrase and the other details of the story show us a Loki with a dignity and a sense of poetry that one would expect from lordly Odin rather than from a deceitful robber of dwarves. The tale makes clear that Utgard-Loki shares with Odin a wisdom about the limitations of the finite, which circumscribe even a god like Thor.

In their creativity, too, Loki and Odin resemble one another. Odin, the god of poetry and poets, participated in the creation of the world. But there are intimations in the myths that Loki was a partner with Odin in the world's creation; and his adventures and misadventures, however self-ishly begun, frequently result in new creations for Asgard. His thefts, his crossings of boundaries, his taking of things from their "rightful" places, stir up the world of the myths, and cause the new, the unexpected, to germinate. Like a cosmic bee, Loki cross-pollinates the different realms of being. In one tale, he takes the shape of a mare in order to lure away a giant's workhorse. The offspring from that odd seduction is Sleipnir, Odin's eight-legged steed, who can cross between the lands of the living and the dead.

Nevertheless, Loki's creations often differ drastically from those of his putative blood-brothers. Whereas Odin is the sire of shining gods, Loki is the father of fiends—Fenrir, the Midgard Serpent, and Hel. Loki is not, however, the only divine creator of monsters. In the Book of Job, there is another portrait which recalls the one of Loki in the Norse myths. Jehovah speaks in an exultant way of his own monstrous mas-terworks, Behemoth and Leviathan. He directs Job's attention to His awesome and glorious creations, to his own unending pollination of the many realms of the universe, and to the inability of finite creatures to understand the works of the Infinite.

Loki forces us, as Jehovah does Job, to feel how the divine tran-scends our desires and our visions, how the suffering or destruction of the finite is sometimes required by the creative purposes of the Infinite, however cruel it may seem to us. If Utgard-Loki is wise in his knowl-edge of the finite's limitations, if Loki seems connected with every realm and kind of being, if nothing is so consistently true of Loki the thief as that he cannot allow any "rightful" boundary or separation to remain intact, it is because Loki is the active, "aggressive" agent of the Whole, the catalyst by whose action all that seems finite is dissolved in the Infinite.

As for Loki's thefts and fearsomeness, all creativity and growth require the displacement of old forms to create new combinations, the destruction of old boundaries to create new syntheses. And it is certain that new creations often inspire fear and loathing in those who cling to old structures. In the tales of Loki, as when God addresses Job from out of the whirlwind, we see how the purposes of the Infinite overwhelm the conscious interests of finite creatures. Job's terrible suffering is a necessary prelude to his closer union with the divine. At Ragnarök, almost all of the gods, including Loki, are slain, the "Earth sinks below the sea," and Asgard is incinerated; yet Ragnarok clears the way for the rise of new, more peaceful gods and an even more glorious world:

> *I see a hall fairer than the sun*
> *thatched with gold; it stands at Gimli.*
> *There shall deserving people dwell*
> *to the end of time and enjoy their happiness.*[2]

For the denizens of Scandinavian mythology, as for Job and for us, the events which bring the greatest gains in wisdom are often those which, when they occur, seem most puzzling, painful, or destructive.

We might say of Loki what the Book of Job says of Leviathan: "When he raiseth himself up, the mighty are afraid; by reasons of breakings they purify themselves ... he is king over all the children of pride."[3] In "Lokasenna," Loki assails the pride of the "mighty" continually, and frightens the gods with talk of their doom.

The terrible is an integral part of the divine. The punishments which Jehovah metes out to idolators and other transgressors in the Old Testament, however just, are terrible to contemplate. And there are shattering events in our lives which we, as finite beings, never see come to good use. There are tragedies which make us feel as if victimized by some cosmic thief who shakes our security, our sense of justice, our faith. In the face of disaster and suffering, even the uncommonly devout have been compelled at times, by their religious passion itself, to extremes of dejection or anger. Rabbi Levi-Yitzhak of Berditchev, one of the eighteenth-century Hasidic masters, for instance, was moved by the anguish of his people to argue with God, and even to challenge and threaten Him. During the Rosh Hashana services, he is said to have cried out: "If You prefer the enemy, who suffers less than we do, then let the enemy praise Your glory."[4]

Even apart from destruction and apparent evil, the Unbounded can be terrible for a finite creature to bear. In the myths of the ancient Greeks and in the Hebrew scriptures, for instance, we find the belief that no mortal, without special intercession from heaven, can endure the sight of God revealed as He truly is. Such a revelation, received without spiritual preparation and surrender, forcibly dissolves the structures of the finite self in madness or death—as Semele was consumed by the sight of Zeus in his splendor, as Loki brings about the deaths of the imperfect elder gods. The death of the remnants of self, even if it serves as a prelude to illumination, may, like Loki, be frightening and violent. We may think of John Donne's entreaty to the divine

> *... to breake, blowe, burn and make me new. ...*
> *Divorce mee, untie, or breake that knot againe,*
> *Take mee to you, imprison mee, for I*
> *Except you enthrall mee, never shall be free,*
> *Nor ever chast, except you ravish mee.*[5]

In the Torah, it is God, not Satan, who commands the services of Death. And as the Old Testament tells us that Death is not a devil, but rather an angel of the Lord, so the Norse myths tell us that Loki is a god, not a demon. It is, after all, both a terrible and wonderful thief who frees Job from his last bonds of pride by first allowing him to be robbed of his happiness, his health, and his peace; who raises Christ only after stealing his friends' loyalty, his spiritual solace, and his earthly life; who brings about the reign of the just only after breaking into the old gods' kingdom and razing it with demons' fire.

Because this guise of the divine is the most dreadful and difficult to accept, we need its symbols, our Lokis, all the more. Without an image of that which stymies our human comprehension, thwarts our finite desires, and steals from us what we cling to desperately—without Loki, Ragnarök, and the Book of Job—the myths and scriptures would fail us, would fail to reach our deepest sufferings and our greatest hopes. Without Loki and his ilk, the myths would lie.

Notes:

1. *Poems of the Vikings: The Elder Edda*, trans. Patricia Terry (Indianapolis: Bobbs-Merrill, 1969).

2. *Ibid.*

3. The Book of Job 41:25, 34.

4. Elie Wiesel, *Souls on Fire* (New York: Random House, 1972).

5. John Donne, "Holy Sonnets," *The Complete Poetry of John Donne*, ed. John T. Shawcross (New York: Anchor Books, 1967).

•

CHAPTER THREE

DIMENSIONS OF MYTHIC TIME

*Amlodhi [Hamlet] was identified, in the crude and vivid imagery of the
Norse, by the ownership of a fabled mill which, in his own time, ground
out peace and plenty. Later, in decaying times, it ground out salt; and now
finally, having landed at the bottom of the sea, it is grinding rock and
sand, creating a vast whirlpool ... which is supposed to be a way to the
land of the dead. This imagery stands, as the evidence develops, for an
astronomical process, the ... shifting of the sun through the signs of the
zodiac which determines world-ages, each numbering thousands of years.
Each age brings a World Era, a Twilight of the Gods. Great structures collapse; pillars topple which supported the great fabric; floods and
cataclysms herald the shaping of a new world.[1]*

—Giorgio de Santillana and Hertha von Dechend

*Turning and turning in the widening gyre
The falcon cannot hear the falconer;
Things fall apart; the centre cannot hold;
Mere anarchy is loosed upon the world,
The blood-dimmed tide is loosed, and everywhere
The ceremony of innocence is drowned;
The best lack all conviction, while the worst
Are full of passionate intensity. ...[2]*

—W.B. Yeats

*Now turns the swinging of time over on the burnt-out world
Back goes the great turning of things upwards again
As yet sunless the time of shrouded light;*

Unsteady, as in dim moon-shimmer,
From out Makalii's night-dark veil of cloud
Thrills, shadow-like, the prefiguration of the world to be.[3]

—Polynesian

The great mill rises, falls and rises again, like a long breath.[4]

—Martha Heyneman

As is generally admitted today, a myth is an account of events which took place in principio, *"in the beginning," in a primordial and non-temporal instant, a moment of sacred time. This mythic or sacred time is qualitatively different from profane time, from the continuous and irreversible time of our everyday, de-sacralized existence. In narrating a myth, one reactualizes, in some sort, the sacred time in which the events narrated took place. ... In a word, the myth is supposed to happen—if one may say so—in a non-temporal time, in an instant without duration, as certain mystics and philosophers conceived of eternity.*[5]

—Mircea Eliade

At the still point of the turning world. Neither flesh nor fleshless;
Neither from nor towards; at the still point, there the dance is,
But neither arrest nor movement. And do not call it fixity,
Where past and future are gathered. Neither movement from nor towards,
Neither ascent nor decline. Except for the point, the still point,
There would be no dance, and there is only the dance.
I can only say, there we have been: but I cannot say where.
And I cannot say, how long, for that is to place it in time.[6]

—T. S. Eliot

Parabola
Volume: 21.1
Prophets and
Prophecy

NIGHT WINDOWS

William Sullivan

In studying the astronomy of myth, one is, in my opinion,
looking simultaneously at the origins of human scientific
enquiry and at a mode of spiritual perception to which all
the world's major religions make respectful reference. To
cite but a single example, the twenty-eight caves at Ajanta
and their iconography refer specifically to the sidereal
lunar month, a fact which cannot possibly detract from
the power of Buddhism. Clearly myth is never a mere
sub-branch of astronomical observation. Instead, some
myths function, on one level, to encode complex astronomical observations. The astronomical level of myth
appears to me to operate as something like a particular
line of music in a polyphonic score.

Although Virgil's (70-19 BCE) declaration, *"Iam redit
et Virgo, redeunt Saturna regna"* ("Now the Virgin returns,
the reign of Saturn returns"), was meant to note that
the constellation Virgo had come to occupy the autum-
nal equinox opposite her vernal counterpart in Pisces
(the soon-to-be fish-symbol of the Christ), it nonetheless elevated this "pagan" poet to the rank of prophet of
Christianity and earned him the role of Dante's guide
in *The Divine Comedy*. The final "step" which transported
Dante across the Milky Way in Gemini, and into the
land of the immortals, was a *scala* or ladder, which Dante
ascended in order to move from the heaven of Saturn to

the sphere of the fixed stars in Gemini. His patron, incidentally, was Can Grande de la Scala—literally "Great Dog Beneath the Ladder," a reference to Sirius, the Dog Star beneath the "ladder" of Orion connecting the northern and southern halves of the celestial sphere at Orion's Belt. Dante and his circle were, let us say, of the old school. This scala, familiar to students of Gurdjieff as the seven-tone musical scale, and explicated by Ouspensky as the principle of organization of the visible cosmos, was a fixture of medieval musicology where it was understood to represent anagrams from the Latin:

DO
    DOminus • The Lord God
RE
    REgina caelum • The Queen of Heaven
MI
    MIcrocosmos • The Microcosm (Earth)
FA
    FAta • Planets
SOL
    SOL • The Sun
LA
    via LActea • The Milky Way
SI
    SIdera • (All) Stars
DO
    DOminus • The Lord God

This way of thinking was ancient in the time of the Chaldean Magi, who, much like Virgil, saw in the star in the East—that is, the conjunctions of Saturn and Jupiter of 6 BCE in the constellation of Pisces—the long prophesied sign of the coming Christ, and the return of a Golden Age already a bittersweet memory of innocence lost in the oldest myths of Sumer and Egypt.

These shards of arcana suggest some "lost" vessel of human thought, as inaccessible to us as the hope of picking the brain of some long-departed priest astronomer of Erech. In fact, it is not so much that the main outlines of this little potpourri of lore cannot be reconstructed, as it is, apparently, difficult to believe that it is possible to do so. Support for this viewpoint is to be found in the fact that now, some twenty-seven years after its publication, the work of Giorgio de Santillana and Hertha von Dechend, known as *Hamlet's Mill*, still awaits engagement by students of the human legacy.

At the heart of their book lies the proposition that myth, on one level, contains a technical language—antedating the advent of writing and of sophisticated mathematics—designed to record the fruits of complex astronomical observation. So complex, in fact, are these observations that they are difficult for us moderns to visualize from the naked-eye perspective whence they were originally derived.

Among the most important of these was the discovery of the precession of the equinoxes—that is, the slow disjunction between solar dates, such as solstices and equinoxes, and the day of heliacal rise of a given star—a disparity caused by a gyroscope-like wobble of the earth's axis of rotation within the sphere of fixed stars, a motion of such magisterial slowness that it requires some 26,000 years to complete a single cycle. From the point of view of naked-eye observation, precession causes the date of heliacal rise of a star (the first day that a given star clears the sun's obscuring brilliance sufficiently that it may be glimpsed rising at dawn in the gathering light) to occur in relation to a solar date (such as vernal equinox) one day "late" every seventy-two years, or about a human lifetime. It is upon this phenomenon that the notion of successive Ages of the World, apparent in mythical traditions around the globe—and the realization that "the times are out of joint"—is founded. At the time of Christ, the constellation of Pisces rose heliacally at the vernal equinox. Now, some two thousand springs later, Pisces has "set in the east," due to precession, and is being replaced by the constellation Aquarius "descending." Thus, "this is the dawning of the Age of Aquarius."

As described by de Santillana and von Dechend, there are three "rules" for understanding the astronomical level of myth. First, stars are animals. Our word *zodiac* literally means "dial of animals." Second, topographical references are analogues for the sun's position against the sphere of fixed stars. Even the term "earth" has a particular astronomical meaning. Thus when mythic floods, earthquakes, or other such "earthly" phenomena "destroy the whole world," one might consider looking straight up, rather than to, say, Mount Ararat, for the location of Noah's mountain and his comprehensive zoo. Third, planets are gods, a proposition which has the potency to sort out the pantheon of Native American myth quite as thoroughly as that of Olympus.

Two primary mythical thought-forms were used to "tell" the ages of the world. The first was based upon the "celestial earth," that is, the area of the celestial sphere, running from tropic to tropic, laid out by the oblique swathe of the ecliptic, the apparent annual path of the sun through the band of stars we call the zodiac. This swathe is cut in half by the celestial equator, that is, the earth's equator blown out upon the celestial sphere. We have no "equatorial zodiac" precisely because, as the earth precesses, this place constantly changes. The celestial equator divides the "celestial earth" into wet and dry. From the celestial equator to the southern tropic lies the "sea" of the earth, while "dry land" runs from the equator to the northern tropic, all the way to the top of the "highest mountain," the sun's position at June solstice. Because of the earth's stubborn habit of changing its position within the fixed sphere of stars, "sea-level" is constantly changing, while some parts of the "dry land" are submerged even as other parts arise out of the "sea." Little wonder that myths of the "flood" are ubiquitous.

The second primary thought-form concerns the "world house." In this analogy the earth is supported by four "pillars." These pillars are the four constellations—lying at ninety degree intervals along the ecliptic—marking the solstices and equinoxes. This is the origin of the concept of the "flat earth"—uranography misleadingly characterized by contemporary scholarship as "primitive" geography. When these pillars are "destroyed"—by the passage of precessional time—they are always replaced by a new "structure" upheld by a new set of pillars for a new age. The land of the gods and of the dead lie to the north and south of the northern and southern tropics respectively. Sometimes this house has a central support pillar, the axis of the precessing earth, which too "crumbles" in the fullness of time. In any case, this is why—so far at least—every time the world-house has been destroyed, a new one has risen from the rubble of the old. Just ask Samson.

Not that there are not other analogies as well. In fact, it appears that mythographers employed multiple analogies just to underscore the fact that these were analogies. For example, if the celestial equator represents sea-level, then the ecliptic must be tilted. And this is why, according to the Greeks, when Zeus flew into a rage at a place called Trapezous, he upended a four-cornered table thereby unleashing Deucalion's flood. In turn, this might help one understand Christ's exceptionally vigorous behavior in overturning the tables of the moneylenders. After all, he had come to bring not peace but, like Arthur, a new age, represented by a shining and altogether axial sword.

Few people are aware that the Inca Empire was less than a century old in 1532, when it was destroyed by a handful of Spanish adventurers. The impetus behind its formation was a prophecy, uttered about 1437 by an Inca king who foretold the utter destruction of Andean civilization within five generations. The institutions and activities of this Empire were nothing less than a comprehensive response to this bleak vision, one founded upon a predictable astronomical event. The fundamental aim of the Inca emperors was to stop time, in the sense of precessional motion. The Spanish had wandered into the midst of an experiment in sympathetic magic without known precedent in human history.

This was the last manifestation, and perhaps the logical outcome of a long history of astronomical prophecy in Andean thought—a tradition that Virgil or the Chaldean Magi would have recognized at once. Completely unaware of the common thread running through their own and Native American cultural tradition, the Spanish conquistadors sought to eradicate native religion root and branch. Nonetheless the curiosity of the soldiers, priests, and administrators of the Spanish Crown produced a body of literature known as the Spanish chronicles, which represent a priceless repository of pre-Columbian Native American thought.

Among those papers lie two versions of a myth, the one collected by Cristóbal de Molina, the other, in the original Quechua, by Francisco de Avila. In this myth, a shepherd finds that his flock of llamas, pasturing high in the mountains, has ceased eating. Instead, they contemplate the sky. The llamas, pointing to "a conjunction of stars," inform the shepherd that "in exactly one month" the entire world will be destroyed by a flood. Heeding the llamas, the shepherd takes his family, animals, and seed-stock and flees to the top of the highest mountain in the world. There the shepherd rides out the storm. As the floodwaters rise, so also does the peak of the mountain. With the rest of the world inundated, the wild animals, according to Avila's version, also flee upward. They include Puma and Fox. So crowded has it become on the mountaintop that Fox, scrabbling for a foothold, slips a bit, getting his tail wet. And that is why, to this day, Fox's tail is black. When the waters recede, the survivors on the mountaintop return to repopulate the world.

The idea that "stars are animals" was a given in native Andean thought. Numerous chroniclers recorded the native view that each species of animal had a corresponding celestial object, which functioned as the protector of that species. The celestial Llama, for example, was an enormous cloud of interstellar dust, appearing inky black against the background glow of the Milky Way, and running from the star Epsilon of the Western Scorpius southwards to the stars Alpha and Beta Centauri, known in the Andes as *llamaq ñawin*, or the "eyes of the llama." It was imagined as a female llama with a suckling. The myth portrays llamas staring at the stars, suggesting the motion of the celestial Llama, setting in the west, and looking east towards some rising object. In fact, to this day just this observation is made yearly in the Andes, where people go out to watch the set of the celestial Llama in the west and the simultaneous heliacal rise of the Pleiades. The purpose of this observation involves divination of the proper time for planting crops. The Pleiades are called *coto*, literally "pile," and the relative dimness or brilliance of their first reappearance, likened to a pile or handful of seeds, suggests whether to plant early or late. In Avila's myth, the name of the mountain where the shepherd took refuge from the flood was Villcacoto, from the sacred term *villca* for "sun," and coto, the Pleiades. The term "sun-Pleiades" is about as clear a reference to a heliacal rise event as one might expect to find anywhere.

Now what sort of precessional event might have appeared sufficiently significant to be crafted into myth? It's a fact that, at the moment of heliacal rise at June solstice in 650 CE, the Milky Way had ceased, due to precession—for the first time in about 850 years—to be visible "on the earth," that is, in contact with the horizon at the point on the horizon where the solstice sun rose. The gates to the land of the gods had slammed shut.

How did Virgil manage to "prophesy" the advent of Christ? What did the *return* of the Virgin, the constellation Virgo, imply? Two of the pillars of the new age would lie at the equinoxes—Pisces and Virgo. But it was the other two—Gemini and Sagittarius—which, in the gently teasing manner of any decent mythographer, Virgil neglects to mention. The keys lie here, because these constellations occupy the two areas in the sky where the zodiac (ecliptic) crosses the Milky Way, that is, the plane of our galaxy. Such an event, in the technical language of mythological discourse, represented a "window of opportunity" when the great celestial causeway of the galaxy came to "earth," opening the "bridges" or "ways" to the land of the gods and the land of the dead. It is a historical curiosity that, as Gemini began to take its place as the constellation ruling summer solstice, aligning the entrance to the land of the gods with the celestial causeway, a succession of saviors came to earth beginning about 500 BCE They were Buddha, Lao-tse, Zoroaster, Christ, and finally Muhammad, who died—in 632 CE shortly before, due to precession, the galaxy and the June solstice point once again parted company—saying, "After me, no more prophets."

Further, the return of Virgo was Virgil's way of alluding to the time depth of this system of thought. The last time Virgo had occupied so important a position had been some six thousand years earlier at June solstice in an era when Gemini and Sagittarius "came to earth" at the equinoxes. This Golden Age was celebrated as an already distant memory in the first written myths, impressed on the clay tablets of Sumer and the Pyramid texts.

The staggering antiquity of these ideas is matched only by their equally staggering ubiquity. And this is a fact which ought to concern historians and students of religion.

Were it possible to state that the vast interlocking hologram of mythic astronomy, uniting heaven and earth in a dramatic pageant of successive ages of the world, represents a sort of archetypal thought-form accessible in the collective unconscious to all people in all times, then it would, of course, be unnecessary to explain the ubiquity of the hologram all around the planet. While there is no reason to suppose that different peoples might not have discovered the disjunctive nature of precession, it is quite another matter to understand how they would have developed precisely the same, highly idiosyncratic technical language to express the discovery.

An excellent example of this problem—one which possesses the additional utility of explaining just what Virgil meant by "the reign of Saturn returns"—is found in the very title *Hamlet's Mill*. The "mill" in question was an image—a circular grindstone hafted upon an axle—of the relationship of the axis of the celestial sphere (the earth's axis of rotation blown out onto the celestial sphere) to the celestial equator, the "millstone." "The mills of the gods grind slow, but they grind exceeding fine." And, in fact, the gods are involved because the mill has an owner, and he is Saturn.

Just how a planet, confined in its orbital path to the ecliptic, might have anything to do with shifting a mill whose axis is lodged at the pole star of a given era is not an example of confusion amongst early mythographers but a question of positing relationships. The relationship in question was between planetary periodicities and the flow of precessional time. Conjunctions of Saturn and Jupiter take place very regularly every twenty years. As Johannes Kepler showed in a famous diagram of the points of these conjunctions plotted against the circle of the zodiac, taking the conjunction at the June solstice as a starting point, the next conjunction will occur almost exactly one-third the way round the ecliptic against the background of the fixed stars. After sixty years the conjunction will occur about nine degrees past its original spot. Connecting these three points forms an equilateral triangle whose vertex advances about nine degrees every sixty years, so that after eight hundred years, or forty conjunctions, one vertex of this moving equilateral triangle will have moved one third of the way through the zodiac while one of its companions will have "returned" to the original spot. To trace the path of one vertex through the entire zodiac back to its point of departure would take about 2400 years, very close to one-twelfth of a precessional "tour" through the twelve constellations of the zodiac.

And so planets were gods, what Plato called "the instruments of time": because they "controlled" the motions of the "mill" in the sense that they gave to the mythographers a way of controlling their own data, a means of monitoring the flow of precessional time. As the visible planet with the longest orbital period (thirty years), Saturn was assigned the role of king, of "ruler" of the stars in both senses of the word. This conceit is no more intentionally abstruse than a differential equation. Rather, the idea of a "mill" and its "owner" demonstrates how, despite the lack of writing or complex mathematics, ancient thinkers were able to place their observations in myth by means of kinetic images sympathetic to the apparatus of human memory: the creakings of the mill; the crashing of mountains; rains that lasted forty days and nights.

Virgil's celebration of the "return" of the reign of Saturn—the return after eight hundred years of the conjunction of Saturn and Jupiter to

Pisces even as Pisces "descended" to occupy its position at vernal equinox, locking, as it were, the galaxy into contact with the "earth" at the solstice points in anticipation of the return of the gods to earth—was a prophecy based upon ancient skills in predicting the advent of synchronous events.

Those familiar with the I Ching know that its usefulness lies not in predicting the future, but in revealing the pattern of constraints and opportunities in the present, in order to suggest courses of appropriate action. Similarly, the ancient mythical perception of a rhythm in human history corresponding to successive World Ages issued from a concern for future generations rather than a desire to dazzle the ignorant with feats of mechanistic astrology. Such myths exist to alert us to "future-presents," those rare, millennial times when humankind is called upon to undertake a particular kind of creative action—to fashion a new world from the remains of one that is dying. The gathering ripple of anticipation of the coming millennium indicates that this perception still lies deep in our cultural bones.

Yet we know virtually nothing of that very history of our planet which our most compassionate ancestors intended us to hear. Myth is the ark which carries this perception, the knowledge of what it takes to remain human, set loose upon the vast sea of time. And this is a history which appears to include the fact that for millennia before Columbus, the ark sailed to every corner of the earth. So long as its techniques of transmission remain unrecognized, this great powerhouse of ancient wisdom will continue to gather dust on dark library shelves, catalogued under the heading "primitive beliefs."

William Sullivan is a historian with a doctorate from the Center for Amerindian Studies, the University of St. Andrews, Scotland. He is the author of *The Secret of the Incas: Myth, Astronomy, and the War Against Time* (New York: Three Rivers Press, 1996).

Parabola
Volume: 23.1
Millennium

Völuspá

The Seeress's Prophecy

The Völuspá *tells the story of Ragnarök, the fall of the Norse gods and of the World-Tree Yggdrasil. The story does not end with destruction, however, but turns instead to rebirth and renewal, the dawn of a new golden age. The poem speaks of nature's ceaseless flow into being and back to the unknown source—a far grander vision of the universe than simple annihilation.*

Hear me, all ye holy kindred,
Greater and lesser sons of Heimdal!
You wish me to tell the ancient tales,
O Father of seers, the oldest I know.

I remember giants born in the foretime,
They who long ago nurtured me;
Nine worlds I remember, nine trees of life,
Before this world tree grew from the ground.

An ash stands, I know, by name Yggdrasil;
That tall tree is watered by white icicles daily;
Thence comes the dew that drops in the dells;
It stands ever green above Urd's well.

Thence come maidens who know much,
Three from that hall beneath the tree:

One was named Origin, the second Becoming.
These two fashioned the third, named Debt.

They established law,
They selected lives,
For the children of ages,
And the fates of men.

She remembers the first slaying in the world,
When Gullveig was hoist on a spear;
Thrice was she burned and thrice reborn,
Again and again—yet still she lives.

Heid was her name.
To whatever house she came
She prophesied well and was versed in spells.
She was much sought by evil peoples.

She sat outside alone when the Old One came;
The fearsome Áse looked her in the eye:
"What ask you of me? Why do you tempt me?
I know all, Odin. I know where you hid your eye—

"In the redoubtable Mimer's well.
Mimer quaffs mead each morning
From Allfather's forfeit."
Know you as yet, or what?

The Father of Hosts gave her rings
And gems to gain
Wisdom and lore from her.
Far and wide she scanned the worlds.

She saw Valkyries ready to ride: Debt bore armor.
So also did War, Battle, and Spearwound.
Thus are the Hero's maidens named,
Valkyries mounted to ride over earth.

She saw the one bound beneath the court,
Where the caldron is kept.
The wretch resembles Loki.
Unhappy Sigyn remains by her spouse.
Know you as yet, or what?

A hall she sees standing far from the sun
On the shores of death, with its door to the north.
Venomous drops fall in through the weave,
For that hall is woven of serpents.

Therein wading the streams she saw
Oathbreakers, murderers, adulterers.
There Nidhögg sucks cadavers,
Wolves tear men.
Know you as yet, or what?

Garm howls at the Gnipa-hollow of Hel.
What is fast loosens, and Freke runs free.
She grasps much; I see more:
To Ragnarök, the Victory-gods' hard death struggle.

Brothers shall battle and slay one another.
Blood ties of sisters' sons shall be sundered.
Harsh is the world. Fornication is rife,
Luring to faithlessness spouses of others.

Axe time, sword time, shields shall be cloven;
Wind time, wolf time, ere the world wanes.
Din on the fields, trolls in full flight;
No man shall then spare another.

Mimer's sons arise. The dying world tree flares
At the sound of the shrill trump of doom.
Loud blows Heimdal, the horn held high.
Odin confers with Mimer's head.

With a roaring in the ancient tree
The giant is loosened.
The ash, Yggdrasil,
Quakes where it stands.

Garm howls at the Gnipa-hollow of Hel.
What was fast loosens, and Freke runs free.

Rymer steers westward; the tree is o'erturned;
In titanic rage
Iörmungandr writhes,
Whipping the waves to froth.

How is it with Aesir? How is it with elves?
The giant world roars; the Aesir hold council.
Dwarfs groan before their stone portals,
Masters of mountains.
Know you as yet, or what?

Fire fares from south with flaring flames.
The embattled gods' sun is skewered on the sword.
Mountains burst open. Hags hurry hence.
Men tread Hel's road; the heavens are sundered.

Then comes Lin's second life sorrow,
As Odin emerges to war with the wolf.
The bane of Bele flashes forth against Fire:
There shall Frigga's hero fall.

Victory-father's son, Vidar the mighty,
Comes forth to battle the beast of death.
He plunges his sword from mouth to heart
Of the Son of Completion. The Sire is avenged.

Approaches the shining scion of Earth:
Odin's son meets with the wolf.

In raging wrath he slays Midgárd's woe.
Then do all men turn homeward.

Nine steps only away from the monster
Staggers the son of Earth.
The sun grows dim; earth sinks in the waters;
The sparkling stars fall from the firmament.
Fire entwines the Life-supporter;
Heat rises high to the heavens.

Garm howls at the Gnipa-hollow of Hel.
What was fast loosens, and Freke runs free.

She sees rising another earth from the sea,
Once more turning green.
Torrents tumble, eagle soars
From the mountains, seeking fish.

The Aesir met on the Ida sward
To judge of the mighty Soil-mulcher;
There to recall their former feats
And the runes of Fimbultyr.

She sees a hall more fair than the sun,
Gilded, glowing on Gimle.
There shall the virtuous hosts abide
And joy in serenity during long ages.

Then comes the dragon of darkness flying,
Might from beneath,
From the mountains of night.
He soars o'er the fields in a featherguise.

Parabola
Volume: 15.1
Time and Presence

OBSERVING SACRED TIME

Mircea Eliade

As is generally admitted today, a myth is an account
of events which took place *in principio*, that is, "in the
beginning," in a primordial and non-temporal instant, a
moment of *sacred time*. This mythic or sacred time is qualitatively different from profane time, from the continuous and irreversible time of our everyday, de-sacralized
existence. In narrating a myth, one reactualizes, in some
sort, the sacred time in which the events narrated took
place. (This, moreover, is why the myths, in traditional
societies, are not to be narrated however or whenever
one likes; they can be recited only during the sacred seasons, in the bush and at night, or around the fire after or
before the rituals, etc.) In a word, the myth is supposed
to happen—if one may say so—in a non-temporal time,
in an instant without duration, as certain mystics and
philosophers conceived of eternity.

This observation is important, for it follows that the
narration of the myths is not without consequences for
him who recites and those who listen. From the mere
fact of the narration of a myth, profane time is—at least
symbolically—abolished: the narrator and his hearers are
rapt into sacred and mythical time. The abolition of profane time by the imitation of exemplary models and the
re-enactment of mythical events constitutes, as it were,
a specific mark of all traditional societies; and this mark

is, of itself, enough to differentiate the archaic world from that of our modern societies. In the traditional societies men endeavored, consciously and voluntarily, to abolish Time—periodically to efface the past and to regenerate Time—by a series of rituals which, as it were, re-enacted the cosmogony. Myth takes man out of his own time—his individual, chronological, "historic" time—and projects him, symbolically at least, into the Great Time, into a paradoxical instant which cannot be measured because it does not consist of duration. This is as much as to say that the myth implies a breakaway from Time and the surrounding world; it opens up a way into the sacred Great Time.

Merely by listening to a myth, man forgets his profane condition, his "historical situation" as we are accustomed to call it today, and is projected into another world, into a Universe which is no longer his poor little universe of every day.

It should be remembered that for each individual, the myths are *true* because they are *sacred*, because they tell him about sacred beings and events. Consequently, in reciting or listening to a myth, one resumes contact with the sacred and with reality, and in so doing one transcends the profane condition, the "historical situation." In other words, one goes beyond the temporal condition and the dull self-sufficiency which is the lot of every human being simply because every human being is "ignorant"—in the sense that he is identifying himself, and Reality, with his own particular situation. And ignorance is, first of all, this false identification of Reality with what each one of us *appears to be or to possess*. A politician thinks that the only true reality is political power, a millionaire is convinced that wealth alone is real, a man of learning thinks the same about his studies, his books, laboratories and so forth. The same tendency is equally in evidence among the less civilized, in primitive peoples and savages, but with this difference, that the myths are still alive among them, which prevents them from identifying themselves wholly and completely with non-reality. The periodic recitation of the myths breaks through the barriers built up by profane existence. The myth continually reactualizes the Great Time, and in so doing raises the listener to a superhuman and suprahistorical plane; which, among other things, enables him to approach a Reality that is inaccessible at the level of profane, individual existence.

Certain Indian myths furnish particularly happy illustrations of this function of "breaking-through" individual and historical time and realizing the mythical Great Time. We will give one famous example from the *Brahmavaivarta Purāna*, of which the late Heinrich Zimmer gave a summary and commentary in his book, *Myths and Symbols in Indian Art and Civilization.*[1] This text has the merit of beginning straight away with the Great Time as an instrument of knowledge, and thence of deliverance from the bonds of Māyā.

After his victory over the dragon Vritra, Indra decides to rebuild and embellish the residence of the gods. Visvakarman, the divine artificer, succeeds after a year's labor in constructing a magnificent palace. But Indra seems not to be satisfied; he wants the building to be enlarged and to be made still more majestic, unparalleled in all the world. Visvakarman, exhausted by his effort, complains to Brahmā the Creator god, who promises to help him and intercedes with Vishnu the Supreme Being, of whom Brahmā himself is but an instrument. Vishnu undertakes to bring Indra back to his senses.

One fine day, Indra in his palace receives a visit from a boy dressed in rags. This is Vishnu himself, who has assumed this disguise to humiliate the King of the Gods. Without at first revealing his identity to the latter, he calls him "my child" and begins to tell him about the innumerable Indras who, up to that very moment, have peopled the innumerable universes.

> *The life and kingship of an Indra endure seventy-one eons [a cycle, a mahāyuga, consists of 12,000 divine years or 4,320,000 years!], and when twenty-eight Indras have expired, one day and night of Brahmā have elapsed. But the existence of one Brahmā, measured in such Brahmā days and nights, is only one hundred and eight years. Brahmā follows Brahmā; one sinks, the next arises; the endless series cannot be told. There is no end to the number of those Brahmās—to say nothing of Indras.*
>
> *But the universes side by side at any given moment, each harboring a Brahmā and an Indra: who will estimate the number of these? Beyond the farthest vision, crowding outer space, the universes come and go, an innumerable host. Like delicate boats they float on the fathomless, pure waters that form the body of Vishnu. Out of every hair-pore of that body a universe bubbles and breaks. Will you pre-*

sume to count them? Will you number the gods in all those worlds—
the worlds present and the worlds past?

While the boy was speaking, a procession of ants had appeared in the great hall of the palace. Deployed in a column four yards wide, this mass of ants was parading across the floor. Noticing them, the boy stops, and then, struck with astonishment, suddenly bursts into laughter. "What are you laughing at?" inquires Indra. And the boy replies:

I saw the ants, O Indra, filing in long parade. Each was once an
Indra. Like you, each by virtue of pious deeds once ascended to the
rank of a king of gods. But now, through many rebirths, each has
become again an ant. This army is an army of former Indras.

This revelation brings home to Indra all the vanity of his pride and ambition. Sending for the wonderful architect Visvakarman, he rewards him royally, and gives up forever his wish to aggrandize the palace of the gods.

The intention of this myth is transparent. The bewildering evocation of innumerable universes arising from the body of Vishnu and disappearing again is enough of itself to awaken Indra—that is, to make him transcend the limited and strictly conditioned horizon of his "situation" as King of the Gods. One might even be tempted to add "his historical situation," for Indra happened to be the great warrior Chief of the Gods at a certain historic moment, in a definite phase of the great cosmic drama. What Indra hears from the mouth of Vishnu is *a true story*; the true story of the eternal creation and destruction of worlds, beside which his own history, that of his countless heroic adventures culminating in the victory over Vritra, seems, indeed, to be "false"—its events are without transcendent significance. The *true story* reveals to him the Great Time, mythic time in which is the true source of all beings and of all cosmic events. It is because he can thus transcend his historically conditioned "situation," and succeeds in piercing the veil of illusion created by profane time—that is, by his *own* history—that Indra is cured of his pride and ignorance: in Christian terms he is "saved." And this redemptive function of the myth applies not only to Indra, but also to every human being who listens to his adventure. To transcend profane time and re-enter into mythical Great Time is equivalent to a revelation of ultimate reality—reality that is strictly metaphysical, and can be approached in no other way than through myths and symbols.

This myth has a sequel, to which we shall return. For the moment, let us note that the conception of cyclic and infinite Time, presented in so striking a manner by Vishnu, is the general Indian conception of cosmic cycles. Belief in the periodic creation and destruction of the Universe is found as early as in the *Atharva Veda* (X, 8, 39-40). And as a matter of fact it belongs to the *Weltanschauung* of all archaic societies.

India, however, has elaborated a doctrine of cosmic cycles by amplifying the number of periodic creations and destructions of the Universe to ever more terrifying proportions.

A complete cycle, a mahāyuga, ends in a "dissolution" or *pralaya*, and this is repeated in a still more radical way at the *mahāpralaya*, or "Great Dissolution," at the end of the thousandth cycle. The 12,000 years of one mahāyuga have been counted as "divine years" of 360 years each, which gives a total of 4,320,000 years for a single cosmic cycle. A thousand of such mahāyugas constitute one *kalpa*; one kalpa is equal to one day in the life of Brahmā, and another kalpa to one night. A hundred of these "years" of Brahmā, say 311 thousand billion human years, make up the life of the god. But even this considerable length of Brahmā's life does not exhaust the whole of Time, for the gods are not eternal, and the cosmic creations and destructions go on without end.

All we need retain from this cataract of numbers is the cyclic character of cosmic Time. In fact, what we have here is the repetition to infinity of the same phenomenon (creation-destruction-new creation) prefigured in each *yuga* ("dawn" and "dusk") but completely realized in a mahāyuga. From this cycle without beginning or end, which is the cosmic manifestation of *māyā*, man can extricate himself only by an act of spiritual freedom (for all Indian soteriological systems are reducible to a previous deliverance from the cosmic illusion, and to spiritual freedom).

The sole possibility of escape from time, of breaking out of the iron ring of existences, is to abolish the human condition and attain Nirvāna. Moreover, all the "incalculable" and all the countless eons also have a soteriological function: the mere contemplation of such a panorama terrifies man, compelling him to realize that he will have to recommence this same transitory existence billions of times over, and endure the same sufferings without end; the effect of which is to stir up his will to escape—that is, to impel him to transcend his condition as an "existant" once and for all.

Let us consider for a moment this vision of infinite Time, of the endless cycles of creations and destructions, this myth of the eternal return, as an "instrument of knowledge" and a means to liberation. In the perspective of the Great Time every existence is precarious, evanescent and illusory. Seen in the light of the major cosmic rhythms, not only is human existence, and history itself with all its countless empires, dynasties, revolutions, and counter-revolutions, manifestly ephemeral and in a sense unreal; the Universe itself vanishes into unreality; for, as we saw, universes are continually being born from the innumerable pores of the body of Vishnu, and disappearing like the bubbles of air that arise and break on the surface of the waters. Existence *in* Time is ontologically a nonexistence, an unreality. That is how one has to understand the affirmation of Indian idealism, and of the Vedānta first and foremost, that this world is illusory, wanting in reality. It lacks reality because of its limited duration; in the perspective of the eternal return it is non-duration. This table here is unreal, not because it does not exist in the strict sense of the term, not because it is an illusion, for it is no illusion that at this precise moment it does exist. But it is illusory in that it will no longer exist ten thousand years hence. This historic world, the societies and civilizations painfully built up by the efforts of countless generations, are all unreal because, in comparison with the cosmic rhythms, they last only for an instant. The Vedantin, the Buddhist, the rishi, the yogi, the sadhu, etc., draw the logical conclusions from the lessons of infinite Time and from the Eternal Return; they renounce the world and seek the absolute Reality; for it is only knowledge of the Absolute that can help them to free themselves from illusion, to pierce the veil of Māyā.

But renunciation of the world is not the only consequence that an Indian is entitled to draw from the discovery of infinite, cyclic Time. As we are now beginning to understand better, India has not known *only* negation and total world-refusal. Starting from this same dogma of the fundamental unreality of the Cosmos, Indian thought also mapped out a way that does not necessarily lead to asceticism and abandonment of the world. Such is the way preached, for instance, by Krishna in the

Bhagavad-Gītā[2], the *phalatrisnavairāgya*, which means the "renuncia-tion of the fruits of action"—that is, of the advantages one might gain by one's action, without renouncing the action itself. This is the way illus-trated by the sequel to the myth of Vishnu and Indra, whose adventure we have recounted above.

Humiliated by Vishnu's revelation, Indra renounces his vocation of warrior-god, and withdraws into the mountains to practice the most terrible asceticism. In other words, he prepares to draw what seems to him the only logical conclusion from the discovery of the unreality of the world. He finds himself in the same situation as Prince Siddhārtha immediately after having abandoned his palace and his wives at Kap-ilavastu and having entered upon his rigorous mortifications. But it is a question whether a King of the Gods and a husband has the right to draw such conclusions from a metaphysical revelation; whether his renunciation and asceticism might not endanger the equilibrium of the world. And indeed, shortly afterwards, his consort the queen Saci, in despair at having been abandoned, implores the help of their spiritual guide Brihaspati. Taking her by the hand, Brihaspati approaches Indra, and speaks to him at length, not only about the virtues of the contempla-tive life, but also of the life of action, the life that finds its fulfillment in this world of ours. Indra thus receives a second revelation: he now under-stands that everyone ought to take his own path to the fulfillment of his vocation, which means, in the last reckoning, doing his duty. And, since Indra's vocation and his duty were to continue to be Indra, he resumes his identity and carries on his heroic adventures, but without pride or delusion now that he understands the vanity of all "situations," even that of a King of Gods …

The gnoseological and soteriological function of such a change of perspective, obtained by reference to the major rhythms of time, is admi-rably illustrated by certain myths about the Māyā of Vishnu.

Here is one of these myths, in the popular modern version narrated by Sri Ramakrishna.[3] A famous ascetic named Nārada having obtained grace of Vishnu by his numberless austerities, the god appears to him and promises to do for him anything he may wish. "Show me the magical power of thy māyā," Nārada requests of him. Vishnu consents, and gives the sign to follow him. Presently, they find themselves upon a desert road in hot sunshine, and Vishnu, feeling thirsty, asks Nārada to go on a few hundred yards farther, where there is a little village, and fetch him some water. Nārada hastens forward and knocks at the door of the first house he comes to. A very beautiful girl opens the door; the ascetic gazes upon her at length and forgets why he has come. He enters the house, and the parents of the girl receive him with the respect due to a saint. Time passes, Nārada marries the girl, and learns to know the joys of marriage and the hardships of a peasant life. Twelve years go by: Nārada now has three children, and, after his father-in-law's death, becomes the owner of the farm. But in the course of the twelfth year, torrential rains inundate the region. In one night the cattle are drowned and the house collapses. Supporting his wife with one hand, holding two of his children with the other and carrying the smallest on his shoulder, Nārada struggles through the waters. But the burden is too great for him: he slips, the little one falls into the water; Nārada lets go of the other two children to recover him, but too late; the torrent has carried him far away. While he is looking for the little one, the waters engulf the two others and, shortly afterwards, his wife. Nārada himself falls, and the flood bears him away unconscious, like a log of wood. When, stranded upon a rock he comes to himself and remembers his misfortunes, he bursts into tears. "My child! Where is the water you were going to bring me? I have been waiting for you more than half an hour!" Nārada turns his head and looks: instead of the all-destroying flood, he sees the desert landscape, dazzling in the sunlight. And the god asks him: "Now do you understand the secret of my māyā?"

Obviously Nārada cannot claim to understand it entirely; but he has learned one essential thing: he knows now that Vishnu's cosmic māyā is manifested through time.

The myth of cyclic Time, of the cosmic cycles repeating themselves *ad infinitum*, is not an invention of Indian speculation. The traditional societies conceive man's temporal existence not only as an infinite repetition of certain archetypes and exemplary gestures, but also as an *eternal recommencement*; the world is successively created and destroyed, and the lunar symbolism of "birth-death-resurrection" is present in a great many myths and rites. It was out of such an immemorial heritage that the pan-Indian doctrine of the ages of the world and of the cosmic cycles was elaborated. The important point for us to note is that the Indians, in magnifying ever more audaciously the duration and the numbers of the cosmic cycles, had a soteriological aim in view. Appalled by the endless number of births and rebirths of Universes accompanied by an equally vast number of human births and rebirths ruled by the law of *karma*, the Indian was in a sense *obliged* to seek a way out of this cosmic rotation and these infinite transmigrations. The mystical doctrines and techniques that are directed towards the deliverance of man from sorrow and from the frightful successions of "life, death and rebirth," take over the mythic images of cosmic cycles, amplify and utilize them for their proselytizing purpose. By the Indians of the post-Vedic epoch—that is, by the Indians who had discovered the "suffering of existence"—the "eternal return" was equated with the infinite cycle of transmigration ruled by karma. This present illusory and transitory world, the world of *samsāra*, of sorrow and ignorance, is the world that unfolds itself under the sign of Time. Deliverance from this world, and the attainment of salvation, are equivalent to deliverance from cosmic Time.

"When a hen has laid eggs," says the Buddha, "eight, ten or a dozen; when the hen has sat upon them and kept them warm long enough—then, when one of those chicks, the first one to break the shell with the point of its claw or its beak, comes safely out of the egg, what will they call that chick—the eldest, or the youngest?"—"They will call him the eldest, venerable Gautama, for he is the first-born among them."—"So likewise, O brahman, I alone, among all those who live in ignorance and are as though enclosed and imprisoned in an egg, have burst through this shell of ignorance; I alone in this world have attained to the blessed, the universal dignity of the Buddha. Thus, O brahman, I am the eldest, the noblest among beings."[4]

Thus the act of transcending time is formulated by a symbolism that is both cosmological and spatial. To break the shell of the egg is equivalent, in the parable of the Buddha, to breaking out of the *samsāra*, out of the wheel of existence—that is, to the transcending *both of cosmic Space and cyclic Time*. In this case too, the Buddha makes use of images analogous to those that the Vedas and the Upanishads have accustomed us to. The sun's standing still at the zenith (in the Chandogya Upanishad) is a spatial symbol that expresses the paradoxical act of escaping from the Cosmos, as forcibly as does the Buddhist symbolism of breaking out of the egg.

All the images by means of which we try to express the paradoxical act of "escaping from time" are equally expressive of *the passage from ignorance to enlightenment* (or, in other words, from "death" to "life," from the conditioned to the unconditioned, etc.) A mystic of the eminence of Meister Eckhardt never ceases to repeat that "there is no greater obstacle to Union with God than Time," that Time hinders man from knowing God, etc. And in this connection it is not without interest to recall that the archaic societies periodically "destroy" the world in order to "remake" it, and thereafter to live in a "new" Universe, without "sin"—meaning without "history," without *memory*. A great many periodic rituals are also directed to collective "purging" from sins (by public confessions, the scapegoat ceremony, etc.), in the last analysis to the *abolition of the past*. All this proves, I think, that there is no break in continuity between the man of the archaic societies and the mysticisms attaching to the great historic religions: both are striving with the same strength, though by different means, against *memory* and Time.

Notes:

1. Heinrich Zimmer, *Myths and Symbols in Indian Art and Civilization*, edited by Joseph Campbell (New York: The Bollingen Series VI, 1946), pp. 3 ff.

2. Cf. for example, Bhagavad-Gītā IV, 20; see also our *Yoga, Immortality and Freedom* (New York, 1958), pp. 158 ff.

3. *The Sayings of Sri Ramakrishna*, Madras edition, 1938, book IV, Chap. 22. See another version of this myth according to the *Matsya Purāna*, recounted by H. Zimmer, *Myths and Symbols*, pp. 27 ff.

4. *Suttavibhanga*, *Pārājika* I, I, 4; cf. H. Oldenberg, *Le Bouddha* (Trans. A. Foucher), pp. 364-5; see Paul Mus, "La Notion de temps reversible dans la mythologie bouddhique," an extract from *l'Annuaire de l'École Pratique des Hautes Études*, Section des Sciences religieuses, 1938-1939, Melun, 1939, p. 13.

Parabola
Volume: 7.1
Sleep

TIME OUT OF TIME

Paul Jordan-Smith

Once upon a time, "while the country was yet a province of Great Britain," there lived in a little village, at the foot of the Catskill Mountains, a simple, good-natured fellow of the name of Rip Van Winkle. Washington Irving—or perhaps one should say, Diedrich Knickerbocker (his pseudonym for this and other early tales)—tells us that Rip was "a kind neighbor, and an obedient, henpecked husband." To escape the endless haranguing of his termagant wife, who even broke in upon the reveries of Rip and his fellow idlers in front of the tavern, Rip one afternoon took to the mountains, with dog and gun, and there, as the story tells us, he met with a strange adventure.

It was late in the day when Rip met a fellow sojourner in those mysterious hills, a man in dress and manner not of Rip's time. Rip and his companion joined other men of even stranger appearance, playing at ninepins, the sound of which rolled through the valleys like thunder. Rip drank of their flagons and watched their game, and little by little fell into a deep sleep. When he awoke the following morning, his dog had disappeared, and in the place of the well-oiled fowling piece he had carried with him there was nothing but an old rusty firelock. Rip returned to his village, only to find himself a stranger in a strange land. He had gone to the mountains a loyal subject of King George; he now finds himself branded a Tory spy. Those he knew of old are now dead or gone away. In desperation he cries, "Does nobody here know Rip Van Winkle?"

> *"Oh, Rip Van Winkle!" exclaimed two or three. "Oh, to be sure! That's Rip Van Winkle yonder, leaning against the tree."*
>
> *Rip looked, and beheld a precise counterpart of himself as he went up the mountain: apparently as lazy, and certainly as ragged. The poor fellow was now completely confounded. He doubted his own identity, and whether he was himself or another man. In the midst of his bewilderment, the man in the cocked hat demanded who he was, and what was his name?*
>
> *"God knows," exclaimed he, at his wit's end. "I am not myself— I'm somebody else—that's me yonder—no—that's somebody got into my shoes—I was myself last night, but I fell asleep on the mountain, and they've changed my gun, and everything's changed, and I'm changed, and I can't tell what's my name or who I am!"[1]*

Following this, Rip encounters his daughter, and old neighbors confirm the identity of the man who went into the mountains and slept for twenty years, and awakened to a new generation.

Rip Van Winkle was not the only sojourner to stumble upon a timeless sanctuary: he belongs to a company of far-flung wanderers that include Oisin, the son of Fionn mac Cumhail, the Seven Sleepers of Ephesus, King Mucukunda, the Valkyrie Brünnhilde, and the Sleeping Beauty. Each of these—and many others as well, as we shall see— stepped for a moment out of the ken of mortal men, and out of mortal time as well. When they returned, the world had aged—in the case of King Mucukunda, eons had passed—though to themselves it seemed that they had been gone for the briefest moment.

For some of these adventurers, sleep was little more than a refuge from the torments of the world: no call or affirmation led to their suspension in Time, but in each case a denial of the world. For Rip Van Winkle, the result was simply relief from his marital anguish, and perhaps a career in his dotage as the town philosopher. For the Seven Sleepers, sleep was a refuge from persecution, an escape from martyrdom, and a revelation, in their last moments, of the grace of God. After his long sleep, King Mucukunda still seeks release from the wheel of rebirth, and from the illusion that has been the torment of his life: he retires into the mountains an ascetic, to await the end of the final age and the rebirth of the world. Like Utnapishtim, he goes beyond the mortal world, as the Master of Time, an exemplar of the all-but-unattainable virtue of detachment.

The sojourn out of mortal time may be something else than simply a refusal or flight, however, for "yes" can sometimes lead to the same place as "no." And perhaps there is an affirmation that lies underneath the most emphatic denial, one that emerges as the response to one's destiny.

Only twelve of the thirteen fairies in the land were invited to the christening of the Sleeping Beauty, or Briar-Rose as she is sometimes called. After eleven fairies had blessed the child with gifts of beauty and grace, the thirteenth fairy swept in, enraged at not having been invited (due to an oversight on the part of the king), and laid a curse on the child: at fifteen, when all the gifts of beauty and grace were at their moment of fulfillment, she would prick her finger upon a spindle and die. The palace was aghast, but fortunately, the twelfth fairy had not yet spoken. The curse was mitigated to a hundred-year sleep. In vain the king tried to protect his daughter by banning spindles from his kingdom: but a curse is a call, of a sort, which cannot be so easily escaped. Willy-nilly, the call must be obeyed; even the King and Queen conspire in its fulfillment: when the Princess has come of age, her parents neglect their vigil for one moment, a sliver of time that suffices to bring the Princess to the tower where the one remaining spindle is waiting to fulfill its destiny, and hers.

In an instant, "in the twinkling of an eye," everything is changed: the Princess falls asleep, and so does the whole palace, from the King and Queen themselves down to the cook and scullery boy, the dogs, the horses, the pigeons on the roof, and the flies on the wall. Even the wind itself died down, and around this suddenly silent microcosm a hawthorn hedge began to grow. So for a hundred years the Princess slept in the room at the top of the tower, and all around her slept as well. Beyond the protecting thicket the story of the Sleeping Beauty passed from father to son and from mother to daughter, and though from time to time (that is, in our mortal time) young men tried to penetrate the hedge, still she slept on, and the hedge became "hung with the corpses of those who had tried to break through before the hundred years were up," as P. L. Travers writes, "thus pointing an admonitory finger at the truth that to choose the moment when the time is ripe is essentially a hero deed."[2] At last, of course, the day of awakening arrived, and the prince came, the one and only hero before whom the thicket would open of its own accord. Drawn to the tower by the inevitability of his quest, he found the Sleeping Beauty. "There she lay and was so beautiful that he couldn't turn his eyes away and stooped down and kissed her." Then, of course, she awoke, and so did the whole palace, right down to the scullery boy, the dogs, horses, pigeons, and the flies on the walls. For mortal time began to flow again, and when the prince and his lady love were married, "they lived happily until their death."

Here the sojourn out of time is connected with what might be termed the "nuptial call," For the joint action of the two forces of the twelfth and thirteenth fairies set into motion a destiny not only for the newborn princess, but also for a prince who would not be born for a hundred years. As inevitably as she is drawn to the room in the tower, so is he drawn to the hawthorn hedge, that sea of thorns surrounding the island in which the palace sleeps.

When the prince who is the son of the King of Erin and the Queen of Lonesome Isle sets out on his quest for the fiery water from the well called Tubber Tintye, he is told that the Queen of Tubber Tintye sleeps, with all her retinue, for seven years—and then all wake for seven years. At the moment he begins his quest, the Queen has just begun her sleep, but the journey is not an easy one. With the aid of a little shaggy horse, the prince must cross over a river of fire, so that not one thread of his clothes should be scorched, and after that pass safely over a grove of poison trees, and in mid-flight leap from the horse's back through a window in the palace of Tubber Tintye. Through twelve chambers he makes his way toward the center of the palace, though each chamber holds a sleeping maiden each more beautiful than the one before. At last he enters the thirteenth chamber, and his eyes are dazzled by the flash of gold.

> He stood awhile till the sight came back, and then entered. In the great bright chamber was a golden couch, resting on wheels of gold. The wheels turned continually; the couch went round and round,

never stopping night or day. On the couch lay the Queen of Tubber Tintye; and if her twelve maidens were beautiful, they would not be beautiful if seen near her. At the foot of the couch was Tubber Tintye itself—the well of fire. There was a golden cover upon the well, and it went around continually with the couch of the Queen.[3]

The Prince of the Lonesome Isle spends six days and nights with the sleeping queen, and then leaves with three bottles of water from the flaming well. But their destinies are still to be fulfilled, for he leaves a letter behind identifying himself. And after her seven-year sleep, the queen awakes to find that she has given birth to a boy. Then begins her quest for her husband to be; at last they are united and the spell of sleep is lifted from the island and its eternal inhabitants.

The Lady of the House of Sleep, as Joseph Campbell calls her in *The Hero With A Thousand Faces*, "is the incarnation of the promise of perfection. ... Time sealed her away, yet she is dwelling still, like one who sleeps in timelessness, at the bottom of the timeless sea." Indeed, it is at the bottom of the sea that Urashima Taro finds his fairy princess in a well-known Japanese folk-tale. But the hapless fisherman does not fare so well as the Prince of the Lonesome Isle. After a few years, he grows homesick for his earthly village and wishes to return. His bride gives him a box to take with him, which, provided that he does not open it, will enable him to return to her in the kingdom beneath the sea. When he comes to his village, he learns that hundreds of years have passed, and that he himself is a centuries-old legend. He forgets the warning of his fairy wife in his bewilderment, and opens the box she had given him. At once, all his years escape from the box and descend upon him, and he vanishes into dust.

A similar fate befell Oisin, son of the Irish hero, Fionn mac Cumhail. After the disastrous battle of Gabhra, in which the Fianna were overcome, a woman came riding over the sea from the west. Niamh of the Golden Hair was her name, and she declared her love for Oisin, taking him away to Tir na n'Og, the Land of the Young. He spent a year in that happy place, "where the grass was always green and fruit and flowers could be picked together, where feasting, music, love, hunting and joyous fighting went on all day and death made no entry."[4] After a year had passed, however, Oisin longed to visit his homeland, and made ready to do so when he was told that time in Tir na n'Og was not reckoned by mortal measure, and that not one year had passed in Eire, but a hundred, or perhaps a thousand. Nevertheless, he might visit his homeland and return, so long as he never let his foot touch the ground. So he journeyed back and saw that, indeed, all had changed, and the Fianna were no more. So sorrowed was he by all this that he forgot the warning of the fairies and alighted from his horse. At once the weight of mortal years fell upon his shoulders and he became an old, old man. His horse rushed back at once to Tir na n'Og, and Oisin spent his last days mourning the passing of Fianna and the loss of his eternal youth.

In a Tyrolean version of the story, cited by Katherine Briggs in her *Encyclopedia of Fairies*, a peasant "followed his herd under a stone and into a cave, where a lady met him, gave him food and offered him a post as a gardener." After several weeks, the peasant grew homesick and wished to return. He was allowed to go, but everything in his former world had changed, and no one recognized him except one ancient woman, who asked him "Where have you been? I have been looking for you for two hundred years." Then she took him by the hand and he fell dead, for she was Death.

The story of King Herla has a slightly different ending—or rather, no ending at all. Herla, king of the ancient Britons (that is, before the Saxon invasion), was once challenged by the king of the fairies each to be a guest at the other's wedding. Sure enough, at the marriage of King Herla with the King of France's daughter, the fairy king arrived, with all his retinue, and a feast was served out of fairy provisions, "of a quality beyond anyone's thoughts." A year later, the fairy king arrived and bid Herla to his own wedding, and Herla followed him into a cave in a high cliff. There the wedding was celebrated, and King Herla and his men were honored with gifts and offerings of "all things pertaining to hunting and falconry." Then they were given a hound, small enough to be carried, and were cautioned not to dismount when they arrived in their own world until the hound leapt from his carrier. When Herla and his men emerged from the cave, they found few who could understand their speech, for two hundred years had passed, and the Saxon tongue had replaced that of the Britons. "The king was astonished," the twelfth-century historian Walter Map tells us, "for he imagined that he had been away for three days only." Some of King Herla's men alighted from their horses, forgetting the warnings of the fairies, and instantly they crumbled into dust. The king and the rest of the men vowed not to descend until the hound leapt down, and since he has not yet done so, it must be supposed that King Herla and his men ride still: and indeed, the sound of his eternal hunt may sometimes be heard to this day in the lonely valleys of Herefordshire.

The hero of an Italian variant of the Oisin tale pursued his Swan Maiden to the Isle of Happiness, and stayed with her there for two months—or so he thought. He wishes to visit his mother, and like Oisin, is given a beautiful black horse to carry him over the sea. He too is warned not to descend from the horse, but in this case his bride goes with him to make sure. They meet an old woman with a load of shoes which she has worn out looking for him, but when she slips and falls and he bends down to assist her, his fairy bride warns him, "Beware! That is Death!" They next come to a great lord on a leg-weary horse, but before the hero comes to his aid again his bride warns him, "Beware! That is the Devil!" Finally, the hero is convinced that his mother is dead and forgotten: for two hundred years have passed in the time he has been away, and so the two return to the Isle of Happiness, where they have lived ever since.

Though the endings differ from tale to tale, the laws governing the return of the hero from time out of time are constant: one may visit the mortal world, but to tarry there and then to go again into merciless time, is to meet death at once. The price of immortality is eternal vigilance—or are they one and the same thing? To dine with the immortals—or drink with them, like Rip Van Winkle—bestows a partial immortality: but since that is a quality only the gods possess, it is plain that immortal man lives not by fairy bread alone. Something else is needed, which only the hero himself can supply, particularly if he is to return to the world from which he sprang. But what world is that? Or is man of another world as well as this one? —the "two worlds of life and death" that Shelley speaks of in *Prometheus Bound*, where one might meet, as did the Magus Zoroaster, "his own image, walking in the garden."

Dug-From-Ground is the name of a truly autochthonous hero of the Hupa Indians of California. He came into being not by natural birth, but from the earth, as a forked root. After performing various deeds by which he was recognized and accepted by his earthly mother and grandmother, he decided to visit the home of the immortals, at the eastern edge of the world. In that world also he was accepted, and married the daughter of the sun. He played the game of shinny with his brothers-in-law, including Wildcat, whose face he smashed into its present shape; Fox, whose face he pinched; Earthquake, and Thunder. Eventually, he went home to his grandmother to find that "as many nights as it seemed to him he had spent, so many years he had really been away." Both his mother and grandmother had worried about him, and kept a kind of vigil during his absence. Then Dug-From-Ground repaired their house, picked it up with a stick and went away, with his earthly family, to the end of the world. They are all living there still.

In this tale the hero explicitly journeys to a sacred place, namely the home of the immortals, the dwelling-place of the sun and of various natural forces and clan totems. He succeeds not only in retaining immortality, but even in conveying it to his mortal family: the difference here is that he comes into the mortal world already marked as being of another nature. The idea of two natures, or two destinies, of man can be seen in stories of a kind usually referred to as "Friends in Life and Death," a fine example of which can be found in Italo Calvino's retelling of "One Night in Paradise," from his collection of *Italian Folktales*.

Once upon a time two friends made a pledge that the first to get married would call on the other to be his best man, even if he should be at the ends of the earth. One of the friends died, however, and when the surviving friend was to be married, the priest told him to visit the grave of his friend and invite him to be the best man. "It will then be up to him whether to come to your wedding or not." As soon as this was done, the earth opened and the dead friend came up at once to keep his word.

The wedding was held, and a marvelous banquet as well, but it was plain that the living friend wanted to know all about the afterlife. After the feast, the dead man rose and said, "Friend, since I've done you this favor, would you walk me back a part of the way?" The living friend agreed to do so, kissed his bride and told her that he would return immediately. But his curiosity got the better of him, and after asking numerous times about the hereafter, he agreed to go on a short visit beyond the grave. So the two friends set off for Paradise, where the living friend saw many marvels that mortal eyes have never (or seldom) beheld. After a few hours of this delightful journey, the living friend remembered that it was his wedding night, and that he should return, though he wanted very much to stay and see more. Reluctantly, his dead friend conducted him back to the grave, and then vanished from sight, and he returned to the world from which he had come. But how changed everything was! The small village had become a great city, the parish church was now a cathedral, and everything was changed. When he went looking for his bride, he was told that no one had been married the day before. Then he told his story to the sacristan, and finally to the bishop, who recalled an old story of a similar nature that he had heard as a boy. The bishop took down the parish books and began looking through them, searching for the name of the bride and bridegroom.

> Finally, on a yellowed, crumbling page he put his finger on those very names. "It was three hundred years ago. The young man disappeared from the cemetery, and the bride died of a broken heart. Read right here if you don't believe it!"
> "But I'm the bridegroom myself!"
> "And you went to the next world? Tell me about it!"
> But the young man turned deathly pale, sank to the ground, and died before he could tell one single thing he had seen.[5]

When his friend Enkidu dies, Gilgamesh sets out to find immortality, the elixir of life. Eventually, he encounters an old man: Utnapishtim, the Far-Away, the Sumerian Noah, who was saved from the Flood, and dwells forever in Dilmun, the garden of the gods, at the mouth of all rivers. The old man puts the hero to the test of staying awake for six days and seven nights, but immediately, sleep, like a fog, blows around him and his eyes shut fast. After the time of his waking had passed in sleep, Utnapishtim awakens Gilgamesh, who insists that he had only just closed his eyes. But Utnapishtim's wife had baked a loaf of bread each day that the hero had slept, and the old man points them out:

> "Count these loaves and learn how many days you slept, for your first is hard, your second like leather, your third is soggy, the crust of your fourth has mould, your fifth is mildewed, your sixth is fresh and

your seventh was still over the glowing embers when I touched and woke you." Gilgamesh said, "What shall I do, O Utnapishtim, where shall I go? Already the thief in the night has hold of my limbs, death inhabits my room; wherever my foot rests, there I find death."[6]

So we come at last, by the elliptical method of fairytale and myth, to the heart of the matter: for what else is it that the hero seeks if not immortality? And what danger faces him when he attains the garden of the gods except precisely those mortal coils which he cannot shuffle off? After failing the test put to him by his ambiguous guru, Gilgamesh is given a boon that he might not go away empty-handed after all that he has endured. He is told of a plant which, if he can pick it from the bottom of the sea, will confer eternal youth. He plunges into the sea and takes the plant in triumph. But on his return to Uruk, he stops to bathe, leaving the plant by the side of the pool. A serpent, smelling the plant, snatches the plant and immediately sheds its skin; through inattention, for a moment's earthly joy of a good bath, Gilgamesh loses everything. The story seems hardly a myth at all, but a parable of our lives, so direct and explicit is the search and the result.

Whence comes the call to such a search, when so much—all the world, even Nature herself, and even the gods—seem opposed to it? Is it an unattainable dream, born of insatiable thirst or persistent dissatisfaction? But then we are thrown back to the question again, for whence that thirst, that dissatisfaction? Is it the product of a confused mind, or what Mircea Eliade calls "nostalgia for Paradise"? There is a story by Sholem Aleichem, called "Elijah the Prophet," which touches on just this point. It is the time of the Passover, and the house is being made ready for the Seder. The narrator is a young boy whose father tells him to sleep, so that he will be able to sit up at the Seder and ask the Four Questions. "Remember," his father tells him, "you must not sleep at the Seder. If you do, Elijah the Prophet will come with a bag on his shoulders. On the first two nights of Passover, Elijah the Prophet goes about looking for those who have fallen asleep at the Seder and takes them away in his bag." This acts as a challenge to the young boy, who even drinks a full cup of wine, to the very dregs. And, of course, he falls asleep. He dreams that in fact Elijah does come, with his bag, and silently comes to the sleeping boy. "Now, little boy," says Elijah the Prophet, "get into my bag and come."

> *I asked him, "Where to?" and he replied, "You will see later." I did not want to go, and he said to me again, "Come." And I began to argue with him. "How can I go with you when I am a wealthy man's son?" Said he to me, "And as a wealthy man's son, of what great value are you?" Said I, "I am the only child of my father and mother." Said he, "To me, you are not an only child." Said I, "I am fretted over. If they find that I am gone, they will not get over it; they will die, especially my mother."*
>
> *He looked at me, the old man did, very kindly and he said to me, softly and sweetly as before, "If you do not want to die, then come with me. Say goodbye to your father and mother, and come."[7]*

But what, or who in us will obey that call? Is it the world without that stands opposed to the quest for eternal life, or the world within? And who, or what, will wake us?

It is said that King Arthur, the Once and Future King, did not die of his wounds, but sleeps to this day in a cave on the Isle of Avalon. A shepherd once encountered a strange and mysterious man, who told him of a hoard of treasure that lay beneath the tree from which the shepherd's crook was cut. Within the cave, he was warned, there hung a great bell, and he must not touch it, or else the Sleepers in the Cave would wake.

The stranger vanished, so the shepherd took his encounter, and its information, for nothing more than a dream. But some time later, while seeking for a lost sheep, he came to a valley and recognized the tree from which his staff had been cut. There under the roots he found the entrance to a cave, and went in. It was dark, so he lit a candle which he happened to have in his pocket, and by its light he beheld warriors sleeping in a circle, each clad in armor, with a sword by his side. In their midst was a king who wore a golden crown and held in his hand a shining sword. The shepherd, dazzled by what he saw, stepped back, and as ill luck would have it, struck his head against the bell which hung over the doorway. As its deep chime sounded through the cavern, the king woke slowly and asked, "Is it time?" The poor shepherd had only just enough wit left to reply, "No, it is not yet time." "Well have you said," replied the king, "for only will I wake when Britain is at its hour of greatest need. Now take of the treasure which lies before you and be gone with God speed, lest my knights awaken and slay you." The shepherd did as he was bidden, and Arthur returned to his long rest.

Within the Smith's Rock on the Isle of Skye lie sleeping the Fenian Men and Fionn mac Cumhail himself sleeps with them. By their side is a great wooden crier, or horn, which if blown, will wake the Fianna to the Last Battle. A smith of the island once found them there, and tried to wake them, giving two blasts on the whistle before fleeing in mortal terror at their fearsome aspect. The heroes are still half awake, propped up on their elbows, awaiting the third blast of the horn to summon them forth.

It is a strange sort of sleep that we encounter in these tales: a sleep of readiness and attentiveness, a kind of vigil, not the sleep of oblivion that characterizes our lives. There is in that state an escape from the ravages of Time, like the third state of being, the *susupta-sthana* of the Mandukya Upanishad. It is spoken of as sleep, but it is as much like sleep as we know it as the wakefulness which it implies is like our waking state.

In each of the stories examined, there are certain consistencies which stand out. The first and most obvious is that the heroes in each story experience a kind of time which flows differently from that to which we are accustomed. As Niamh of the Golden Hair tells her beloved Oisin, "time is not reckoned by mortal measure." The second is that this other order of time is connected in every instance with a specific place which can be termed sacred: mountains, caves, islands, towers, palaces—all these are places set apart from the ordinary run of life. To strengthen the image there is usually a barrier or difficulty to be surmounted in order to gain entrance: a hedge of thorns, river of fire and poison trees, the grave, or simply the sundering sea. These are the architectonic emblems of the Center, the foot, as it were, of the Cosmic Tree, the *axis mundi*, the Sacred Mountain, where heaven and earth meet. At the Center, wherever that is, time is different, values are reversed, sleep is waking, and waking sleep. Here the hero encounters his destiny, that for which he is in quest, and the very element which serves to strengthen the image of Center—danger—serves also as a reminder that once the threshold is crossed between these two worlds (or perhaps they are the two natures of man) a new set of laws applies. Joseph Campbell writes that once the hero's mortal parts are "brought into accord with the powers and forms of timelessness," the least fluctuation of the heroic will, the briefest moment of forgetfulness places him in great peril, and that "all of him [stands] to be refuted, blasted, by the impact of the forms and powers of time."[8]

The return of the hero is fraught with so much danger that the tales of failure seem to far outnumber those of successful return. A moment of forgetfulness—that is, of the waking sleep that characterizes our lives—suffices for all to be lost. The Living Friend and the Seven Sleepers begin to tell their tales to mortal ears and crumble away into dust, Urashima Taro opens the box of his years, Oisin slips to the earth and into mortal time. These are the heroes who lost everything through their own forgetfulness. The eternal vigils of King Arthur and the Fianna are disturbed, though not broken, by forgetful or thoughtless mortals. The deliberate (one might say, lawful) awakenings lead to less disastrous results: King Mucukunda is awakened through Krishna's trickery to the last battle and ultimate retreat into the mountains to complete his victory over Time; the Sleeping Beauty and the Queen of Tubber Tintye, like the Valkyrie Brünnhilde, awake to an immortal hierogamy. Dug-From-Ground returns to mortal time only long enough to find his grandmother and bring her back to the land of the immortals. The return is not, therefore, impossible—only extremely difficult and dangerous, as is any crossing of the threshold between the "two worlds of life and death."

"Go I know not where, bring back I know not what" is the hero's task in one Russian folktale. Could anything more precisely express the dilemma in which those in search find themselves? To fetch the apples of the Hesperides may seem explicit enough a task, but how will one recognize them? It is the dilemma of all heroes in all quests, however exactly the object of the quest may be described. Will they, like Tiltil and Mytil in Maeterlinck's *The Blue Bird*, mistake a thousand mortal birds for the one and only which will endure for all time? How is the "sleep" of true consciousness to be distinguished from the other kinds of sleep in which we pass our lives? There is an ambiguous image in these references to sleep, a hint perhaps that our evaluations are topsy-turvy. What could be more pleasurable, more rewarding for the labors undergone, more refreshing for the labors to come, than sleep: yet Gilgamesh dozes off and loses everything at the exact moment that he could have become the master of sleep, and therefore the master of time. Rip Van Winkle may have slept for twenty years, or watched the mountain revelers for twenty years and slept but a single night: but what knowledge, what boon did he bring back? Only a curious story to titillate the curious. Perhaps the image of the Sleeping Beauty, the Queen of Tubber Tintye, the Lady of the House of Sleep, in those nuptial journeys of sleep signifies that to master time—that is, to master mortality—requires a marriage of our two natures: only first, one of them must be awakened.

Where is Tir na n'Og, the Land of the Young? At the Center, apparently. But where is that, and how will we recognize it? The myths call it the Sacred Mountain, and folktales call it Fairyland sometimes, but that doesn't tell us much. Perhaps the clearest clue occurs in a story by George MacDonald called "The Golden Key": "Things that look real in this country look very thin indeed in Fairyland, while some of the things that here cannot stand still for a moment, will not move there." Is Time one of those things?

> *There was a boy who used to sit in the twilight and listen to his great-aunt's stories.*
>
> *She told him that if he could reach the place where the end of the rainbow stands he would find there a golden key.*
>
> *"And what is the key for?" the boy would ask. "What is the key of? What will it open?"*
>
> *"That nobody knows," his aunt would reply. "He has to find that out."[9]*

Notes:

1. Washington Irving, "Rip Van Winkle," in *The Sketchbook of Geoffrey Crayon, Gent.* (New York: New American Library, 1961), p. 50.

2. P. L. Travers, *About the Sleeping Beauty* (New York: McGraw-Hill, 1975), pp. 58-59.

3. Jeremiah Curtin, *Myths and Folk-Lore of Ireland* (Boston: Little, Brown & Co., 1890), pp. 101-106.

4. Katherine Briggs, *An Encyclopedia of Fairies* (New York: Pantheon, 1976), p. 400.

5. Italo Calvino, *Italian Folktales* (New York: Harcourt Brace Jovanovich, 1980), p.121.

6. N.K. Sandars, *The Epic of Gilgamesh* (Harmondsworth: Penguin Books, 1971), p.112.

7. Sholem Aleichem, "Elijah the Prophet," reprinted in *Jewish Affairs*, March 1969, pp. 24-26.

8. Joseph Campbell, *The Hero With a Thousand Faces* (Princeton University Press, 1973), p. 221.

9. George MacDonald, "The Golden Key," in *The Complete Fairy Tales of George Mac-Donald* (New York: Schocken Books, 1977), p. 210.

Parabola
Volume: 25.1
Threshold

CROSSING INTO THE INVISIBLE

Laura Simms

There was an orphan boy whose job it was to watch the fresh threshed corn on the threshing floor of the barn. But he fell asleep and the hens ate the corn. His stepmother was furious. He exclaimed, "But I had a remarkable dream. I was standing with one foot in this world and one foot in the other. The sun was on my right side and the moon was on my left. I wore a crown and my body was speckled with stars."

"Give me that dream," demanded the stepmother.

"I cannot. It is my dream," he answered, "It came and it went."

Angrily she sent him away. He stepped over the threshold and went out into the world in search of his fortune.

In the literal story, the threshold the dreamer crossed was the barn and the life that he knew. In a more hidden sense, the threshold was the dreamer himself who would not give away his dream. The hidden jewel is the storytelling wherein the listener crosses over the threshold that separates the waking mind from the invisible world within. To bring an audience into an abiding present is as significant and far-reaching as understanding the narrative text or the psychological travels instigated by a story's images. It is what awakens us and lets us step again and again over the threshold of our own limited perceptions.

Writing about performance, Peter Brook says, "The essential thing is to recognize that there is an invisible world which needs to be made visible."[1] The experience of being swept into the ritual of ongoing story teaches us that the ground of the visible world is the invisible world out of which it arises.

As the characters in the fairy tale cross thresholds into other realms, we listeners are drawn inward past the boundaries of our logical minds into vast space and communal presence. The words beguile our minds with profuse detail as our imaginations recreate the story. The habitual patterns of thinking that usually patrol the borders of this familiar world are engaged, and thus the door falls open inward—we feel the ever-present timeless space of mind that has always existed beneath consciousness.

The teller frees us to dream awake. "We must pass through dreams in order to perceive the supernatural dimensions of the natural," writes Helene Cixous.[2] The story and the telling provide doorways to be opened. The process of the telling provides the push that sends us across.

The first doorway opens onto the threshold of longing. Then, we cross the threshold of no return followed by the unrelenting threshold of death. In the middle of the journey we sink through the threshold of mystery until we ascend again over the threshold of return.

The threshold of longing: From the moment the storyteller begins to speak, our attention is focused by his or her presence and voice and by the beginning of the story. We hover half in and half out of our world, longing to find out more about the world of the story. If the voice is trustworthy, we shift our attention seemingly outward, while setting the ground for an inner visualization. A Turkish storyteller's proverb says, "The voice is half the wisdom." And the tale itself slowly seduces our minds into wanting to know what is going to happen next. ...

The Dreamer came to a Palace. The King was outside and inquired what he was doing. The boy explained how he had lost his home and work because of his dream. "Give me your dream!" ordered the King. When the boy refused he was placed in a dungeon.

But the princess, who was being forced to marry a King that she hated, took pity on the Dreamer and brought him food. Night after night he solved impossible riddles posed by her father until he won her freedom. At last she was married to the Dreamer, which caused the rejected King to declare war upon their Kingdom. The Dreamer said, "I will battle the King" and went off to fight without an army. He was armed with his dreaming mind.

Moved forward by the storyteller's living voice, we construct a basic landscape within which the characters of the story can perform without constant reconstruction. We are moved to inquire about what will happen next. The longing opens our hearts with a different kind of desire. This is the passage over the first threshold.

Such longing is akin to entering the grounds that surround a sacred temple, a place where one will have the opportunity to come face to face with the Divine: the pilgrim "is within a temenos, or precinct, a place 'cut off' from the common land and dedicated to a god."[3] The threshold of no return is both a state of mind and an uninterrupted involvement in the co-creation of the narrative. Longing releases our discursive mind while imagination rises up from the heart and inner eye to conduct the unfolding drama of the story.

The listener is literally carried away—it is as if a little trap door in the inner world falls open, and we hardly notice that our listening activity is propelled onward like a natural waterfall. We would be disappointed and disturbed if we were to be interrupted. What is it that holds us so fast? Beneath the response to the spoken narrative, the natural space of mind rests in a vast ocean of silence that is reassuringly familiar and wholesome. "The door opens," as Cixous tells us of stories, "directly into the soul."

Another example of catapulting across the threshold of no return is exemplified in the tale of the warrior princess. An eldest and a middle brother took up the challenge of a foreign princess who would marry whatever man could defeat her in single combat. Who would not want to know what was going to happen next?

Each brother traveled over seven mountain ranges, and each came to an old man standing alone in a valley. The old man said, "Tell me what you value most, advice from me or rushing off to battle the princess?" Each brother refused his advice, saying, "I don't need an old man's advice. I am going to marry the princess." Each brother was beheaded in the battle, bedazzled by the armored warrior who tricked them by baring her breasts just as the battle began.

When the third and youngest prince rode out, we, like him, are pre-pared to take the old man's advice: "She is not strong. She tricks those who meet her heedlessly. When she lifts her spear to start the battle, look away and do not be distracted." The wisdom of the old man reflects our inner state of knowing, as well as the composure in listening that supports the audience. Later we learn that her ruse of baring her breasts is not as magnetizing as opening the heart.

The threshold of death awaits us all. There is no avoiding it, and the story allows us to taste its insistence.

A soldier, who had carried a princess-turned-snake around his neck for seven years with the promise of bliss at the end of the journey, arrived at a copper palace. The snake informed him that he must only stay in the court for seven days and under no condition pass over the threshold to leave, and she will return as a woman to marry him.

How simple seven days seem after seven years. However, his soldier's mind had not been tested well enough. He gave in to insecurity and need, chased a wish-fulfilling cask of food over the threshold, and lost everything. He watched the castle crumble to dust and the princess soar away on the back of a hideous dragon. He confronted his death over and over again in seeking the dragon's realm known only to Baba Yaga, the unbiased, fierce mother of nature herself. Disappointment, terror, and total surrender were necessary. In some fairy tales the hero or hero-ine must make the journey with no protection on a three-legged horse. The most serious threshold in every story calls forth our greatest fear or attachment to the world as we know it.

In a Norwegian fairy tale, the hero came to a crossroads where there are three signs: "He who travels down this rode will return unharmed"; "He who travels this path may or may not return"; and "He who travels here will never return." Of course, he chose the third. How else would we discover the outcome of this journey? But it is just a story—and we are not aware that the characters, the feeling, the landscape, and the task are created by ourselves, since we have crossed over into the becoming of everything with no return. The road imagined is ours. The fear felt is conjured from our own experience.

> *He met a wolf whose body was so thin from hunger that his ribs shone through his fur like crystals. The starving beast said, "If you feed me, I will take you where you have to go." The prince replied, "But I have no food myself."*
>
> *The wolf howled pitifully, "Then kill the horse you ride on and let me eat your beast." Having come this far, the youth, weeping, killed his horse and fed it to the wolf. The wolf took him across the uncrossable border of his father's kingdom to the realm of a heartless giant.*

In the invisible world of our inner drama we have killed our only conscious vehicle of travel, our sweetest companion, and passed over the threshold of death. Here, in the exercise of imagination, we murder the safe path, killing our own limited vehicle of travel. What is most terrible or feared must be done in the mind in order to meet our terror and contain it in our waking lives. The vastness of listening contains all the fear of the universe.

The hero or heroine sometimes dies and is reborn, like the shaman who sheds his skin and loses his bones in order to journey to the other world to retrieve health, lost souls, or information unavailable to us. We too in hearing shift our allegiance from the ways of this world to a magical listening that arises from the mind before thought emerges. We let go of our expectations and preconceptions, defying all logic in our pilgrimage toward the end of the story.

The threshold of mystery: having crossed so far, we no longer question the logic of the story or spring back into conceptual thinking. We are committed to going forward with the events because they are of our own making. All the while, we sink deeper into the sensuousness of total presence. The experience is of a lush inner relaxation, familiar and vast. No one thinks about it while it is happening because to think about it would be to lose it. Later it is called enchantment or trance. But it is wide awake.

> *A youngest prince discovered that his two sisters had disappeared in a supernatural whirlwind before his birth. He set off to find them. He refused his father's army and wealth, instead taking only a harp that had no strings, which he had found in the basement. He learned to play. His music was stunning, and all who heard him wept for joy. He tricked demons and stupefied monsters, winning a cloak of invisibility.*

The journey of this prince crossed four worlds, and our imagination goes with him freely. He traveled in uncanny ways, beyond conception or visibility, to the incomprehensible realm of the Queen of Everything, who had turned her back to our world. Her island was surrounded by hundreds of thousands of warriors. Their spears held the heads of everyone who had attempted to pass into her garden by conventional means or force.

The prince put on his cloak of invisibility and entered the Queen's garden. He saw twenty white doves fly to earth and turn into twenty women, and in the center stood the Queen. Without thinking, he took off his cloak, revealing himself, and called her name. He no longer cared if he lived or died.

The opening of the heart without fear takes place in the crossing of this threshold. We have learned to alight and ascend from a groundless place, trusting that we contain all possibilities. Needless to say, we are held by the presence of the storyteller, our guide on this holy excursion, although each of us enters the temple of our own design.

> *The Queen was taken by surprise. "How did you get here?" she inquired. The prince told his entire story, and she invited him to dine with her. "I will allow you to enter into my palace because you came with a good heart and did not attempt to enter with force."*

It is not surprising that we who listen to stories do not want the tale to end at this point. To remain in the Garden of the Queen, to enter her palace is the culmination of the journey—one that is most pleasurable, with none of our everyday concerns of rent and worry, responsibilities or illness, death and loss. Her palace is not described.

The threshold of return is necessary and most poignant. The storyteller knows the story will soon end and in a thousand unspoken ways is gently preparing us for re-entry, holding the reins of attention while letting out its taut line slowly—by sound of voice, by intention, by the knowledge that our lives are social, responsible, and that the story event was only the practice. How we live our ordinary lives is what is essential.

In truth, the storyteller knows that the timelessness found in listening is always the ground of all existence. And the true challenge to the listener, and to the storyteller, is to acknowledge this in waking life.

In the most moving of Scottish fairy tales, the hero Diarmud ("No Envy") passed through three worlds and gave up everything to save his dying otherworldly wife. He went where no man had ever gone to retrieve the Cup that Heals. However, as he was about to offer her the drink, a red dwarf appeared:

> *"I forgot to tell you that when she finishes the drink you will not love her any more. Do not pretend. She will know. The King will hold a celebration in his world beneath the sea. Accept no gift. Ask only for a ship to return to your world."*

When he sailed back to his companions and all the people of the world, they awaited him on the shore with great joy. They had feared that he, greatest hero and poet, lover of the feminine and hunter of the sacred, who alone had crossed three thresholds into other worlds, would stay in the other world forever. And we would have been left without his story.

The prince who played the harp that had no strings returned to his world to free his sisters from wrathful forces of the supernatural and become a great King. He understood the intricate relationship between nature and human beings and how it had fallen out of balance. He also knew the necessity for the Queen to be part of our world in all her power.

> *And the Dreamer traveled back to his wife after five years. The old King had died, and she sat the Dreamer on a throne. Because of his journey, one foot was planted in each world. She sat beside him like*

the sun, the other King's daughter sat beside him like the moon, and the water from a golden bowl his five-year-old son held shimmered on his chest like the stars in the sky. "You did not give away your dream and it has come true," said the Queen.

The storyteller returns us to our ordinary perceptions, letting us come back gently: "And so the story ends and they all lived happily ever after."

This lie that we will all live happily ever after is a lie only in a world concerned solely with the visible. For knowing that the invisible world is ever-present and ever-nourishing in the visible world, we do indeed live happily ever after, regardless of the ceaseless manifestations of the world and the truth of death.

The real journey of these spoken fairy tales takes us to a place that does not exist but must be reached, and then brings us back again. Like the heroine or hero adorned with wisdom and story, we bring back a secret treasure of awareness that is priceless. For the stepping over is a "seeing, as the Hindu would say, the *darshan* ... the viewing of the sacred itself."[4] The story ends like pilgrimage, having brought us to the inner chamber in the temple where one might view a statue of a deity or discover nothing at all. The journey was the crossing.

Notes:

1. Peter Brook, *The Open Door* (New York: Pantheon, 1993).

2. Helene Cixous, *Three Steps on the Ladder to Writing* (New York: Columbia University Press, 1993).

3. Jane Harrison, *Ancient Art and Ritual* (Bradford-on-Avon, England: Moonraker Press, 1978).

4. Michael Wood, *The Smile of Murrigan* (London: Penguin, 1996).

CHAPTER FOUR

•

ALL OUR RELATIVES

A mythology is not an ideology. It is not something projected from the brain,
but something experienced from the heart, from recognitions of identities
behind or within the appearances of nature, perceiving with love a "thou"
where there would have been otherwise only an "it."[1]

—Joseph Campbell

" … within this bundle there is a sacred pipe. With this you will,
during the winters to come, send your voices to Wakan Tanka,
your Father and Grandfather."

After the mysterious woman said this, she took from the bundle
a pipe, and also a small round stone which she placed
upon the ground. Holding the pipe up with its stem to the
heavens, she said: "With this sacred pipe you will walk upon
the Earth; for the Earth is your Grandmother and Mother, and
She is sacred. Every step that is taken upon Her should be
as a prayer. The bowl of this pipe is of red stone; it is the Earth.
Carved in the stone and facing the center is this buffalo calf who represents
all the four-leggeds who live upon your Mother.
The stem of the pipe is of wood, and this represents all that
grows upon the Earth. And these twelve feathers which hang
here where the stem fits into the bowl are from Wanbli
Galeshka, the Spotted Eagle, and they represent the eagle and
all the wingeds of the air. All these peoples, and all things of
the universe, are joined to you who smoke the pipe—all send their
voices to Wakan-Tanka, the Great Spirit. When you pray with
this pipe, you pray for and with everything."

The wakan woman then touched the foot of the pipe to the round stone which lay upon the ground, and said: "With this pipe you will be bound to all your relatives: your Grandfather and Father, your Grandmother and Mother. This round rock, which is made of the same red stone as the bowl of the pipe, your Father Wakan-Tanka has also given to you. It is the Earth, your Grandmother and Mother, and it is where you will live and increase. This Earth which He has given to you is red, and the two-leggeds who live upon the Earth are red; and the Great Spirit has also given to you a red day, and a red road. All of this is sacred and so do not forget! Every dawn as it comes is a holy event, and every day is holy, for the light comes from your Father Wakan-Tanka; and also you must always remember that the two-leggeds and all the other peoples who stand upon this earth are sacred and should be treated as such."[2]

—Black Elk

… Andean culture enlists nothing less than the faculty of feeling to serve as the organizing field for memory. One feels myth first, and understands it later.[3]

—William Sullivan

Parabola
Volume: 29.2
Web of Life

Ours Is Not a Dead Universe

Seyyed Hossein Nasr

When we turn to religions and traditional civilizations all over the world, we see a remarkable unanimity in regards to consciousness. It is something that *is*, like Being itself, which at its highest level of reality is at once luminous and numinous. Universally, consciousness is regarded as not only a state or a process, but a substance. Consciousness at its elevated levels is at once knowing and knowing that it knows, knowledgeable of its own knowledge. It is at once the source of all sentience, of all experience, and beyond all experience of the knowledge that something is being experienced.

In the Rig Veda, the oldest of all Hindu sacred scriptures, we read, "When alone is the dawn beaming over all this, it is the one that severally becomes all this." The one is *Sat*, *Chit*, and *Ananda*, the three states of being, consciousness, and bliss.

In reality it is Chit, consciousness, that is Sat, or being, and is also Ananda, or bliss. We find the same idea in the *Tao Te Ching*, the primary text of Taoism, which also influenced Neo-Confucianism. The nameless Tao is the beginning of heaven and earth, and the same Tao is the mother of the ten thousand things. So at the origin of the universe you have the Tao, which in fact is also consciousness. We all know the opening of the Book of John: "In the beginning was the Word. And the Word was with

God, and the Word was God." In chapter 6 of the Book of John, Christ says, "The words I have spoken to you are spirit and they are life." So this Word is not simply word in the ordinary sense, but it is the spirit and life; it is consciousness. Finally, in the Koran, in chapter 36, the surah *Yasin*, it is said, "But His command when He intendeth a thing is only that He sayeth unto it, be and it is." So the origin is very explicitly stated in the Koran to be the command of God, who is the knower (*al-'Alim*) and is supreme consciousness.

I believe that it was only with the Scientific Revolution that "in the beginning was consciousness" was seriously challenged. Once the new worldview was established in which God became at best only the creator of the world, two issues arose. First, all the levels of consciousness were reduced to a single level. That is, the multileveled structure of the world of consciousness—from the Divine Consciousness, to the angels, the great intellects, the great saints, and sages, all the way to the consciousness of ordinary human beings (not to speak of animals)—was reduced to a single level of reality. People began to speak of consciousness in the world as being confined to ordinary human consciousness alone.

The second consequence was even more devastating. While it is true that most of the architects of the Scientific Revolution accepted that God created the world and that God had consciousness, they believed that after creating the world he had nothing further to do with it. In other words, they understood "in the beginning" only temporally. This is the deistic position, and during the last forty years we have been hearing about something like the same idea in new clothes—the Big Bang theory. It has been related to the perspective of the book of Genesis, or the Koran, and the Abrahamic vision of a creator God. But the consciousness of God within his creation is still seen as being irrelevant, because once the Big Bang has taken place, and the universe is here, there is no reference to a consciousness in the universe, and in fact the predominant scientistic view denies such a reality. Only energies and material particles are spoken of, so consciousness again remains outside of God's creation.

It is this denial of the primacy of consciousness that led to the method of explanation by reduction. This reductionist outlook is one of the most important characteristics of modern thought. One example is found at the doctor's office. We are reduced to what the MRI shows, and our chart, and the rest of us does not count. We are reduced to our biological aspect, and the biological aspect to chemistry, the chemistry to physics, and so forth. This is reductionism at work in our personal lives. It is only recently, in fact, that Harvard University has started a spirituality and healing program at the Medical School, because some medical doctors have come to realize all too well that our consciousness does affect our body in remarkable ways, even if we cannot explain it according to the prevalent scientistic paradigm.

In the Hindu view (to name one example) everything manifests a level of consciousness. A stone's being is a form of stony consciousness; the same holds true up the line, all the way to the level of human beings and beyond. The consequence of cutting human consciousness off from the higher levels of consciousness in the prevalent scientistic worldview is the weakening of access to the transcendent. Although the higher levels do not go away by our denying them, taking away the ladder or stairs to the third floor in this building means that one does not try to go up to the third floor any longer, and gradually the existence of the third floor is denied. Therefore, the quest for transcendence—for the empowering and illumination of our consciousness, which was the goal of all traditional civilizations—becomes irrelevant, and is ignored as an illusion. The desire for the transcendent and for the gaining of perfection, which defines what it means to be human, is horizontalized. The human search is reduced to gaining more and more information but not luminous knowledge, and this has resulted in a negative transformation of human consciousness.

This loss has put into serious doubt the truths and realities of religion itself. These truths have become either lost entirely, or reduced to meaningless metaphors or historical curiosities for modern man. It is no accident that many of the philosophies of religion from the nineteenth century onward have been based on reducing religious realities to what can be understood temporally and materially and denying everything that cannot be demonstrated by positive historical methods or proven in a laboratory. Since we cannot walk on water, then Christ could not have walked on water either, and people who say he did were either blind or had not been as well educated as us, or the event had some other meaning and must, on the basis of our truncated view of reality, be interpreted metaphorically.

An important consequence of this change is the loss of the meaning of being human. What does it mean to be human? This is not just an academic matter. A Christian or Muslim would say the human being has an immortal soul, but what does "soul" mean in the generally accepted view of the cosmos? And what about our attitude toward and relation to the rest of God's creation? What does that entail? Furthermore, what is the relationship between our being human as an immortal soul and our body? Since the establishment of the mechanistic worldview there has been an indifference to the body as a source of wisdom. In the 1960s, what appeared to be a sudden rediscovery of the body, expressed through sexuality and new kinds of music, was in fact a reaction to the reductionist view prevalent in Western society, an attempt to reassert the reality of the body.

All this brings us back to what happened to us as a result of the loss of the sense of the presence of consciousness throughout reality. Not only was the sense of the sacredness of human life put into question—the word "sacred" does not mean anything in the context of modern science—but we became homeless in a cosmos that is seen as nothing but energy and matter. Historically, humanity knew its position in the universe and felt at home in it. In the West the Ptolemaic system placed the earth in the middle and all of the heavens above; this did not cause hubris because humanity was seen to dwell on the lowest level of the cosmic hierarchy. The Mesoamericans in the Amazon feel they know where they are ontologically, but we do not know where we are; we do not have a home in the cosmos, and we have lost our sense of orientation.

The result has been a very profound sense of alienation, which is one of the maladies of the modern world. Alienation, like AIDS, is really a modern ailment, and it comes, to a large extent, from the fact that if we accept this reductionist worldview that came into being in the seventeenth century, and take seriously this cutting off of consciousness from the world in which we live, then we become very lonely here. The cosmos is no longer a hospitable place for us, and we are alienated from the world in which we live. Of course, when you calculate the probabilities for our being here from a scientific point of view, and it comes out to be extremely small, then that makes it even stranger that we are here at all. That is why in our normal lives we do not take these probabilities seriously—our human psyche, in order to remain sane, has to feel somewhat at home in the world. Any person who walks in the street and smells a flower, and sees how beautiful it is, will not take this point of view seriously, because if our human psyche is to remain sane, it must feel somewhat at home in the world in which we live.

As the world around us becomes increasingly alien, it also becomes spiritually worthless and is valued only in so far as it gratifies our own immediate impulses and so-called needs. The result is catastrophic for the world of nature. In the early 1960s, when I was teaching at Harvard, I spent a summer doing research on the book that became *Man and Nature: The Spiritual Crisis of Modern Man*, first given as the Rockefeller Lectures at the University of Chicago in 1966. These lectures foretold the environmental crisis, and spoke of its spiritual and inner causes. Practically none of the Christian theologians were interested in the issue at the time. The theology of nature was a non-existent category then. Some were angry at me for even speaking about the fact that the environmental crisis has a religious, theological, spiritual basis, and is not just a result of bad engineering. The crisis has a deep root; it has everything to do with what we think of the world around us. What is this tree that I am looking at through the window? If it is just wood for my fireplace, or if a fox is just fur to put around my wife's neck, or a mountain is just the place from which to extract iron ore and make cars, that is a very different attitude than if I look upon these things as sharing my own reality, including consciousness.

Our abominable treatment of nature is, I believe, a direct consequence of our alienation from a world in which there is no participation in a shared reality beyond the material. Even if you say, "My body is made of stardust, and I share the dust of the stars," this is a nice poetic utterance, but it does not mean anything in the prevalent scientistic paradigm. Stardust is dead matter in a dead universe.

We have so much marginalized ourselves that we find ourselves at a loss when something happens that goes outside of the definition that we have determined, and either seeks or claims to find consciousness somewhere else in the cosmos. Take for example the question of UFOs or alien abductions. All civilizations have marginalized and rejected people who have had a worldview contrary to the dominant one; today we do it in the name of science. John Mack, a professor at Harvard, has studied hundreds of cases of UFO sightings—clinically and scientifically. Even if you do not accept that these people are telling the truth, this phenomenon is related to a deep urge for connectedness with an intelligence or consciousness beyond our immediate human terrestrial sphere. This matter is not irrelevant; it is now part and parcel of our common pop culture. Children are brought up with movies about aliens and other types of science fiction.

What function does this fill? The "beings" involved in such experiences have taken the place of all the non-human intelligences and forms of consciousness that we see in traditional civilizations, in traditional philosophies as well as within folk and fairy tales. These tales were told to children by their elders, and satisfied a very deep yearning of the human soul for companionship in the world, and they were not considered mere fiction. When you cut human beings off from that cosmic world of consciousness—when it is no longer considered relevant—myth is converted to science fiction, and the vision of angels to the experience of aliens and UFOs. Myth then becomes something unreal instead of a sacred reality, and in its place have come all kinds of pseudo-myths which surround us.

Desacralization and the ensuing alienation have also made a sham of the metaphysical and philosophical basis of ethics. In all periods of human history, ethics was related to a vision of reality, and had a cosmic aspect. We think of the battle between the good spirits, the *ahuras*, and the bad, the *divs*, in Zoroastrianism, or of St. Augustine's treatise on the good. Whatever traditional world you enter, there is a permanent set of ethical norms that are never only human ethics linked to the human world; rather, they have a cosmic aspect. Through this depleting of the cosmos of consciousness, we have made ethical acts toward the world of nature contrived and without a metaphysical and cosmological basis. In the Ten Commandments, for example, we adhere to being respectful toward our neighbor: "Thou shalt not kill." But within the scientistic paradigm, where is the reason for not cutting down a tree or not killing an animal, except sentimentality or expediency?

In the sacred scriptures, explanations were given for an ethics encompassing the world of nature as well as that of human beings. Animals and plants were seen as God's creation, with spiritual value, as were rivers and mountains. Those notions are now scientifically meaningless, and any environmental ethics based on that view of the world is based on mere sentimentality. What is sacred about DNA if it is just molecules banging against each other in certain configurations? If we reject the sacred, reject that it is the wisdom of God that is imprinted upon the DNA, that all creation bears the imprint of God—a meaningless statement in modern biology—where then does the sacredness of human life come from?

The withering away of traditional ethics is related to the extension of the desacralized view of nature into the domain of human life itself. This is especially notable when it comes to environmental ethics, which we need to create in a serious way if we are to continue to survive. For now, animal activists and others like them are outside the mainstream— "crazy" people who tie themselves to trees. These acts are not part of the mainstream of society, a society which is not able to develop an effective environmental ethics that is in accord with the worldview that dominates our lives. A similar disjunction occurs in our hospitals because of the purely mechanical treatment of the human body, and the tensions that are created by the belief of many that they have a soul and that the body is not just a mechanical gadget. These tensions present great challenges to the dominant worldview and are signs that this paradigm is now falling apart.

The rejection of the idea of consciousness as the beginning not only of time but also of the universe, shatters all the deepest hopes of human beings. The hopes of immortality become mere dreams. That is why, for the first time in human history, we have a society in which many people do not dare to harbor these hopes that relate to the deepest needs of our souls, for they are no longer meaningful or realizable within the framework of a worldview based on the primacy of the material rather than consciousness.

These are the deepest aspirations of human beings—aspirations for immortality, that is, for an experience beyond time and space, for we are the only beings who are aware that we shall die. The diversions that we create for ourselves cannot completely veil this truth from us. Hence the significance of the hope for immortality, which is inseparable from the deepest nature of our souls. If we have come into being only from the matrix of time and space, we cannot transcend time and space. The reality of human life, whose terminus is the call of death, and what that implies spiritually, has, of course, been very strongly challenged by the reductionist worldview. I believe the time has come for us to take this challenge seriously, to rethink what consciousness is in relation to our life, to the manner in which we live, to the world in which we live, and to our way of knowing—our sentience, our experience. It is also time to realize fully the consequences of the negation of the primacy of consciousness in all its import.

I believe that ultimately consciousness will have the final say. But it is for us, while we have this great gift of consciousness, to use it properly, to understand what it means to live consciously, to live fully with awareness, to know where we are coming from, where we are going, and why we are here.

Adapted from "In the Beginning of Creation Was Consciousness," the Dudleian Lecture at Harvard University for 2002–03, given by Seyyed Hossein Nasr.

Parabola
Volume: 8.4
Sun and Moon

FIELDS OF FORCE

Martha Heyneman

Et le soleil n'est point nommé, mais sa puissance est parmi nous ...

—St. John Perse, *Anabasis*

The moon hangs over me as I sleep: eighty-one million million million tons above my head. And the earth, upon whose surface I lie like a speck of dust, hangs on to the moon as they swing around each other, reflecting each other's reflected light, on their annual trip together around the sun. No other planet except Pluto has to support a satellite so large in proportion to its own size. The moon pulls the earth now toward the inside, now toward the outside of the smooth elliptical path traced by their common center of gravity, which lies some one thousand miles within the earth—three thousand miles moonward from our planet's true center—veering around inside earth's body as she makes her almost twenty-eight day-and-night spins within a single month-long circle of the moon. Spinning has made earth thick around the middle. Sun, moon, and planets tug at the bulge on her equator as if trying to bring it into the plane of her orbit, but she holds her angle, so that the rhythmic seasons continue to sweep over her, and her axis only wobbles in a slow circle, always 23.5 degrees from the vertical, her north pole pointing to one star after another, the equinoxes sliding slowly backward around the zodiac, coming full circle in twenty-six thousand years. Asleep and too small, I feel none of these pulls and tugs upon the earth. Only four times the diameter of the moon (but eighty-one times heavier), earth continues on her weaving, spinning, wobbling way, held on course by the sun's great gravity.

Through the moon, when it approaches closest to the earth, there passes a delicate shiver, always the same. No one was aware of this until the astronauts left supersensitive seismometers on the moon's surface. Something inside her moves. She is not as dead as we thought. On her surface, however, except for an occasional soundless pock and puff of dust as a meteorite strikes her, nothing whatever happens. The astronauts' footprints are still there in the moondust, and will be there in a million years.

As I sleep, the moon is tugging at everything on her side of the surface of the earth. She sucks on the very rocks. As she passes overhead the earth's crust rises a few inches beneath her and is elsewhere compressed, kneaded as a cat kneads your stomach. The water level in wells far inland rises and falls in opposite phase to the tides of the sea. Moon and sun raise tide waves sometimes three miles high in the ionosphere. As the streams of conductive ions move through earth's magnetic field, electric currents are induced, and attendant tides of magnetism, which for all I know are ebbing and flowing through my motionless body on the bed.

As I sleep, the solar wind is streaming out of the sun. The earth holds her magnetosphere before her like a shield. It streams out behind her like the garments of a mother in a hurricane. Except for a few hours at the full, when it passes through the earth's magnetotail, the moon stands naked in the full blast, recording the sun's history in her rocks, trailing behind her a cone of absence which may be the most nearly perfect vacuum in the solar system.

As I sleep, sun and moon—working together or at cross-purposes—are dragging on all the oceans of the earth, to their seamed and jagged depths, moving billions and billions of tons of water, creating the conditions for the world between the tides: that world that so possessed us through the long summer days, as we stood gazing out to sea, following the exhalation of the ebbing tide; or squatted over pools in the rock, looking down at the display of earth's inexhaustible imagination: starfish, hermit crab, sea urchin, sponge, the delicate perilous tentacles of the sea anemone; or, suddenly noticing furtive fingers of sandy water coming and going under our feet, stood up and ran before the grumbling, rock-leaping mass of the tide's return.

Tidal friction is slowing the earth down. The night grows longer. As she slows earth down, the moon, like a growing child, moves farther away.

I stir in my sleep. A tide of awakening, its advance edge bordered with birdsong, is moving over the continent. The sun, our only savior from entropy, slowly infuses its musical energy into everything on this side of the earth. Suddenly I feel like getting up, like going to work, like lifting up out of the mess of chaos some measure of order and beauty. If the weight of my body and the aimless drift of my psyche are overcome, it is a triumph of the sun. I sit up. I sing no hymn. I dress and go down to breakfast.

As I sit down, a photon of light, having wandered fifty million years finding its way from the sun's hot heart to its photosphere, has sped in eight minutes from there to the earth and arrived at the gentle surface of a leaf. A molecule of chlorophyll is delicately enticing it into the dance of photosynthesis. I say no grace. I eat the sun with my toast. I breathe the labor of the leaves exhaled in oxygen.

As I lift my coffee cup, the sun lifts tons of water from the oceans into the sky. Air warmed at the equator rises and moves toward the poles, is cooled, moves down and under. Spinning within her envelope of air, the earth deflects the currents, sending the clouds in great white swirls across her face. As I swallow, curtains of rain are somewhere sweeping the earth. Parched soil, like a woman at last encountering love, is relaxing, absorbing, softening, beginning to feed the myriad seeds within her. I eat the earth with my egg. The white has the taste of the sea. I do not notice.

When I go to my study, the sun has arrived there before me. Summer sunlight rests quietly on the desk. Books about the solar system are scattered over it. I pull one toward me and open it to the photograph of the earth as seen from the moon. No wonder the moon circles around her, keeping its smooth side, sculptured by meteorites, always towards her, hiding its thick, rough back. The earth is beautiful—alive. Everything on her face is moving and changing in the delicacy, complexity, intelligence of her response to the sun. She is like Scheherazade telling endlessly diverting tales to the king (so that he will not kill her), while her little sister, the moon, with her expressionless face, sits silently by. The earth intercedes for us with the source of our life so that he will not kill us. Most of the time, I do not think about the earth.

She is wary with the sun, keeping her distance, neither too near nor too far, fending off his killing corpuscular radiation (the solar wind) with her magnetic field, filtering the blaze of his light through her atmosphere, selecting, sorting, and releasing just those kinds and amounts of energy that will maintain our lives, keeping out lethal ultraviolet rays with a thin veil of ozone, incinerating like fleas the millions of meteorites that each day come hurling in our direction. Protected by the earth, we live inside the sun: the solar wind—hot, ionized gas and its attendant magnetic fields, streaming radially out of the sun, thrown into a spiral by the sun's rotation, traveling at an average speed of two hundred and fifty miles per second almost irrespective of distance from the sun (but subject to surges when faster streams, shot out by solar flares, overtake slower ones), filling interplanetary space to the outermost reaches of the solar system—is an attenuated extension of the sun's corona, where, although the temperature is two million degrees Kelvin, the gas is so rarefied that you would freeze to death if you could go there with some shield to protect you from the direct light of the sun

Sunlight rests upon my arm. A faint warmth penetrates my skin. A breeze from the window stirs the hairs on my arm. I cannot conceive of the sun. It is too bright, too great, maybe too intensely alive for me to encompass and comprehend, even in the elastic vessel of imagination. If I try to take it into that space behind the solar plexus where we can feel and sense the life of a thing and not just take facts about it into our heads, it annihilates me. It flashes out in all directions beyond the bounds of my body.

I turn again to the photograph of the earth. You and I are in this picture. We were on the earth that day. Yet we cannot see ourselves, any more than I can see the bacteria on my arm—who, for all I know, may now be waking up, feeling the warmth of the sun, hearing something like the ripple of wind through a forest or a great field of wheat. To the earth, you and I are microorganisms. To the sun, we are viruses on a tick—or maybe even less: electrons or quarks.

I read the facts about the sun: if the earth were the size of an ordinary marble, the sun would be the size of a weather balloon large enough for a man to turn around inside with arms outstretched. The sun radiates some hundred thousand tons of light per second. Its total energy output is 3.83 x 10²⁶ watts, of which the earth intercepts 2 x 10¹⁷ watts, about half of which (that is, approximately one four-billionth of the energy streaming out of the sun) gets through the atmosphere. According to current theory, the source of this energy is nuclear fusion in the sun's core: four protons (hydrogen nuclei) combine in a series of steps to make one atom of helium, with a loss of 0.7 per cent of the proton mass, which is converted to energy in accordance with Einstein's equation, $E=MC^2$. If mass could be converted to energy with one hundred per cent efficiency (which it can't), one gram of matter would be energetically equivalent to thirty million kilowatt hours, enough electric energy to keep an average home going for ten thousand years at the present annual rate of consumption. For every fusion of a new helium nucleus, two neutrinos (among other things) are released, for a total of 2 x 10³⁸ neutrinos per second. Having no electrical charge and negligible mass, neutrinos interact with hardly anything and so, unlike the photons of electromagnetic energy, which take millions of years to get out of the sun, they zip straight out from the core at the speed of light. Billions of them are passing through your body at this moment and straight on through the earth underneath you. (At the time of the writing of these books, however, attempts to detect the presence of the predicted numbers of neutrinos had been unsuccessful.) The sun has maintained essentially the same energy flow for about five billion years.

These enormous numbers zip through my head like neutrinos. In order to get some feeling for the sun I have to turn to Lewis Thomas:

> *Morowitz has presented the case, in thermodynamic terms, for the hypothesis that a steady flow of energy from the inexhaustible source of the sun to the unfillable sink of outer space, by way of the earth, is mathematically destined to cause the organization of matter into an increasingly ordered state. The resulting balancing act involves a higher and higher complexity, and the emergence of cycles for the storage and release of energy. In a nonequilibrium steady state, which is postulated, the solar energy would not just flow to the earth and radiate away; it is thermodynamically inevitable that it must rearrange matter into symmetry, away from probability, against entropy, lifting it, so to speak, into a constantly changing condition of*

rearrangement and molecular ornamentation. In such a system, the outcome is a chancy kind of order, always on the verge of descending into chaos, held taut against probability by the unremitting, constant surge of energy from the sun.[1]

I look up. The book is now in shadow. The earth has moved. Afternoon sunlight now enters the southern windows and slants across the floor. Sunlight, slanting across a windowsill like this, or resting upon a wall, has sometimes rescued me (when I noticed it) from despair. Does the sun know what it's doing? Could that which has lifted us up out of chaos be less intelligent, less conscious than we are? Is all this towering largesse—even prodigality—only a manifestation of automatic processes? Or do we suffer from a kind of chauvinism of scale, which blinds us to the presence of awareness in any creature much greater or smaller, much longer- or shorter-lived than ourselves?

We owe our lives to the sun. Nothing in the facts of science contradicts this assertion. How is it, then, that we feel no gratitude?

I know this is a naive question. We hardly send a thank-you note to a ball of burning gas or a nuclear furnace. It is not only its greatness but also the prevailing world view that prevents me giving thanks (at least in public) to the sun. When I was a child, I looked at the stars, and the stars were looking back. That was the way I saw them. After I had been to school, I no longer saw them that way. They no longer seemed worth looking at. I forgot all about them.

Now, long out of school, I examine the roots of the world view I so docilely and unconsciously absorbed with my education until it seems to have altered the very molecular structure of my retina. (Our concepts determine our percepts.) I reflect: In the battery of human faculties employed in doing science, that one by which we are able to detect the presence of a "thou" is not included. The "thouness" of a thing is not even a "secondary quality." There can be, therefore, no "thous" included in the world view arrived at by this method. (And the holographic paradigm is no improvement in this respect.) But since doing science is not my aim, do I have to be confined by this world view?

At the same time, I do not want to kid myself. I want (at least at this moment in the sun) to arrive at the most complete picture of reality possible to me with all my faculties (such as they are) working in concert, none despised or repressed.

I do sometimes come face to face with a "thou" in the world, at least in a creature of my own approximate size and nature, though it seems to be more and more difficult for me to wake up to its presence. I have to make a conscious effort even under my own roof, even with a member of my own family, to feel that he, too, thinks, feels, suffers, aspires, longs for he knows not what in the context of our desolate world view. With the person sitting next to me on the subway I don't even try. The power to perceive a "thou," long since fallen from respect as an instrument for arriving at useful knowledge, has atrophied for lack of exercise.

The person in the heart is the same as the person in the sun—so the Upanishads tell us. Since we no longer conceive of the latter, the former seems to be fading out in direct proportion—an unexpected side effect. If we could revive the former, would we start to see the latter?

St. Francis saw a person in the sun—and in almost everything else, though I have never heard him accused of primitive animism. William Blake saw not just one person, but a multitude of the heavenly host singing Holy, Holy, Holy; and I myself, as a child, assumed that the sun, although I was not allowed to look at it, had a big smile on its beaming face, as in the storybooks. I could plainly see for myself that the moon looked down benignly, like St. Anne in Leonardo's painting, which hung in sepia reproduction over my bed. If we began to feel the presence of a person in the sun, there would be no need to look for life in outer space. The facts of science would compel us to be wholly occupied in adoration.

If I told you now that I saw a person in the sun, you might question my judgment. Don't worry. I am unable. Standing up to go down and make dinner, I forget all about the sun.

But his power is among us.

Note:

1. Lewis Thomas, *The Lives of a Cell: Notes of a Biology Watcher* (New York: Bantam Books, Inc. 1974), pp. 27-28.

Parabola
Volume: 32.3
Holy Earth

A SENTIENT UNIVERSE

Everett Gendler

It is taught: R. Jose says:
Alas for creatures who see but know not what they see,
Who stand but know not upon what they stand.
—Talmud, Hagigah 12B

Moses saw the divine face to face. Still, God had to remind him, "Remove the sandals from your feet, for the place on which you stand is holy ground" (Exod. 3:5). Considering that Moses, the greatest of all prophets, did not fully comprehend the nature of the ground upon which he stood, it is not surprising that we, too, remain oblivious to the underlying mystery of nature.

A tree stands in front of us: it appears solid. But the molecular physicist, examining it with utmost scrutiny, observes that there is more open space than substance in the tree. What else might we miss upon first observation? This tree is clearly alive, but by ordinary human measure, it is without will, desire, emotion, or spirit. Perhaps we lack adequate senses to perceive the nature of the tree's inner life. Does the tree "feel" as we do? Consider the grass beneath our feet, the sand, the soil, the stones. Consider the stars overhead. Does sentience or panpsychism, in any sense, characterize the rest of the universe?

These terms need not alarm us. *Sentient*, though solemn sounding, simply means "sensing, feeling, having some degree of awareness." And as for *panpsychism*, which is a near synonym for *sentience*, it is neither a New Age notion nor an ancient Greek practice connected with the god Pan. It is simply the idea "that the basic physical constituents of the universe have mental properties, whether or not they are parts of living organisms."[1] In other words, every "material" particle, however small, is not only "matter" but to some degree "mind," even if it remains forever beyond our experience.

Genesis 9: The Covenant with the Earth

Everyone knows that the Bible does not claim that independent, distinct spirits or souls are found in nature. In this way, Judaism differed from other faiths of its time. This does not mean, however, that Judaism understands nature as lifeless and lacking all spirit or feeling. After all, one can have spirit without spirits. In the biblical account of Creation, God, while connected with nature, is not entirely limited to it. The Divine is, in some significant way, more than nature. Yet, this does not necessarily mean that Creation is lacking in spirit or mind. In fact, a fresh look at Gen. 9:8-17 will quickly confirm that the Bible itself presupposes some degree of sentience in Creation, even in the earth itself (emphasis added):

> And God said to Noah and to his sons with him, "I now establish *My* covenant *with you and your offspring to come, and with every living thing that is with you—birds, cattle, and every wild beast as well—all that have come out of the ark, every living thing on earth. I will maintain my* covenant *with you: never shall again flesh be cut off by the waters of a flood, and never again shall there be a flood to destroy the earth."*
>
> God added, "This is the sign *that I set for the* covenant *between Me and you, and every living creature with you, for all ages to come. I have set my bow in the clouds, and it shall serve as a* sign *of the* covenant *between Me and the earth. When I bring clouds over the earth, and the bow appears in the clouds, I will remember My* covenant *between Me and you and every living creature among all flesh, so that the waters shall never again become a flood to destroy all flesh. When the bow is in the clouds, I will see it and remember the everlasting* covenant *that I have established between Me and*

all flesh that is on earth." Then God said to Noah, "This is the sign of the covenant *which I have established between Me and all flesh that is upon the earth."*

In this passage, both the terms *brit*, "covenant," and *ot*, "sign," apply to all living creatures and to earth, not only to humans. Upon first consideration, the reader, who tends toward rationalism, is likely to dismiss the wording as a mere figure of speech. Yet, the sevenfold repetition of brit and the three-fold repetition of ot prevent easy dismissal. (Seven and three are, in many traditions, sacred numbers.) Their repeated use and their specific references to living creatures and the earth imply that the notion of divine covenant in relation to earth and its life must be taken seriously. While the covenantal references do in four instances specify human beings, in those same four instances the other living creatures are included as well. Two covenantal references pertain generally to all living creatures, while the seventh speaks exclusively of God's covenant with the earth.

To accept seriously God's covenant with other living creatures as well as with the earth itself raises questions that are disconcerting, yet exciting. A covenant is reciprocal. It involves an exchange of responsibilities and duties. What does this imply about the status of earth and its living creatures? If the earth can participate in a covenant, then the earth has some qualities of a living being. Johannes Pedersen, one of the twentieth century's greatest biblical scholars, argues that

> *... The Israelites do not acknowledge the distinction between the psychic and the corporeal. Earth and stones are alive, imbued with a soul, therefore able to receive mental subject-matter and bear the impress of it. The relation between the earth and its owner ... is a covenant-relation, a psychic community, and the owner does not solely prevail in the relation. The earth has its nature, which makes itself felt and demands respect.*[2]

Therefore, according to Pedersen, the important thing is to "deal kindly with the earth, to uphold its blessing and then take what it yields on its own accord."[3] When Pedersen uses the term *soul*, he does not mean something immaterial and unrelated to the physical composition of an object or person; he means the collection of innate tendencies or inclinations of that entity, or what we would call its nature or character. "Earth and stones are alive," concludes Pedersen. They are "able to receive mental subject-matter."[4] In this perspective, some element of the mental or spiritual characterizes all of Creation.

Similarly, Professor Monford Harris, a philosophy professor at Spertus College, argues that the natural world is alive for the ancient Hebrews. It could be used, it could be appropriated, but it could not be violated. "Man has covenental relationship, community, with the natural world,"[5] writes Harris, adding that in the terms of Martin Buber, an "I-Thou" approach to the natural world must complement and constrain our more ordinary, more instrumental "I-It" approach.

Psalm 148: The Sound of Nature's Symphony

The fact that earth and all living beings are bound by covenant to God implies that Judaism takes universal sentience for granted: all of Creation must be alive with feeling. Yet rarely do we think of the Bible as making such a claim. Why is this? How did we come to see all the world—except our species—as essentially inert, lifeless, and lacking sentience? We are not lonely soloists in this world, the only ones capable of experiencing and expressing. There is a vast symphony singing, if we could only hear. Grasses whisper and animals sing the praises of God. The Bible tells us this again and again.[6]

Psalm 148, which is included in the daily morning service of the Hebrew prayer book, is particularly rich in this regard. Observant Jews recite it 365 times a year.

> *Praise God, sun and moon;*
> *praise God, all you shining stars!*
> *Praise God, you highest heavens,*
> *and you waters above the heavens! ...*
>
> *Praise the Lord from the earth,*
> *you sea monsters and all deeps;*
> *fire and hail, snow and frost,*
> *stormy wind fulfilling God's command!*

Mountains and all hills,
fruit trees and cedars!
Wild animals and all cattle,
creeping things and flying birds!

Kings of the earth and all peoples,
princes and all rulers of the earth!
Young men and women alike,
old and young together!

Let them praise the name of the Lord ...

Among those summoned to "praise the Lord" are sea monsters and the deeps of the oceans, fire and hail, snow and frost, and stormy wind. So, too, are mountains and hills, fruit trees and cedars, wild animals and cattle, creeping things and flying birds—together with kings, peoples, princes, rulers, men, and women. The wording of the psalm is clear: the same praise asked of humans is asked of the other natural elements.

Yet, rarely do these words touch our hearts. Rather, we defend ourselves from the fantastic possibilities suggested here. First, we tell ourselves that the psalms are not referring to *literal* praise. Instead, the authors are implying that the orderly functioning of nature is itself a kind of praise for the Creator. What could be more of a hymn to God than the dance of crackling fire? Doesn't a hummingbird hail the Creator simply by hovering near a flower? Surely, nothing more than this is meant by the repeated phrase, "praise God." Alternatively, we reason that to "praise God" is simply a figure of speech and need not be taken literally.

If we think about it, however, we might as well ask: Why do we overlook what is written? Isn't such a denial of the simplest meaning of the text illogical? In fact, such a reading is contrary to the principles of Jewish scriptural interpretation.

If orderly functioning is all that the term "praise" implies, then it is superfluous to ask for such praise; it *already* exists. In Ps. 19:2-5, for example, the alternations of day and night, the regularity of the sun's circuit, and the patterns of the heavens are deemed sufficient praise of their Creator, without words to embellish them:

The heavens are telling the glory of God;
and the firmament proclaims His handiwork.
Day to day pours forth speech,
and night to night declares knowledge.
There is no speech, nor are there words;
their voice is not heard;
yet their voice goes out through all the earth,
and their words to the end of the world.

But Psalm 148 demands more. It asks for *intentional* praise of the Creator not only from humans but from all realms of nature. It asks for praise *beyond* simple existence. The psalm presupposes a response from nature. Why ask for praise from something that is not capable of giving it?

As for the second way we defend ourselves from feeling the wonder of the psalmist, we dismiss the praises of nature as metaphorical. It is disappointing that even so distinguished a scholar as Nahum Sarna, the preeminent biblical commentator, avoids the issue of sentience by using precisely this device. Commenting on Psalm 19, in which "the poetic notion of nature's constituents [extol] their Maker," he cites Psalm 148 and Job 38:7. He admits that in Psalm 148 all heavenly beings and objects are called upon to "rhapsodize God" and that in Job "we are told that at the creation of the world, 'The morning stars chanted in unison, and all divine beings shouted for joy.'" Sarna then blunts the sharpness of the language by declaring, "We are dealing, of course, with figurative language."[7]

"Of course" is hardly a compelling argument. It is, in fact, no argument at all, but circular reasoning, an appeal to commonly held beliefs. Confident that the psalmist or Job was either in error or carried away by human emotion upon contact with "the timeless magnificence of the celestial scene," Sarna seeks to explain the dynamics underlying the figurative language. Obviously sensitive to "the inward, spiritual experience" that the starry skies can evoke in us, Sarna can only suggest that the psalmist "projects this situation onto the heavens and the heavenly bodies, which are now all personified."[8] Thus Sarna, like many other commentators, succumbs to the post-Cartesian intellectual fashion that asserts the radical distinction, the total difference, between minds and matter.[9]

In fact, Sarna departs from the principles of traditional Jewish interpretation when he denies what the text is plainly saying. The Talmud says, "A verse cannot depart from its plain meaning."[10] Guides to the Talmud reiterate this point: "The text does not lose its literal meaning."[11]

One rabbinic authority, Rabbi Kahana, held that this rule applied only when Torah lays down laws and principles of behavior, but not to "proverbial or poetical passages." But another authority, Mar b. R. Huna, argued that the rule applied to the poetic passages as well, and it was this view that prevailed.[12] The plain, the literal, the natural meaning of a text is what is meant. Therefore, whatever further interpretations of the language may stimulate, there is good reason to insist on the literal meaning of Psalm 148: Creation is being called to praise God.

It seems that the early rabbis also interpreted Psalm 148 literally:

> *As Scripture says,* The Lord hath made everything to bear witness to His glory *(Prov. 16:4). He created the heavens to sing His praises, and so they sing them, as it is said,* The Heavens declare the glory of God, and the firmament showeth His handiwork *(Ps. 19:2). And even as the heavens and all that is in them sing praises of God, so also the earth and all that is in it sing His praises, as it is said* Praise the Lord from the earth. ...
>
> *After God's praises are sung from the heavens, who ought to be the first on earth to sing His praises? He that is larger than his fellow creatures. And who are the largest? The sea-monsters, of whom it is said* And God created the great sea-monsters *(Gen. 1:21). Therefore, the first on earth to sing God's praises are the sea-monsters, to whom it is said* Ye sea-monsters, and all deeps *(Ps. 148:7).[13]*

Here, the literal meaning presupposes that, to some degree, all of Creation is sentient, feeling, and able to respond to this encompassing cry of "Halleluyah, Praise the Lord!"

Notes:

1. Thomas Nagel, *Mortal Questions* (Cambridge: Cambridge University Press, 1979), p. 181.

2. Johannes Pedersen, *Israel: Its Life and Culture* (London & Copenhagen: Oxford University Press, 1959). I-II, p. 479.

3. *Ibid.*

4. *Ibid.*

5. Monford Harris, "Ecology: A Covenantal Approach," *CCAR Journal*, (Summer 1976): 103-04.

6. For example, Ps. 19, 96:11-12, 98:7-9; Isa. 44:23, 55:12; Job 38:7.

7. Nahum M. Sarna, *Songs of the Heart* (New York: Schocken Books, 1993), p. 78.

8. *Ibid.*

9. Cf. "All that is either spatial or conscious. ...What is spatial is not conscious: what is conscious is not spatial. ... All things are either bodies or minds; substances are either spatial or conscious. ... The world falls thus into two completely different and completely separated realms; that of bodies and that of minds." W. Windelband, *A History of Philosophy* (New York: Macmillan, 1901), p. 405.

10. *Soncino Talmud* (London: Soncino Press, 1936), Shabbat 63a; cf. Yebamot 116, 24a.

11. Z. H. Chajes, *The Students Guide Through the Talmud* (New York: Philip Feldheim, 1960), p. 177.

12. *Ibid.*

13. *Ibid.*, 148:5.

Excerpt is from *Ecology and The Jewish Spirit: Where Nature and the Sacred Meet* © 1998 by Ellen Bernstein (Woodstock, VT: Jewish Lights Publishing).

Parabola
Volume: 8.2
Animals

COME INTO ANIMAL PRESENCE

Denise Levertov

> Come into animal presence
> No man is so guileless as
> the serpent. The lonely white
> rabbit on the roof is a star
> twitching its ears at the rain.
> The llama intricately
> folding its hind legs to be seated
> not disdains but mildly
> disregards human approval.
> What joy when the insouciant
> armadillo glances at us and doesn't
> quicken his trotting
> across the track into the palm brush.
>
>
> What is this joy? That no animal
> falters, but knows what it must do?
> That the snake has no blemish,
> that the rabbit inspects his strange surroundings
> in white star-silence? The llama
> rests in dignity, the armadillo
> has some intention to pursue in the palm-forest.
> Those who were sacred have remained so,
> holiness does not dissolve, it is a presence
> of bronze, only the sight that saw it

faltered and turned from it.
An old joy returns in holy presence.

•

CHAPTER FIVE

The Great Goddess

About the first watch of the night, when as I had slept my first sleep, I awaked with sudden fear, and saw the moon shining bright as when she is at the full ... and by and by ... appeared to me from the midst of the sea a divine and venerable face, worshipped even of the gods themselves. Then, by little and little, I seemed to see the whole figure of her body, bright and mounting out of the sea and standing before me ... she had a great abundance of hair, flowing and curling, dispersed and scattered about her divine neck; on the crown of her head she bare many garlands interlaced with flowers, and in the middle of her forehead was a plain circlet in fashion of a mirror, or rather resembling the moon by the light that it gave forth. ... Thus the divine shape, breathing out the pleasant spice of fertile Arabia, disdained not with her holy voice to utter these words unto me:

"Behold, Lucius I am come; thy weeping and prayer hath moved me to succour thee. I am she that is the natural mother of all things, mistress and governess of all the elements, the initial progeny of worlds, chief of the powers divine, queen of all that are in hell, the principal of them that dwell in heaven, manifested alone and under one form of all the gods and goddesses. At my will the planets of the sky, the wholesome winds of the seas, and the lamentable silences of hell be disposed; my name, my divinity is adored throughout all the world, in divers manners, in variable customs, and by many names. For the Phrygians that are the first of all men call me the Mother of the gods of Pessinus; the Athenians, which are sprung from their own soil Cecropian Minerva; the Cyprians, which are girt about by the sea, Paphian Venus; the Cretans which bear arrows, Dictynnian Diana; the Sicilians, which speak three tongues, infernal Proserpine; the Eleusians their ancient goddess Ceres; some Juno, other Bellona, other Hecate, other Rhamnusia, and principally both sort of the Ethiopians, which dwell in the Orient and are enlightened by the morning rays of the sun, and the

Parabola
Volume: 5.4
Woman

Innana:
Queen of Heaven and Earth

Diane Wolkstein and Samuel Noah Kramer

For over a year Diane Wolkstein worked with Sumerian authority, Samuel Noah Kramer, on a cycle of poems about the goddess Inanna. The scholar supplied all the available deciphered texts on The Goddess; the storyteller worked and reworked the materials. Together they filled in the gaps, question marks, and paraphrases and provided explanatory notes and bibliographi-cal references; together they are telling her story in the book Innana, Queen of Heaven and Earth.

The following excerpt is from the very end of the cycle. After Inanna has brought the world order (the me*) to her people and begun her reign on earth, has loved her earthly king, Dumuzi (Ushumgalanna), and has left him to descend to the underworld, she returns to Sumer, and the people sing her praises:*

Honored Counselor

Honored Counselor, Ornament of Heaven, Joy of An!
When sweet sleep has ended in the bedchamber
You appear like bright daylight.

When all the lands and the people of Sumer assemble,
Those sleeping on the roofs and those sleeping by
　　　　the walls,

When they sing your praises, bringing their concerns to you,
You study their words.

You render a cruel judgment against the evildoer;
You destroy the wicked.
You look with kindly eyes on the straightforward;
You give that one your blessing.

My Lady looks in sweet wonder from heaven.
The people walk before the holy Inanna.
The Lady Who Rises Into the Heavens, Inanna, is radiant.

To you, Inanna, I sing!
The Lady Who Rises Into the Heavens is radiant on the horizon.

Lady of the Evening

At evening, the Radiant Star, the Great Light that Fills the Sky,
The Lady of the Evening appears in the heavens.
The people in all the lands lift their eyes to her.
The men purify themselves; the women cleanse themselves.
The ox in his yoke lows to her.
The sheep pile up the dust in their fold.
The beast of Sumugan, the numerous creatures of the steppe,
The four-legged creatures of the high steppe,
The lush orchards and gardens, the green reeds and trees,
The fish of the deep, the birds of heaven—
My Lady makes them hurry to their sleeping places.

The living creatures and the numerous people kneel before her.
Those selected by the matriarchs prepare immense quantities of food.
The Lady refreshes herself in the land.
There is festive play in the land.
The young man makes love with his beloved.

My lady looks in sweet wonder from heaven.
The people walk before the holy Inanna.

Inanna, the Lady of the Evening, is radiant.

The Lady of the Evening is radiant on the horizon.
I sing your praises, holy Inanna.

The Amazement of the Land

The Amazement of the Land, the Lone Star, the Evening Star,
The Brave One Who Appears in the Heavens—
All the lands fear her.

The faithful people of Sumer bow to her.
The young man on the road makes his way to her.
The ox raises his head in his yoke to her.
The people hasten to the pure Inanna.

They prepare with care for My Lady.
Everything is made abundant for her in the storehouse of the land.

In the pure places of the steppe
On the high roofs of the dwellings
On the platforms of the city
They make offerings to her:
Heaped up incense like sweet smelling cedar;
Fine sheep, long haired sheep, fat sheep.
They purify the earth for My Lady;
They celebrate her in song.

The fill the table of the land with the first fruits—
Butter, dates, cheese, fruits of all kinds.
They pour dark beer for her.
They pour light beer for her.
Dark beer, *emmer* beer,
Emmer beer for My Lady.

The *sagub* vat and the *lamsari* vat make a bubbling noise for her.
They make *gug* bread in date syrup for her.

They pour out honey and wine for her at sunrise.
Beer at dawn, flour, flour in honey.

The gods and people of Sumer go to her with food and drink.
They feed Inanna in the pure clean place.

The Joy of Sumer

The people of Sumer assemble in the palace,
The house which guides the land.
The king builds a throne for the queen of the palace.
The king sits with her on the throne.

In order to care for the life of all the lands
The exact first day of the month is closely examined.
And on the day of the disappearance of the moon
The *Me* are perfectly carried out
So that the New Year's Day, the Day of Rites, may be properly
    determined
And a sleeping place be set up for Inanna.

The people can cleanse the rushes with sweet smelling cedar oil.
They arrange the rushes for the bed.
They spread a coverlet over the bed,
A coverlet to sweeten the bed,
A coverlet to rejoice the hearts.

The queen bathes her holy lap.
She bathes for the lap of Dumuzi.
Pure Inanna washes with soap.
She sprinkles fragrant cedar oil on the ground.

The king goes with lifted head to her holy lap.
Dumuzi goes with lifted head to the lap of Inanna.
Ushumgalanna lies down beside her.
Tenderly he caresses her holy lap.

After the queen has rested on his holy lap
After they have held each other in love
The queen murmurs softly, "O Dumuzi, you are surely my beloved."

Piling up offerings, performing laving rites,
Heaping up incense, burning juniper resin,
Bearing food offerings, bearing bowls,
The people enter the Egalmah at the king's request.

He embraces his beloved wife.
The king embraces the pure Inanna.
Inanna, seated on the royal throne, shines like daylight.
The king, like the sun, sits radiantly by the side of Inanna.
He arranges abundance, lushness, and plenty before her.
He assembles the people of Sumer before her.

The musicians play upon their instruments—
The loud instrument which drowns out the south storm,
The sweet *algar*-instrument, the ornament of the palace,
The stringed instrument, the source of joy of all people.
They play for Inanna a song which rejoices the heart.

The king stretches out his hand for food and drink.
Ushumgalanna stretches out his hand for food and drink.
The palace is festive. The king is joyous.
In the pure clean place they celebrate Inanna in song.
She is the Ornament of the Assembly, the Joy of Sumer!

The people spend the day in plenty.
The king stands before the assembly in great joy.
The king hails Inanna with the praise of the gods and the assembly:
"You are the Holy Priestess fashioned with heaven and earth."

Inanna, Oldest Daughter of Nanna, Lady of the Evening!

My Lady looks in sweet wonder from Heaven.
The people of Sumer parade before the holy Inanna.

The Lady Who Rises Into the Heavens, Inanna, is radiant.

Mighty, trustworthy, radiant, and ever youthful—
To you, Inanna, I sing!

From *INANNA, Queen of Heaven and Earth* by Diane Wolkstein and Samuel Noah Kramer (New York: Harper & Row, 1993).

Parabola
Volume: 1.3
Initiation

The Seven Gates of the Great Below

Inanna, the queen of heaven, goddess of heaven and earth, has set her mind on the Great Below: from the Great Above, she has set her heart, the sister of Shamash, on the dark kingdom, the realm of her sister Ereshkigal. Heaven and earth she abandons, directs her step towards the underworld; seven cities the queen of heaven abandons, to descend to the nether world.

To her side she fastens the seven divine decrees, on her head places the holy *shugurra*, the crown of the plain. Radiance she places upon her countenance, a sweet ointment upon her face. The rod of lapis lazuli she grips in her hand, small lapis lazuli stones she fastens about her neck. Sparkling and bright are the stones at her breast, a ring of red gold she puts on her hand. About her breast she fastens a breastplate, and all the garments of her ladyship she arranges around her body. Now fully bedecked with the seven decrees at her side, with the seven bright ornaments of her royalty adorning her body, the queen of heaven walks toward the nether world, her faithful messenger at her side, the loyal Ninshubur.

To Ninshubur she gave her instructions, she warned him of her peril: "O Ninshubur, my constant support! Faithful one, bearer of supporting words, listen to me, hearken to my need. Now I descend to the nether world, to the realm of my sister Ereshkigal I now direct my steps. When I shall have come there, when I shall have been there three days, fill heaven with supplications for me, in the house of the gods pray for me. Lower thine eyes for me, bow thy head for me. In a single garment, dressed as a pauper, go to the house of Enlil at Nippur. Bow low before Enlil, weep before him, with the words I shall give thee, pray for me.

"If Enlil will not stand by me, go to Ur.

"In the house of Nanna at Ur, bow low before Nanna, weep before him, with the words I shall give thee, pray for me.

"If Nanna will not stand by me, go to Eridu.

"At Eridu, in the house if Enki, bow low before Enki, weep before him, with the words I shall give thee, pray for me. Surely will Enki, the father, the lord of wisdom, who knows the secrets of the food and water of life, come to my aid."

To Ninshubur she has given her instructions; the queen of heaven walks toward the dark kingdom, sending her messenger from her to bear her words against her return.

At the gate of blue stone, the door of the underworld, Inanna asked entry; she demanded to be let in, she threatened the gatekeeper:

"Open the house, gatekeeper, open the house. Throw open the gate, allow me to enter. I, Inanna, queen of heaven, would enter the underworld: open the house! If thou dost not, darker than night will be my wrath, like a storm it will fall upon thee. I will smash the door down, shatter the bolt. I will crush the doorposts, tear down the lintel. I will raise the dead, eating the living, so that the dead will outnumber the living, will abandon their kingdom and come up to the earth."

To lofty Inanna, the gatekeeper Neti bowed down, begging her patience, appeasing her anger. "I will go," he said to her, "I will go to my queen, to the lady Ereshkigal I will go. To her I will bear thy words, awesome and terrible. I will tell her that her sister Inanna stands before the blue gate and demands admittance." Neti bowed low before the goddess, he bowed low and departed.

When Ereshkigal had heard the words of Inanna which the gatekeeper Neti had brought to her, her face turned pale as tamarisk wood, her lips became dark as a bruised reed. "Why does she come here?" asks Ereshkigal. "What has brought the queen of heaven, my sister, to my empire, the land of the dead? Shall we give up our empire? Shall I be made to drink water with the Anunnaki? Shall we eat clay instead of bread, drink pond water for beer? Shall the queen of the dead be made to mourn for her subjects? Go, gatekeeper, return to the blue gate. Admit my sister according to the ancient rules. Let her be brought low before me, abiding by the rules of the gates of the empire of eternal night."

Then Neti returns to the gate, and comes again before the queen of heaven. He unlocks the gate and allows her to enter by the rules of the gate. By the rules of each gate Inanna enters the underworld.

At the first gate, as he enters, the crown of the plain, the fair shugurra, is taken from her.

"O gatekeeper, why have you taken the crown from my head?"

"Extraordinarily have the rules of the Nether World been perfected, O Inanna! O Inanna, do not question the rites of the Nether World!"

And at each of the gates, by the rules of the Nether World, another of her royal ornaments is taken from her—the rod of lapis lazuli, the necklace, the sparkling stones, the ring of red gold, and the breastplate. Finally, at the seventh gate, as she enters, the garments of her ladyship are taken from her. Now, naked and bowed low, the Lady of Battles is taken before her sister, the dreadful Ereshkigal, queen of the Nether World. In the palace of dust she reigns, the dread queen, she oversees the realm of the dead. In that place is no light, they are blind who reside there. Clothed as birds, with drooping wings for raiment, the inhabitants of that world go about mournfully. Over all that is there lies dust: dust is upon the latchbolt and lintel, upon hearthstone and floor. In all the chambers of the dead there is darkness and dust. To that place now has come the queen of heaven, before the throne of the seven deadly judges, where Ereshkigal rules among the Anunnaki.

Upon Inanna they fasten their eyes, the Anunnaki, the eyes of death. Misery of the eyes they unleash against her eyes, misery of the sides against her sides, misery of the heart against her heart, misery of the feet against her feet, misery of the head against her head. The sixty miseries they unleash against her, those whose words torture the spirit. In misery is Inanna bound, hand and foot. The healthy queen is turned into a sick woman; the sick woman is turned into a corpse. The corpse is hung upon a stake.

Three days and three nights have passed since Inanna went down to the Great Below. On the morning after the third night Ninshubur the faithful raises himself up. Like a pauper, he puts on a single garment. He anoints his head with dust, with ashes he adorns his face. Tears streak the ashes. With supplications and prayers he goes before the gods, all heaven he fills with complaints for Inanna. He lowers his eyes for Inanna, he bows low his head. Dressed as a pauper he journeys to Nippur, to the house of Enlil. He bows low before Enlil, he weeps before him. With the words of Inanna he prays for her:

"O Father Enlil, let not thy daughter be put to death!
Let not thy good gold be ground into the dust of the Nether World;
    Let not thy daughter be put to death.
Let not thy good stone, the fair lapis lazuli, be crushed into powder
    in the Nether World;
    Let not thy daughter be put to death.
Let not thy sparkling stones become dull pebbles in the Nether World;
    Let not thy daughter be put to death.
Let not thy good boxwood be cut up for kindling in the Nether World;
    Let not thy daughter be put to death.
O Father Enlil, let not thy daughter, the fair Inanna, be put to death;
    Let not thy daughter be put to death!"

To Ninshubur he answers, Father Enlil:
"My daughter Inanna, queen of the Great Above, directed her mind to the Great Below, to the realm of her sister she turned her heart. The seven decrees she fastened at her side, the seven adornments she put about herself. With threats and curses she came to the gates of the Nether World, but by the rules of the gates was she made to enter. What, shall I gainsay the rites of the Nether World? Shall I turn back the judgment of the Anunnaki? For what shall the rules of the Nether World have been perfected if they may be turned aside?"

Father Enlil stood not by his daughter Inanna; Ninshubur when to Ur.

Dressed as a pauper, he journeys to Ur, to the house of Nanna. He bows low before Nanna, weeps before him, and makes the selfsame prayer. But again his supplication is cast aside.

Father Nanna stood not by his daughter Inanna; Ninshubur went to Eridu.

To the First City, Eridu, dressed as a pauper, comes Ninshubur, to the house of Enki, the Lord of Wisdom. He bows low before Enki, weeps before him, and prays once more with the words of Inanna.

"Let not thy daughter be put to death!" he pleads once more.

And to Ninshubur he answers, the Lord Of Wisdom, Father Enki:

"What has my daughter done!
What has the queen of heaven done!
My heart is troubled for her.

From the Great Above she is absent!
To the Great Below she has descended!
My heart is troubled for her.

Stripped of her adornments, she has been brought low!
With the sixty miseries she has been bound!
My heart is troubled for her.

Her corpse hangs upon a stake!
My heart is troubled for her.
My heart is troubled for my daughter Inanna."

Then Father Enki brought forth earth and water and fashioned the *kurgarru*, and with earth and water he made the *kalaturru*. Two creatures did he make, neither man nor woman did he make them. To them he entrusted the food of life. To them he entrusted the water of life. And into their ears he poured his instructions.

"To the Great Below direct your steps, bow not before Neti. To the gate of blue stone bear your trust, bow not down before it. Without life and without death have I made you, the gates of the Nether World will open before you. Neither man nor woman have I made you, you will not be brought low. To the center of the Nether World direct your steps, there find the stake on which a corpse hangs. Upon the corpse hung from the stake, direct the fear of the rays of fire. Sixty times sprinkle the food of life upon it, sixty times sprinkle the water of life. Truly, when you have done this, Inanna will arise."

To the Great Below they journey, the two creatures. The kurgarru bears the food of life, the kalaturru bears the water of life. Before Neti they do not bow low, neither do they brush him aside. To the great gate of blue stone they bear their trust. They bow not down before it, neither do they show it disrespect. Through the seven gates of the Nether World they go, the two creatures, to the center of the dark kingdom they go. Before Ereshkigal they have come, before the eyes of the Anunnaki. They do not fear the eyes of death, for neither living nor dead has Enki made them. Miseries of the eyes have no power over them, miseries of the sides have no power. Miseries of the heart have no power over them, miseries of the feet have no power. Miseries of the head have no power over them, the sixty miseries have no power. Upon the corpse hanging from a stake they direct the fear of the rays of fire. Sixty times they sprinkle upon the corpse of Inanna the food of life, sixty times they sprinkle the water of life.

Inanna arises.

To the world above she directs her step, the queen of heaven. From the Great Below, she turns her heart again to the Great Above. Through the seven gates of the Nether World she goes back:

> At the first gate she is given her garments of ladyship,
> At the second gate she is given her breastplate.
> How beautifully they adorn her!

> At the third gate she is given her ring of red gold,
> At the fourth gate she is given her sparkling stones.
> How beautifully they adorn her!

> At the fifth gate she is given her necklace of lapis lazuli,
> At the sixth gate she is given her rod of lapis lazuli.
> How beautifully they adorn her!
> Beautifully adorned with the seven treasures, Inanna goes forth.

> At the seventh gate she is given the shugurra, the crown of the plain. How beautifully it adorns her!
> Beautifully adorned with the seven treasures, Innana goes forth.

The Anunnaki flee before her, the souls of the peaceful hide them-selves. Before her and after her hasten the dead, clamoring around her in procession: the small demons like reeds, the large demons like tablet styluses walk at her side. With the company of the dead, Inanna comes forth from the Nether World, the Star of Lamentation ascends to the Great Above.

Paul Jordan-Smith's retelling of material traditionally referred to as "Inanna's Descent into the Netherworld" (Sumerian), or "Ishtar's Descent" (Acadian); both sources were used.

Parabola
Volume: 5.4
Woman

THE PERENNIAL FEMININE

Helen M. Luke

One can scarcely open a magazine nowadays—let
alone read any of the innumerable brochures announcing lectures, seminars, group therapy, or conferences
on psychological matters—without being struck by
the preponderance of the theme of the "new woman."
When this degree of interest arises we may be sure that
it springs from an overwhelming need for a new attitude.
As always in the modern world, there is danger that, in
the very urgency of that need, the tender new growth of
consciousness may be swamped, in many, by the spate of
theories and opinions poured out upon us.

The safeguard for the individual woman lies in her
ability to connect the theories expounded and the emotions aroused in her with her symbolic life; for only when
this connection is made do the changes in her actual life
become real. Without it, however things may appear on
the surface, the theoretical changes merely create a deeper
and more destructive conflict in her soul.

Where, however, is a woman to look for nourishment
for her inner imagery as her new personality struggles
for birth? The changes in the way of Eve have come with
staggering swiftness in the last one hundred years, but it
seems to me that only recently has the realization broken
through that a deeper awareness of the nature of these
changes is now essential. If we are to stop the wreckage

caused by the disorientation of women, by their loss of identity under the stresses of the new way, then the numinous meaning of the great challenge they face must break through from the unconscious; for no amount of rational analysis can bring healing. Only so can the images of the masculine and feminine, which have become more and more dangerously mixed in this century be discriminated once more, so that they may come to a new synthesis in both woman and man.

It is important that we attempt to arrive at some degree of clarity about various attitudes and assumptions which are currently prevalent when people talk about woman. Those who assert that the only difference between men and women is biological, and that in every other way they are equal and have the same inborn potentialities, have disastrously missed the point. Equality of value between individuals is an eternal truth, beyond all comparisons, whereas "superior" and "inferior" are relative terms defining abilities or degrees of consciousness. Equality of opportunity for women has indeed to be fought for, but equality of value can never be understood until we have learned to discriminate and accept *difference*. The biological difference between man and woman is never a "nothing but"; it is a fundamental difference, and it does not stop with the body but implies an equally fundamental difference of *psychic* nature. No matter how consciously we may develop the contrasexual principle within us, no matter how strong our intuition of the ultimate union between the masculine and feminine elements in each individual, yet as long as we remain in our bodies here in space and time, we are predominantly either male or female, and we forget this at our peril. Disaster awaits a woman who imitates a man, but even a woman who aims at becoming half man, half woman, and imagines she is thereby achieving archetypal "androgyny" will certainly be inferior on both counts. A woman is born to be essentially and wholly a woman and the more deeply and consciously she is able to know and live the spirit, the Logos, within her, the more surely she will realize this truth. One of the most frightening characteristics of our present *Zeitgeist* is the urge to destroy difference, to reduce everything to a horrible sameness in the cause of "equality."

Whether a woman is efficient or brilliant in spheres hitherto deemed masculine, or whether she remains in a traditionally feminine role, modern woman must discriminate and relate to the image of the spirit, while at the same time maintaining her roots in her basic feminine nature—that which receives, nourishes, and gives birth on all levels of being through her awareness of the earth and her ability to bring up the water of life from under the earth. All her true creativeness springs from this.

As we look back on the extremely rapid emergence of women in this century into the masculine world of thought and action, it is not surprising that she has fallen into increased contempt for her own values. It has surely been a necessary phase, but its effects have been devastating not only on woman herself but also on the men around her. For the animus—the unconscious masculinity in a woman—when he has taken possession of her femininity, has a terrifying power, charged as he is with the numinosity of the unconscious—and most men in their turn, when faced with this power in their women, either retreat into an inferior passive femininity, seeking to propitiate the animus power, or else react with brutal aggressive masculinity. Small wonder that women thus possessed, having lost their true roots in nature, are constantly beset by the anxious feeling of being useless, however outwardly successful. The dreams of modern women are full of this basic insecurity.

It is time then for woman to turn from this hidden contempt for the feminine values so that she may cease to identify creativity solely with the productions of thought and with achievements in the outer world. It is exceedingly hard for us to realize, in the climate of Western society, that the woman who quietly *responds* with intense interest and love to people, to ideas, and to things, is as deeply and truly creative as one who always seeks to lead, to act, to achieve. The feminine qualities of receptivity, of nurturing in silence and secrecy are (whether in man or woman) as essential to creation as their masculine opposites and in no way inferior.

But these are rational thoughts *about* the situation. What of the images without which, as I said at the outset, no change is possible? How is a woman, when she feels the immense fascination of the power of the spirit stirring in her, to welcome it and yet remain true to her womanhood, or how is she to rediscover her femininity if she has lost it? How is a man to realize the values of the heart without losing the bright sword of his spirit in the fogs of emotion? There are no intellectual answers. Only the images by which we live can bring transformation. The future hangs on this quest for the heart of love by both sexes.

Each of us has a well of images within, which are the saving reality, and whence may be born the individual myth carrying the meaning of a life. That new images are now emerging in the tales and poetry of our time is now beyond doubt. But any truly valid "new myth" cannot be rationally invented. It must be born out of the crucible of our own struggles and suffering as we affirm our new freedom without rejecting the perennial truth of the feminine way.

There is one story written in this century that speaks with particular power to the predicament of women in our time. C. S. Lewis, towards the end of his life, wrote *Till We Have Faces*—a story based on the myth of Psyche and Eros and told from the point of view of one of the ugly sisters. I have written elsewhere a detailed commentary[1] on this beautiful tale of a woman's quest for her lost femininity, and I mention it here because it is an example of how an old myth grows into contemporary relevance through the imagination of an individual expressing the unconscious need of his or her time.

However, the still more ancient myth of Demeter and Kore is a seedbed of feminine experience for women of all times and places, and I shall now try to explore some of its unchanging wisdom.

The story, taken from the Homeric Hymn to Demeter, is as follows.

Demeter's lovely daughter, Persephone, was playing with her companions in the meadows and, wandering off by herself, she saw a flower, a narcissus with one hundred blossoms, which Zeus himself with help of Gaia, goddess of Earth, had caused to grow as a snare for her. Fascinated by this flower, with its intoxicating scent, she reached to pick it. At that moment the earth opened, and the Lord of the Dead himself appeared from the depths with his immortal horses and, seizing her in spite of her cries, carried her off to the underworld, unseen and unheard by any except the goddess Hecate who, as she was thinking "delicate thoughts," heard the cry from her cave. Otherwise only Helios the Sun himself witnessed the act. Persephone cried out to Zeus to save her, but he took no notice at all, for he himself had planned the whole thing.

The mountains and the depths of the sea, however, carried the sound of her voice, and "her lady mother heard her." For nine days the sorrowing mother, the great goddess Demeter, wandered over the earth carrying burning torches and stopping neither to eat nor to wash, but no one anywhere could give her news of her lost daughter.

But on the tenth day came the goddess Hecate, bearing a torch, and told the seeking mother that her daughter had been ravished away, but that she had heard only and not seen who the ravisher might be. Then together the two goddesses went to Helios, the Sun, as he drove his chariot across the heavens, and Demeter entreated him to tell her what he had seen. He answered that Zeus himself had given Kore to his brother Hades for his wife, and he urged her to cease lamenting as this was a good marriage for her daughter.

But her grief only increased the more and she wandered unknown, and disfigured by sorrow, among the cities of men, until she came one day to Eleusis and there she sat by the wayside beside the Maiden's Well where the women came to draw water. She bore the form of an old woman past childbearing, and she sat in the shade of an olive tree. Then came the four daughters of the King of Eleusis to draw water, and when they saw her, they questioned her, and she told them that she was far from her home in Crete and sought for work—to nurse a child perhaps. Then the princesses led her to their father and mother, for they needed a nurse for a late-born son. With her dark robe and her head veiled she came into the house of the king, and her great height and the light which came from her struck awe into them all. At first she sat sad and speechless, but the ribald jokes of an old woman cheered her. When they offered her wine, she refused it saying she was not permitted to drink it and asking for meal and water mixed. Then she took the child from his mother and held him "on her fragrant heart," and he grew daily stronger and more beautiful on food that was more than mortal. Each night she took the child and laid him in the fire like a brand while his parents slept. But one night the child's mother came in the night and saw what was being done to her child and cried out in terror and anger and snatched him from the goddess, thus depriving him of immortality. The goddess revealed her identity, upbraiding the mother for her "witlessness" in destroying the child's chance of immortality, and she ordered that a great temple be built for her there in Eleusis. When this was done she sat within the temple and mourned for her daughter.

Now she brought a terrible year on mankind, for she withheld growth from the earth, and no seed came up, and all the fruits of the earth were withering, so that mankind would surely have perished, and the gods would have been left without worshipers. So now Zeus in his heaven sent Iris to Demeter and begged and implored her to return among the gods and restore fertility to the earth, but she was deaf to all his pleading, even when each and all of the gods had come one by one to persuade her. And then at last Zeus sent Hermes to his brother Hades to tell him he must release Kore to her mother Demeter so that she might no longer withhold the seed from the earth.

Hades then turned to the still grieving Persephone and said that she might go, but offered her a pomegranate seed to eat as they parted. And she, though she had eaten nothing in the underworld, now, in her joy, took it and ate it, thus ensuring that she must return. Only if she had not eaten could she stay always with her mother. Henceforth she must return always to the underworld for one-third of the year. Then as they rejoiced in each other Hecate came again and kissed Kore many times and from that day was her "queenly comrade." And the Spring burst forth on the earth, but for one-third of each year the trees were bare and the land lay fallow. And as Demeter caused the grain to grow rich and fat again, she taught the meaning of it to all the rulers in Eleusis and gave instructions as to her rites, and the mysteries which should be celebrated there.

In his essay on Kore (the primordial maiden) Jung has said, "Demeter and Kore, mother and daughter, extend the feminine consciousness upwards and downwards—and widen out the narrowly conscious mind bound in space and time, giving it intimations of a greater and more comprehensive personality which has a share in the eternal course of things. ... It seems clear enough that the man's anima found projection in the Demeter cult. ... For a man, anima experiences are of immense and abiding significance. But the Demeter-Kore myth is far too feminine to have been merely the result of an anima projection ... Demeter-Kore exists on the plane of mother-daughter experience which is alien to man and shuts him out."

There is an immense difference between the mother-son and the mother-daughter experience. On the archetypal level the son carries for the mother the image of her inner quest, but the daughter is the extension of her very self, carrying her back into the past and her own youth and forward to the promise of her own rebirth into a new personality, into the awareness of the Self. In the natural pattern of development the boy will feel his separateness from his mother by reason of his masculinity much sooner than the girl and will begin his striving for achievement. Everywhere, however, before the twentieth century, the growing girl remained at home contained in the orbit of her mother until the time came for her to become a mother herself and so reverse her role. Thus she would grow naturally from the passive state of being protected into the vital passivity of opening herself to receive the seed, the transition point being marked actually or symbolically by the violent breaking of her virginity.

Margaret Mead has written, "If women are to be restless and questing even in face of child-bearing they must be made so through education." For better, for worse, she has been made so. It can lead a woman either to disaster or to her great opportunity, and if she is to succeed in bridging the gap it is vital that, in one way or another, she pass through the Demeter-Kore experience in her inner life.

In ancient Greece the Eleusinian mysteries of Demeter bear witness to this overwhelming need of woman in her already growing separation from the natural pattern of the primitive feminine—the need for the Goddess to teach her the *meaning* of the deep transformation of her being from daughter to mother to daughter again. How much greater is that need today, when so often the woman lives almost like a man in the outer world and must find the whole meaning of her motherhood inwardly instead of physically, and when so many of those who do bear children are simply playing at "mothers and babies," never having allowed themselves to experience consciously the violent end of their daughter identification. There is strong evidence that the man initiated into the mysteries also "became" the *Goddess*, not the *God*. He too, in the flowering of Athenian civilization and the growing split between the conscious and unconscious, and between reason and the ancient goddesses of the earth and moon, must go through a profound anima experience and rediscover the meaning of the feminine within, must free his infantile anima from possession by the mother, and then find her again as mature and objective feeling, mother and maiden in one.

Persephone is playing with her companions in the eternal Spring, completely contained in her carefree belief that nothing can change this happy state of youth and beauty. Underneath, however, the urge to consciousness is stirring, and "the maiden not to be named," strays away from her fellows, and, intoxicated by the scent of a narcissus, she stoops to pick it and in so doing opens the door through which the Lord of the Underworld rushes up to seize her. We may notice here that Gaia, mother earth, is clearly distinguished from Demeter in this myth. She is Zeus's fellow conspirator as it were! Kerenyi says, "From the Earth Mother's point of view, neither seduction nor death is the least bit tragic or even dramatic."

It is through the father that the daughter first becomes conscious of her self. When there is no adequate father-image in a girl's life, the identity of daughter and mother can assume a tremendous intensity, or else when the father-image is very negative and frightening, the daughter may unconsciously take on the mother's problem in a peculiarly deep way, sometimes carrying it all her life, long after the mother's death, and so remaining crippled in her effort to face her own fate in freedom. Normally the girl begins to detach from the mother, and to become conscious of her own potential motherhood through love of the father. Thus she is ready for the intoxicating moment of finding the narcissus—seeing *herself* as a person (as Narcissus saw his own face in the water), and the inevitable rape will follow. Dionysos was admiring himself in a mirror when he was set upon by the Titans and torn to pieces, the dismemberment which led to his rebirth. He is a male counterpart of Persephone.

The moment of breakthrough for a woman is always symbolically a rape—a necessity—something which takes hold with overmastering power and brooks no resistance. The arranged marriages of the primitive were often accompanied by a ritual stealing of the woman. The carrying of the woman over the threshold has survived through the centuries, becoming finally a joke, its connection with myth being lost. Any breakthrough of new consciousness, though it may have been maturing for months or years out of sight, comes through a building up of tension which reaches a breaking point. If the man or woman stands firm with courage, the breakdown becomes a breakthrough into a surge of new life. If he cannot stand it and settles for an evasion, then he will regress into neurosis.

The Lord of the Underworld is he who arises, bursts forth from the unconscious with all the tremendous power of instinct. He comes "with his immortal horses" and sweeps the maiden (the anima in a man) from the surface life of her childish paradise into the depths, into the kingdom of the dead—for a woman's total giving of her heart, of herself, in her experience of her instincts is a kind of death. This statement in no way equates this total giving with the outward experience of intercourse with a man. This is a normal part of it and by far the easiest way, but the instincts may be experienced to the full, sometimes perhaps even more profoundly, by a woman whose fate does not bring her the fruition of intercourse on the physical plane. An immature man may experience his instincts in a compartment, so to speak, without deep-seated damage— but not so a woman. If she does so she pays a very great price. It was not merely a man-made piece of injustice that condemned a woman's adultery as so much more shameful than a man's. The horrible cruelty of conventional prejudices should not blind us to the archetypal truths from which these distorted collective judgments spring. The woman who gives herself on the instinctual level without the love of her heart betrays the very essence of her being as woman. A prostitute, so called, whose warmth of *heart* flows out to the man in her every encounter is a far more moral person than the respectable wife who fulfils her "duty" with hidden hatred in her heart.

Persephone cries out in fear and protest as the cord of her tie to her mother, to her unconscious youthfulness, is violently cut, and nearby, Hecate, the goddess of the moon, hears her in her dark cave, though she does not see the abduction. There are three goddesses in the myth, Demeter, Persephone, and Hecate, and they are three aspects of woman. Hecate is the goddess of the dark moon, of the mediumistic intuition in woman of that which *hears* in the dark but does not see or understand. In this myth she appears as beneficent, linked positively to the others, but she has also of course her negative side. Disconnected from the other aspects of woman or from a man's undeveloped feeling she is the goddess of ghosts and witches and of the spells with which the unconscious binds us, or those near to us, from below. Mother earth and the sea, the mother of all, also carry the sound of the daughter's voice, and Demeter, the mother, hears and knows that the daughter is lost but not how. For nine days she wanders over the earth in fear and sorrow, searching for her daughter but not *understanding*. She is wholly identified with her grief, swallowed by it, even her body forgotten so that she does not eat or wash. It is the beginning of the unspeakably painful struggle of a woman to separate from her possessive emotions, the struggle which alone can give birth to love. As Demeter sank into her grief, so every time we are shocked out of some happy identification with another, which we have

fondly imagined to be an unbreakable state, we are beset by the temptation to this surrender, to this despairing search for that which has been
lost, demanding that it be restored to us exactly as it was, without any
effort to discover the meaning of the experience. If we imagine we have
succeeded in restoring the status quo, then the whole story will begin
again and repeat itself endlessly and pointlessly until we can follow the
goddess to the next step—the dawning of her attempt to *understand*.
This cut, this loss, must be experienced by every woman both as daughter
and as mother or, especially in later years, as *both* at the same time, for
in every relationship between two women the mother and the daughter archetypes are constellated; each may mother the other, each may
depend on the other and ask to be mothered—the balance weighted now
one way, now the other.

At this point we will look at the specific experience of the loss of
the daughter in older women. It is the loss of the young and carefree
part of oneself, the opportunity for the discoveries of meaning which
are the task of the second half of life: it is the change from the life of
outer projection to the detachment, the turning inward, which leads to
the "immediate experience of being outside time" in Jung's words. In the
language of this myth Death rises up and takes away the woman's belief
in everlasting spring. The great majority of women today, having no contact at all with the Demeter mystery, have extreme difficulty in giving
up this unconscious clinging to youth, their partial identification with
man's anima image, the unraped Persephone eternally picking flowers
in blissful unconsciousness of the dark world below her. To such women
the menopause brings long-drawn out disturbances of the body and the
psyche as the conflict grows more acute and remains unresolved.

Kerenyi has written, "To enter into the figure of Demeter means to be
pursued, to be robbed, to be raped" (as Persephone), "to rage and grieve,
to fail to understand" (as Demeter), "and then to get everything back
and be born again" (as Demeter and Persephone—the twofold single
reality of Demeter-Kore). There can be no short cuts in this experience.
All through her nine-day search (the symbolic nine of pregnancy) in her
unconscious abandonment to grief the goddess had nevertheless carried
burning torches in her hand, symbol perhaps of that small fire of attention which must be kept burning through the darkness of our journey
when all meaning seems to have left us. On the tenth day Hecate, the

hitherto dormant intuition came, also bearing a torch, and tells Demeter that her daughter had been ravished away, though she does not know who the ravisher may be. Demeter's moon nature brings the first rift in the isolation her absorbing personal grief has created. The stricken mother begins to intuit, to hear for the first time a voice which leads her to reflect upon that which has brought about her loss. She emerges enough from her self-concern to seek the aid of conscious reason. Together the two goddesses approach and question Helios, the sun, and he tells Demeter what has happened—that Zeus himself has arranged this marriage for her daughter and that this should be accepted as a good, a happy fate. But although her conscious mind has seen and understood, she cannot accept this reasonable answer. "She fails to understand" with her essential being and continues "to rage and to grieve."

Strangely enough, a woman is certainly right to reject his all too easy rational solution. "Let us be sensible," we say. "Our loss is good for us." Our grief was nothing but a childish reaction, and so on. Nevertheless the sun's calm reasoning has affected us. We must go on living. We must emerge from this totally self-centered, self-pitying, sorrow and be awake to other people. We must work, we must relate, but we must not deny our grief. And so Demeter comes to the well of the maidens at Eleusis— the place where the woman consciously draws the water up from the depths—listens to the wisdom of the unconscious. There sitting under an olive tree she meets the king's daughters and offers to work as nurse to a child or at any menial task. No longer obsessed with *her* child, she can look again on the beautiful daughters of others and respond.

She goes to the palace. Arrived there she takes a lowly seat and her royal hosts offer her a cup of wine. But this she refuses and asks for a mixed drink of meal and water. It is not time yet for the wine of new life, the wine of full communion. We may remember here the words of Christ before his Passion. "I will not drink henceforth of the fruit of the vine until that day when I drink it new with you in my Father's Kingdom." There is a time when all seeking of release from tension must be refused, and the drink must be plain and tasteless.

The goddess remains deeply sad in her bearing and there follows the delightful image of the first smile appearing on her face as she listens to the crude jokes of Iamba, the serving woman. Her load is not lightened by some lofty thought, but by a most earthly kind of humor. The ancients were not cursed with the puritanical split between earth and the holy.

This then is the next step, after a loss, after any emotional blow, even after a seemingly trivial incident involving hurt feelings. We must return to the well of feminine wisdom. We can always work and we can always serve and we can recover our sense of humor, if we will descend far enough from our goddess-like superiority. Demeter here appears as a woman past childbearing—she has lost her own child, she can never bear another in the flesh. Even the partial acceptance of this means that she can now give of her wisdom to the children of others. Demeter, being a goddess, has the power to bestow immortality, and she feeds the child of the King and Queen with inner wisdom, and at night she thrusts him like a brand into the fire which burns but does not consume.

What is the meaning of this incident for us? It can perhaps be seen from two opposite angles. The fear and the protest of the human mother is on the one hand a warning of how fatal to a child's inner life is the overprotective possessiveness of mother love which tries to prevent all suffering and danger from touching the beloved son. But from another angle, on another level, the human mother's instinct is surely right. This is a human baby and must grow up into a human being, subject to death. If he is to reach immortality, he must reach it on the hard road of human experience and the battle for consciousness—not be given immunity and deprived of the suffering and dignity of manhood by a goddess. She is right, as a mother's instinct so often is, even if for the wrong reasons. It may be noted that the goddess here descends to something like a temper tantrum, throwing the child heartlessly on to the floor and reviling the mother for her witlessness and for her lack of vision.

It could be that the goddess' behavior at this point gives us a glimpse into another danger of the way. After a violent awakening to loss, inner or outer, when already we have been greatly matured by this, and when we have, perhaps with great courage, decided to do our best to serve and to work, it is often a great temptation to seek assuagement for our anger and grief in the satisfaction of passing on to others who are still in a very unconscious state our hard-won wisdom, and then to get very angry when this priceless gift is refused.

In a woman, it would not be so much a matter of preaching ideas, but of being quite sure she can save someone else from having to go through the same agony. To feed the infant the food of divine wisdom is well, but to thrust him into the fire of premature transformation is to deprive him of his choice as a human being. Many women do this when they unconsciously lay on their sons the burden of their own unlived inner quest, thrusting them inexorably into the priesthood or similar "spiritual" vocation at an early age. Of this particular child we are told that all his life long the food of the goddess made him wiser than other men, but thanks to his mother, he remained a man, retained his human fate and his human dignity.

As is the way with myth, this in no way invalidates the other meaning—the danger of overprotection. There are very few mothers who do not react as this one did when they see the Great Mother, life itself thrusting their child—their outer or their inner child—into the fire. Only when she herself will accept the Demeter experience is she strong enough to consent to this. This is why the woman's experience of the dark is so often expressed in myth by the descent of the child, daughter or, more often, son, into hell. It is a more terrible experience for the feminine psyche than her own descent. The woman does not hang on the cross. She stands at its foot and watches the torment of her son. This is an image expressing the truth that immortality can only be realized through the sacrifice of the most precious thing of all—and that for a woman is her child, whether of the flesh or of the spirit. Christ was the Word Incarnate and his life's work was mocked and spurned and came to ignominious failure. Mary was the mother incarnate and her sacrifice was quite simply the complete acceptance of that which happened to her son, which meant the death of every shred of possessiveness. Every archetypal story tells of course of the experience in its pure form. It is the theme upon which the endless variations in the individual psyche are built.

Demeter's effort to transmit immortality to the unconscious child may also be seen as an attempt at a short cut, if we think of the child for a moment as her own new consciousness. After a partial awakening it is easy to imagine that we have already arrived, or that the "baptism of fire" can now take place immediately through some kind of miracle or through self-imposed, dramatic purging—that we won't need to suffer it through in actual experience over the years. Demeter has a long road to travel before she comes to the Holy Marriage of the mysteries and the birth of *the* divine child. Paradoxically it is the failure of this attempt to play the goddess and use her powers on the human child that recalls her to her true goddess nature. She remembers who she is, reveals herself, and immediately begins to prepare for the passing on of her vision, her essence, on an altogether different level—the symbolic level of the mysteries.

Demeter's center of gravity has changed, and she orders a temple to be built for her in Eleusis. It seems totally illogical that at *this* point she orders the temple to be built, for there is still a long road to be traveled before the opposites can be reconciled, before that which is to be worshiped and experienced at Eleusis is understood by Demeter herself. But myth, particularly feminine myth, is not logical. Its truth is of another order. Demeter has emerged from her wholly personal grief; she consciously knows that she is living a great mystery and that no matter how long her suffering may last, the end of it is certain. The *Hieros Gamos*, the Holy Marriage, which is the unity of all opposites, is an established possibility—she *remembers* her true nature. It is a moment of recognition, a kind of remembering of that which somewhere at bottom we have always known. The current problems are not solved, the conflicts remain, but such a person's suffering, as long as he or she does not evade it, will no longer lead to neurosis but to new life. The individual intuitively glimpses who he is.

So the goddess remembers herself and builds her temple, within which she now encloses herself, and in which she sits down again in a grief more terrible than before. It is not regression; it is her cave of introversion. Whereas at first she had simply surrendered to her sorrow, she now enters consciously into it. She is in a ritual, holy place, contained. She does not yet know the solution, but she herself must accept the dark, and inner death, if her daughter is ever to return to the light of day. And as the Goddess withdrew, so the earth dried up and withered, the sap of growth departed, and the land lay dying. The wasteland around the Fisher King in the Grail legend carries the same meaning—when it is time for a transformation of the whole personality, the birth of a totally new attitude, everything dries up inwardly and outwardly and life becomes more and more sterile until the *conscious* mind is forced to recognize the gravity of the situation, is compelled to accept the validity of the unconscious.

The gods now become frantic at what is happening on earth—pretty soon there will be no more men to worship the mighty gods of reason! As always happens, they get busy *bribing* Demeter to emerge from her temple and her sorrow—urging her to settle for a pleasant life of peace and honor on Olympus and to forget about her daughter down below, who can be left to keep the dark powers happy and prevent them from bothering the upper gods. So does reason and the fear of the dark speak to us. "Even if my greatest value does not stay buried forever, it is foolish and arrogant of me to make so much fuss about it. I must conquer my misery, stop thinking about it, make the best of things as they are. Surely the great god Zeus must know best, and he is offering me ease and a position of great importance." But Demeter does not for a moment yield to good sense arguments. There can be no half-way solution, no stopping at the state of separation of the opposites. She is deaf to all the entreaties and appeals of every god in turn. She uses the invincible weapon of the woman who, when something utterly irrational and against all conscious values rises up from the root of her being, simply sits still and refuses to budge. No man can resist this, but unfortunately we too often use this tool when we are moved not by a real intuition from our roots, but by our overpowering emotional possessiveness or an animus opinion.

The gods give in to Demeter, of course, and at last the conscious and the unconscious, the masculine and the feminine begin to pull together. It seems at first simply a capitulation of consciousness to the regressive longing of the mother. Zeus sends Hermes to tell Hades he must give Persephone back and restore the status quo, for Zeus himself cannot produce the solution which reconciles the opposites. Only when Hades the Lord of Death, Zeus's dark brother, will cooperate can the answer come. It is he who gives Persephone the seed of the pomegranate to eat—and she, who has hitherto rejected all food—refused to assimilate the experience—now in the moment when she is full of joy at the thought of not having to accept it, takes the pomegranate seed involuntarily, but voluntarily swallows it. In spite of her protests, she really has no intention of regressing to identification with her mother again. This is an image of how the saving thing can happen in the unconscious before the conscious mind can grasp at all what is going on. There are many dreams in which the dreamer tries to return to an old thing or situation but finds, for example, the doors barred or the telephone broken. The ego still yearns for the status quo but further down the price has been paid, and we *can't* go back. Hence the great value of dreams in making us aware of these movements below. Even Demeter in her conscious planning, still half yearns for her daughter to return as before; but her questioning is quite perfunctory. As soon as she knows the seed has been eaten, there is no more said on the subject—all is joy. Persephone has eaten the food of Hades, has taken the seed of the dark into herself and can now give birth to her own new personality. So also can her mother. They have both passed through death to the renewal of a new spring—the inward renewal which age need never lose—and have accepted the equal necessity of winter and life in the darkness of the underworld.

The two become Demeter-Kore instead of Demeter and Kore. Now, to complete the unity, Hecate joins the others; she too is united to Persephone, becoming from that day her "queenly comrade," mother, maiden, and sibyl—the threefold nature of woman made whole. The images unite; they no longer merge or fight or possess each other, and the woman who knows this experience becomes "one in herself."

The Mysteries

Demeter, united to her daughter, taught the rulers of Eleusis her rites and her mysteries, and these mysteries were for a thousand years a center of the inner religious life of antiquity. It is a measure of the power and depth of experience of the initiates that in all this time the secrets were never revealed by any one of the vast numbers involved. The merest hints leaked out, so that we can only know that certain symbols played a part, but very little about the rituals which led to the final revelation.

It is certain that the rites were not a mystery-drama, not an acting out of the story of the two goddesses, though each element of the myth was *symbolically* experienced. The initiates gathered in Athens on the first day—anyone could be a candidate if he spoke Greek and was not guilty of the shedding of blood—and went through a purification ritual of bathing in the sea. Probably they had already been through the lesser mysteries of Persephone at Agrai in which water and darkness played a major part, and the candidate experienced the passive suffering of the raped Persephone in the underworld through a conscious act of surrender. After the bathing there was a procession to Eleusis of the purified, bearing torches. Various symbolic actions were performed along the way, and on arrival outside Eleusis there was a time of fasting. The journey and the fasting were the symbols of Demeter's nine days of wandering and grief; Eleusis itself was the place of the *finding*.

It is probable that the rites proper began with a dance. Euripides wrote that on the night of the dance round the "fountain in the square of beautiful dances—the stormy heaven of Zeus begins to dance also, the moon and the fifty daughters of Nereus, the goddesses of the sea and the ever flowing rivers, all dance in honor of the golden-crowned maiden and her holy mother." Already the individual is lifted out of his small, rational, personal ego, and the whole universe is dancing with him.

There was also, it is thought, a communion drink—meal and water, probably, as drunk by Demeter in the king's hall, and the rites moved on through we know not what pattern to the climax of a ritual marriage by violence—not, as one might expect, that of Hades with Persephone, but the marriage of Demeter and Zeus. These are the mysteries of Demeter (not of Persephone, except insofar as she is an aspect of Demeter), of the Great Mother, whose experience of loss and finding led her to the *hieros gamos*, the union of the earth with the creator God, which means the birth of the divine child who is the "whole."

After the sacred marriage, a great light shone and the cry of the hierophant rang out "The great goddess has borne a sacred child—Brimo has borne Brimos." The goddess has acquired a new name which means "the strong one," "the power to arouse terror." Without terror, without experience of the terrible face of God, there can be no divine birth. It must be remembered that Persephone also, in her dark, negative aspect, is Medusa, the Gorgon's head, which she herself sends forth from the underworld—"a monstrosity," says Kerenyi, "the nocturnal aspect of what by day is the most desirable of all things." The birth of the child who bears the name, Brimo, alone can resolve the intolerable tension of these opposites, the child who is Demeter, Persephone, Hecate, Zeus, and Hades in one living image. The child is a boy, but also a girl, the androgynous fruit of the holy marriage. It is known that a single child initiate played a part in the mysteries, and that this could be either a boy or a girl, as the omens should decide.

The marriage and the birth, however, were not the final revelation. The most profound vision of all, the actual experience of immortality came in deep silence, when a mown ear of corn was held up and *seen* by the initiate. Nor can words ever accompany such an experience. The ancients said that at this point the idea of immortality "lost everything confusing and became a satisfying vision."

The mown ear of corn is a perfect symbol of immortality, of eternal rebirth. It is the fruit of life, the harvest, which feeds and nourishes, it is the seed which must sink into the earth and disappear in order to give birth again. It is mown down in the moment of its ripeness, as Persephone was mown down and torn from her mother, as every achievement in our lives outer or inner must be mown down in order to give birth to the new. It is the mother who nourishes, it is the seed of the father, and it is the child born of them both, in one image. The elevated Host in the Mass is the same symbol, the same silent epiphany, "showing forth" of immortality, with a tremendous added dimension. Bread is that which has been produced by man from the raw grain. *Consciousness* is added to the purely natural symbol, for Christ has consciously lived the myth. His initiates too must experience the mowing down, the burial and the rising again in a conscious realization of the Christ within. "Unless a corn of wheat fall into the ground and die, it remaineth alone, but if it die, it bringeth forth much fruit." That which must die is not the evil and the ugly but the thing of greatest beauty and meaning, the maiden of stainless innocence, so that we may finally know that over which death has no power.

There is evidence that the final act at Eleusis was the setting up of two vessels which were tipped over, so that the water flowed towards the east and the west, the directions of birth and death. Thus the ritual began and ended with water, symbol of the unconscious beginnings of all life and of the wise spirit of the conscious end—the living water "springing up into eternal life."

It should be stressed that the rites at Eleusis were neither allegory nor a miracle but a mystery. An allegory exists in the realm of ordinary knowledge; it is a metaphor, a story, reflecting, for example, the cycle of the seasons or speaking of the living on of man in his descendants—facts which we all know of but which have for the most part, little power to affect or change our personalities. As Kerenyi says, "There is a vast difference between knowing *of* something and knowing it and being it." Of the difference between miracle and mystery, he writes that a miracle causes people to talk endlessly about it, whereas the true mysteries are kept silent so that they may transform us from within through the symbols which in Jung's words "alone can reconcile the warring opposites, conveying to man in a single image, that which is thought *and* feeling and beyond them both."

The Homeric hymn ends with the words "awful mysteries which no one may in any way transgress or pry into or utter, for deep awe of the gods checks the voice. Happy is he among men upon earth who has seen these mysteries; but he who is uninitiate and who has no part in them never has lot of like good things once he is dead, down in the darkness and gloom." The ancient hymn thus asserts the three essentials of all the mystery rituals of all the religions. First, the rites must not be transgressed, altered in any way; second, they must be accepted without analysis and without question; third, they must not be spoken of, must be kept absolutely secret.

It is immediately obvious that modern man, even in the Roman Church which has been the guardian of the Christian mysteries for so long, is busy breaking all these essentials of a ritual mystery. We are changing it, we pry into everything, and we speak about it all incessantly. The element of awe is being deliberately banished. All this is not something which can or should be avoided. The growth of consciousness inevitably and rightly means that we pry into, we question everything with our hungry minds, and to try to stop this would be futile obscurantism. But it is equally futile and an arrogant folly to imagine that having banished the mystery from our outer cults, we can now dispense with it altogether. Then indeed, we shall end up in the "darkness and gloom" denying reality to the psyche itself and its truths. Without vision, without mystery, all of our fine intellectual understandings and its great values turn to dust.

The hymn refers to the fate of the initiate after death. In this context Kerenyi writes, "The 'eidola' in the realm of the dead ... are the images with which the deceased individual, through his uniqueness, has enriched the world." Only to the extent that a man has lived his unique individual meaning does he attain to immortality. Persephone was called "the eternally unique" because she had united the two worlds, the dark and the light.

Surely the meaning of the dogma *extra ecclesiam nulla salus*, is that there is no salvation without experience of the mystery. It became a cruel and bigoted statement when it was interpreted in the literal outer sense (a kind of interpretation from which all the great dogmas of the Church have suffered immeasurably), and it gave sanction to such horrors as the Inquisition. The Ecumenical movement today is tackling this distortion on its own level with arguments of reason and good sense, but it misses the essential point, which is that man should recognize and experience the level of his being where this dogma is eternally and *individually* true. Outside the "Church," outside the mystery, there is no salvation.

When the outer cult loses its "mana" for a man, then the mystery falls into the unconscious and must there be rediscovered by the individual journeying alone in the dark places to the experience of the symbols within. When images of power and beauty rise up in dreams or fantasies, they make an immediate impact. We are in awe before them. Sometimes there comes a specific dream of initiation which may alter the whole course of a man's life. Such images are not something thought up or pried into, they cannot be altered, and instinctively we sense that they must not be spoken of except to another "initiate." When one does expose them wrongly, the can *feel* the power go out of them. Although their details are individual, unique, they link a man to the whole experience of mankind, and their impact can be immensely increased through a knowledge of the content and meaning of ancient myth, of the eternal themes which have embodied through the ages the truths of the human psyche. Our individual images may invoke perhaps, the dance of the primitive, or the flood or Demeter-Kore, Isis-Osiris, the Buddha's Flower sermon, the Zen Master's koan, and, for us in the West most powerfully of all, the birth and death of Christ, the bread and wine of the Mass. The analyzing mind which has destroyed mystery is thus linked again to the immediacy of the inner experience, and the redeeming symbol is reborn.

Note:

1. Helen M. Luke, *Kaleidoscope: Way of Woman, and Other Essays*, Copyright © 1992, distributed by Morning Light Press, Sandpoint, ID.

THE FIRST TREE / SUMERIAN

Retold by Diane Wolkstein

In the first days, in the first years, when everything
needed was brought into being, when everything needed
was properly nourished; when bread was baked in the
shrines of the land, and bread was tasted in the homes
of the land; when heaven moved away from earth and
earth separated from heaven; when names were given
to all living beings, the Sky God, An, carried off the
heaven. The Air God, Enlil, carried off the earth, and
Ereshkigal, Queen of the Great Below, was given the
underworld for her domain.

At this time, he set sail. Father Enki set sail. Enki,
the God of Wisdom, set sail for the underworld. The
Queen of the Great Below resisted. Small windstones
were tossed up against him; large hailstones were hurled
up against him. Like onrushing turtles, they charged the
keel of his boat. The waters of the sea devoured the bow
of his boat like wolves. They devoured the stern of his
boat like lions.

In the midst of the tempest, one seed, the seed of a
huluppu-tree flew up into the air and entered the moist
earth by the banks of the Euphrates River. The waters
of the Euphrates nourished the tree. The huluppu-tree
grew. Then, the whirling South Wind arose, pulling at the

roots and ripping at the branches until the waters of the Euphrates carried it away.

A young woman who walked by the banks of the Euphrates saw the tree. She reached out and rescued the tree from the river. Inanna spoke. Inanna, the Morning and Evening Star, who had descended from the heavens, Inanna, the daughter of the Moon, spoke and said: "I will take this tree to my city, Uruk. I will plant this tree in my garden."

Inanna took the young tree to her city. She planted the tree in her garden, settling the earth around the tree with her foot, caring for the tree with her hand. She watched her tree, and she wondered, "How long will it be until I have a shining throne to sit upon? How long will it be until I have a shining bed to lie upon?"

Five years passed. Ten years. The tree grew thick but its bark did not split.

Then one day a serpent who could not be charmed made its nest in the roots of the tree. The Great Bird set his young in the branches. And the dark maid Lilith built her home in the trunk.

Inanna wept. The young woman who loved to laugh wept. How she wept. All night Inanna wept. But, the fearful creatures would not leave her tree.

As the birds began to sing at the coming of dawn, Utu, the Sun God, the brother of Inanna, left his royal bedchamber and started across the heavens. Inanna called out to her brother for help. She told him of the first days, the first years, of heaven separating from earth and earth moving away from heaven; of the battle of the God of Wisdom in the underworld; of the planting and rescuing of the tree; and of her hopes and dreams for a throne and a bed.

Utu, the son of the moon, the brother of Inanna, Utu, the Sun God continued in his path across the heavens. He would not help his sister. She wept. The young woman who loved to laugh wept. How she wept. All night Inanna wept. But, the fearful creatures would not leave her tree.

As the birds began to sing at the coming of the second dawn, Gilgamesh, the hero of Uruk, walked across the land. Inanna called to Gilgamesh for help. She told him of the first days, the first years, of heaven separating from earth and earth moving away from heaven; of the battle of the God of Wisdom in the underworld; of the planting and rescuing of the tree; and of her hopes and dreams for a throne and a bed.

Gilgamesh, the valiant warrior, the hero of Uruk, stood by Inanna. He fastened his armor of sixty pounds around his chest; the sixty pounds weighed as little to him as fifty feathers. He lifted the bronze axe of the road, weighing four hundred and fifty pounds, to his shoulder. He entered Inanna's holy garden.

Gilgamesh struck the serpent who could not be charmed. The Great Bird flew with his young to the mountains. The dark maid Lilith smashed her home and fled to the wild, uninhabited places. Gilgamesh loosened the roots of the huluppu-tree. The sons of the city, who accompanied him, cut off the branches.

Then, from the trunk of the tree, he carved for her a shining throne. From the trunk of the tree Gilgamesh carved for her a shining bed. And she from the roots of the tree fashioned for him a drum and from the branches a drumstick. She gave the drum and drumstick to Gilgamesh. Gilgamesh struck the drum. He woke the people of Uruk so that they might follow his command.

Adapted from the book *Inanna, Queen of Heaven and Earth, Her Stories and Hymns from Sumer*, by Diane Wolkstein and S. N. Kramer, HarperCollins, 1983.

CHAPTER SIX

The Hero as Warrior and King

*"If it is true, as I have heard, that poetry reveals mystical
knowledge, let us hear a tale, master poet, worthy of the king
and his forefathers: a tale of gods and fighting men,
a tale of romance, courage, and adventure."*[1]

—Irish

*... there are two types of deed. One is the physical deed, in which the hero
performs a courageous act in battle or saves a life. The other
kind is the spiritual deed, in which the hero learns to
experience the supernormal range of human spiritual life
and then comes back with a message.*[2]

—Joseph Campbell

GILGAMESH

In answer to the prayers of the people of Uruk, the goddess Aruru sent Enkidu as a challenge to Gilgamesh, king of Uruk, to divert his limitless energy from the constant battles and building that were wearing his people out. The goddess took clay and water and fashioned a man and set him down in the wilderness. A temple harlot was sent to seduce Enkidu from the wilderness and bring him to the walls of Uruk, where he was to meet and challenge Gilgamesh. The two heroes were equal in strength however, and in their battle neither yielded. They became fast friends and set forth on all expeditions together.

One day Gilgamesh revealed that he had set his heart upon the cedars growing in the forest known as the Country of the Living. His purpose was twofold: to gather cedar wood, and to slay the monster Humbaba, the watchman of the forest. Enkidu was full of foreboding, but at length they set out, once Gilgamesh had consecrated his task to the sun-god Shamash.

The foreboding in Enkidu's heart grew stronger as their forest journey progressed. When he set his hand to the forest gate, he lost the strength of it, and his nights were full of evil dreams. At last they met Humbaba and joined battle.

With the slaying of Humbaba, the goddess Ishtar presented herself to Gilgamesh and demanded that he be her lover. When he refused, she sent the Bull of Heaven to destroy him, but this monster the heroes also slew, and so incurred the wrath not only of Ishtar but of Enlil, the god of the storm, as well. The judgment was passed among the gods that the two men should die, but the arguments of Shamash prevailed in the judgment against Gilgamesh, and he was spared. Thus it was that Enkidu, who had been to Gilgamesh as a brother, was slain by the gods.

"Hear me, ye elders of Uruk!" cried Gilgamesh, from where he sat by the body of his friend. "I weep for my brother Enkidu, my friend, my companion. All the beasts that ran with you, Enkidu, mourn you as I do: let the elders of Uruk weep for you also. You were the axe at my side, my brother: my hand's strength, my sword and my shield. Listen! the beasts that we hunted, panther and tiger, weep for you; Listen! the mountain we climbed to slay the watchman Humbaba mourns for you. Listen! the rivers of Kullab, Ula of Elam and the blessed Euphrates, weep for you. Listen! the warriors of Uruk, where we slew the Bull of Heaven, mourn for you. Listen! the harvesters weep for you now, and the servants, the women, and the temple harlot who brought you to me. Can you hear them? What is this sleep which lies over you now? What is this darkness which cloaks you so that you cannot hear the words of my mourning?"

For a long time Gilgamesh stayed by the body of his friend: seven days and nights he sat, numbed and silent, until at last the worms, who serve the Annunaki, the judges of the dead, fastened on Enkidu to take him below. Then did Gilgamesh bury his friend and make an offering to Shamash. Then he covered himself with the pelts of wild beasts, and streaking his face with ashes, he set forth to find Utnapishtim.

"At the end of the world lives Utnapishtim, who is called the Faraway," said Gilgamesh to his heart. "Him will I seek whom the gods spared from the Flood. They set him in a land far away, at the mouth of the rivers of the earth, in the garden of the gods. To him they gave eternal life. Him will I seek because I am afraid of death. I will seek him and learn from him the secret of eternal life."

A long path through the wilderness Gilgamesh walked, and when he came at last to the mountain passes, he made his camp. For a time he watched the embers of his fire, and then he slept. But in the night he awoke from a dream and beheld a strange sight. There in the moonlight were lions, and they leapt and played and gloried in their life. Then

Gilgamesh took his sword and fell on them like an arrow from a taut bowstring, and he vanquished them, he destroyed and scattered them.

In the morning he rose and went his way, coming at length to the great mountain Mashu, which guards the rising and setting of the sun. At its gate stand the Men-Scorpions, the dragons who guard the passes and whose glance is death. For a moment only did Gilgamesh shield his eyes; then he went forward.

"Who are you who comes to us without fear, without trembling? Your courage is that of the gods, but you are dressed as a wild man, in pelts. Stand and tell us the reason you come," said the Man-Scorpion, the captain of dragons.

"Gilgamesh is my name," answered that one. "I come for Enkidu, my friend. Him I loved dearly; together we suffered and together we gloried. Now he is dead, and surely that is my lot also. I seek Utnapishtim, the Faraway. To him the gods gave life everlasting. I need to question him about the living and the dead. Open the gate of the mountain and let me pass!"

"No man has done what you have done," replied the Man-Scorpion. "None, not one has made the journey through the mountain. Twelve leagues does the way run under the mountain, all in darkness. Three leagues are in darkness, and three more. Yet three more leagues are in darkness, and yet three more. Would you go that way? There is no light there, the presence of Shamash does not find a way in. Yet if you would go that way, Gilgamesh, I will open the gate to you. Go with the blessing of the gods, may you find what you seek. Go, the Gate of Mashu is open."

Now three leagues under the mountain went Gilgamesh, and darkness cloaked every step. Nothing could he see before him, nothing behind. Three leagues more he went, and yet three leagues. Nine leagues thus he went in darkness, the darkness was thick about him, it enveloped him like a cloak. Nothing could he see before him, and nothing behind. After nine leagues, the end was near, a cool wind blew upon his face, yet he could see nothing. So yet three more leagues he went, and at last he came out from under the mountain and beheld the sun, the light of Shamash, streaming down upon him.

So it was that Gilgamesh came, weary and worn, to the garden of the gods. Golden trees were there, and fruit of gems. Lapis lazuli were the leaves, and grapes of carnelian hung upon the vine. There Gilgamesh sat down by the shores of the ocean, and there Shamash saw him, saw his weariness, saw the labors of this man dressed in pelts of wild beasts. And Shamash spoke to him:

"Gilgamesh, listen to me! To me you dedicated yourself and slew Humbaba, the watcher of the forest; and it was I whose supplications spared your life when you slew the Bull of Heaven. Listen then to me, Gilgamesh! Never will you find the life you are seeking. Better it were that you never came this way, a way no man has gone before."

And to Shamash Gilgamesh replied, "Long have I toiled in darkness, through the wilderness and over the mountain passes. In darkness I came here, to seek Utnapishtim, the Faraway. Am I to cover my head with earth now? Though I may be no better than a dead man, let me at least look upon the glory of the sun."

With her golden bowl she sits by that sea: Siduri, the maker of wine. With a veil she is covered, none can see her face. To her gate came Gilgamesh, and from afar she saw him approach. She saw a man dressed in the pelts of wild beasts, a man with the marks of a long journey on his face, with despair in his heart. To him she barred the way, she drew the bolt across the gate, saying to herself, "Surely this is a thief who comes this way."

But even as the bolt shot home, Gilgamesh lodged his foot in the gate and called in anger, "Woman, wine-maker, who are you to bar the gate to me? I will smash your gate, will tear down your door. I am Gilgamesh, who slew the Watchman of the forest, who slew the Bull of Heaven, who vanquished the lions in the mountain passes. You may not bar the way to me!"

Then Siduri said to him, "This is not Gilgamesh, lord of Kullab, slayer of Humbaba and the Bull of Heaven, vanquisher of lions. This is one who is dressed in the pelts of wild beasts, whose face is weary, whose heart is full of despair. Why do you come this way? Are you looking for the wind?"

"And why should I not be weary and full of despair?" Gilgamesh replied. "My friend Enkidu is dead, whom I loved as a brother. Now I seek Utnapishtim, who lives at the mouth of the rivers, and to whom the gods granted eternal life. I would ask him about life and death. Woman, I have looked upon your face: let me not look upon the face of death, that face I fear so much."

"Gilgamesh," Siduri said to him softly, drawing him inside her hut, "you will never find that life for which you are seeking. The gods have not given that to man. To man they gave the fruit called Death; the fruit called Life they kept for themselves. As for man—as for you—fill your belly with good food and wine. Day and night, feast on the things of life, dance, rejoice in what is your lot. Soon enough all will be taken from you: food and wine, the love of family and friends. Make your garments fresh, Gilgamesh, anoint your hair. Cherish the hand of the child, make your wife happy in your embrace: this is the lot of man."

Now Gilgamesh sat by the fire in Siduri's hut and stared a long while into the embers and was silent. At last he spoke.

"Woman, wine-maker: how can I be silent, how can I rest, how can I be merry, dance, enjoy the things of life, when my brother, whom I love, is dead? Seven days and seven nights I sat by him and wept, and then the worms, the servants of the Annunaki, fastened on him and carried him below. This too is my fate, and I fear it. No, I cannot rest. I will go over this Ocean, to find Utnapishtim. What directions can you give me?—this, not soft words and wine, is the boon I ask of you. How will I cross the Ocean?"

Siduri said to him, "There is no crossing of that sea, Gilgamesh; except for Shamash, who can cross it? Deep are the waters of death that lie between this place and that which you seek. How can you cross? When you come to the waters of death, what will you do? Nevertheless, Gilgamesh, I will tell you this. In the woods, seek out Urshanabi, the ferryman of Utnapishtim. With him are the Sacred Ones, the Ones of Stone. With his help you might cross. But if it is not possible, you must turn back."

Then Gilgamesh leapt up, in a rage. He seized his axe in his hand, and he sped to the woods by the shore like an arrow from a taut bowstring. Swinging his axe wildly, shattering the Ones of Stone in his wrath, he sought Urshanabi the Ferryman. He found him as he sat by his boat, carving the prow in the shape of a bird.

"Who is this who comes wildly, shattering the Ones of Stone, the Sacred Ones who protected the crossing and the landing of the ferryboat?" said Urshanabi as he sat by the beak of his ship. "Surely this is a thief, a brigand who comes thus wildly. Would you shatter me too? I have nothing to give you."

"I am Gilgamesh, lord of Kullab, slayer of Humbaba and the Bull of Heaven. For Enkidu I come, for Enkidu my brother, who is dead. I would speak with Utnapishtim of the secret of eternal life. Take me to him! Take me now in your boat across the Ocean, across the waters of death!"

Urshanabi stood up then and for a long time looked at Gilgamesh in silence. He looked at the clothing of Gilgamesh, the pelts he wore. He looked at the marks of mourning and weariness on his face. Urshanabi looked at the despair in the heart of the lord of Kullab. Then he spoke.

"The crossing is deadly, Gilgamesh. It is doubly deadly now that you have destroyed the Ones of Stone: they protected this harbor, they protected the crossing and the landing. How will we cross now?

"Go into the woods and do this. Go, and cut six score staves, each sixty cubits long. Caulk them with bitumen and cap them with ferrules and bring them here."

At once Gilgamesh turned and went into the woods. There with his axe he cut six score staves of straight wood, caulked them with bitumen, and capped them with ferrules. He brought them to Urshanabi and placed them in the boat.

"Now listen to me again, Gilgamesh, When we come to the waters of death, you must do this. Thrust in a pole, down to very bottom of the sea. When the pole runs out, thrust in another, and another after that, and another. Make sure your hand never touches the water, for that is certain death."

For three days they sailed, they sped across the Ocean in three days, the journey of a month and a half. Then they reached the waters of death and the boat would not move. Then it was that Gilgamesh took up the first staff and thrust it down deep into the water, taking care that his hand did not touch the water of death. When the first pole ran out, he took another, and after that another. So they crossed, pole by pole, until all six score staves had thus been used. Then Gilgamesh raised his arms like a mast and fastened his garments to them like a sail, and so they crossed the waters of death and came to the other side.

From where he sat by the water's edge he saw them coming: Utnapishtim, the Faraway, he to whom the gods gave eternal life. And Utnapishtim wondered to himself, "Who is this who sails with Urshanabi, dressed in the pelts of beasts? This is none of mine, and yet he is. By his clothes and wild appearance he is none of mine. But by his face and heart he might be myself, though not for many, many years."

Then Gilgamesh approached and bowed down before Utnapishtim and prayed to him:

"Utnapishtim, the Eternal, you whom men call the Faraway, you who dwell at the mouth of the rivers, hear me! I am Gilgamesh, lord of Kullab, from the house of Anu, king of Uruk. You wonder at my appearance, but why should I not look thus? My face is of one who has made a long journey in heat and cold, in light and darkness, over the mountain passes and across the waters of death. As for my clothing, it is the raiment of mourning, and I wear it for my friend Enkidu, who is dead. For seven days and nights I watched by his side when he died, and I saw the servants of the Annunaki take him below. I watched his death, and now I fear my own. As for my heart, it is the heart of a man who has seen death a thousand times and never feared it, yet saw death but once and now cowers in despair. O you whom the gods spared, you to whom they gave eternal life, my father Utnapishtim, you who have entered the assembly of the gods, I beg you: how shall I find the life for which I am searching?"

By the sea they sit, Gilgamesh and Utnapishtim, the young king and the old man, the mortal and the deathless. Utnapishtim looks at Gilgamesh and speaks.

"Tell me, what is permanent? Tell me of the works of men, are they permanent? Do houses stand forever? Do brother divide an inheritance to keep forever? What endures? Does the floodtime of the rivers endure? Does the dragon-fly endure forever? From the days of old there is no permanence. To all creation the gods gave death. The sleeping and the dead, how alike they are, like brothers! Yes, sleep is like a painted death. What happens when the Annunaki assemble together, when Mammetun, the mother of destinies, decrees the fates of men? This one shall live, that one shall die. But the day of death they never tell."

To Utnapishtim the Faraway, Gilgamesh now speaks.

"I came here expecting a hero, a warrior like myself, but what do I find? An old man taking his ease in the sun by the water's edge. If nothing is permanent, if nothing endures, if nothing lives forever and all shall die, how do you come to be here, how came you to enter the assembly of the gods, how did you merit everlasting life?"

"Listen to me now," says Utnapishtim. "Listen to me now, Gilgamesh: I will tell you a secret of the gods."

Then Utnapishtim spoke and told of Shurrupak, where it stands by the Euphrates, a city old when the earth was young. The world was filled with people in those days, and their noise went up as a great clamor and offended the gods. They came together in council then, and resolved to destroy the earth by deluge. But Ea, whom Utnapishtim honored, warned him of the flood, and guided the building of a boat. Onto that boat went Utnapishtim and his wife and his servants. Onto that boat went gold and living things, the beasts of the fields and the craftsmen who made the boat. When the time came, the ship was battened down, and the destroying rains came and flooded the earth. The boat of Utnapishtim rode out the storm. It rode out the rains and the rising waters. It rode out the darkness and the thunder. When Enlil, the god of storm, broke the land like a cup, the boat rode out the storm. Great was that flood: even the gods fled before it to the highest reaches of the heavens. And when it was over, nothing was left: over the earth was water only, there was no land to be seen. Then on the mountain of Nisir, the boat of Utnapishtim touched land and held fast. The first day it held fast and the waters receded. The second day it held fast and the waters receded. The third day it held fast, and the waters receded. For seven days the waters receded and the boat held fast. On the seventh day, Utnapishtim let loose a dove, but it found no resting place, and so returned. Utnapishtim let loose a swallow, and it also returned. Then he let loose a raven, and the raven did not return. Then Utnapishtim threw open everything, and made a sacrifice to the gods and gave thanks. And the gods, smelling the sacrifice, swarmed like flies over it. Ishtar was there, and she saw the earth, smashed and broken and the bodies of men and beasts strewn everywhere. Then she took her necklace, made of the jewels of heaven, and set it above the earth. She forbade Enlil to come to the sacrifice, for without reflection he had destroyed her people. Then came Enlil and said in anger, "Has any mortal survived the flood? For none was to survive." Then Ea spoke and told him of Utnapishtim, she told him that it had been she who had warned the man. Then Enlil repented, and took Utnapishtim and his wife, and the god touched his forehead to theirs, and so they became immortal. Then he set them down by the mouth of the rivers, far away at the end of the world, in the garden of the gods, to live forever.

"How then will you find the life for which you seek, Gilgamesh?" said Utnapishtim as he finished. "Who will call the gods to assembly for your sake? But if you are intent, put it to the test: only prevail against sleep for seven days and seven nights. ..." Yet even as he spoke, a mist of sleep stole over Gilgamesh, and his head nodded upon his breast.

"Look at this strong man now," said Utnapishtim to his wife. "Over the wide world he travels, in search of eternal life. High over the mountain passes he came, and over the sea, to escape from death: yet he cannot even hear out my story, but sleep steals over him like a cloak."

"Touch him then, and awaken him," said the wife to Utnapishtim.

"No, let him sleep. And let him know how long he sleeps. Men are great dissemblers: even you he will try to deceive. Therefore bake bread while he sleeps, one loaf for each day he sleeps so."

So Utnapishtim's wife took flour and water and made dough and baked bread, one loaf each day as Gilgamesh slept. And when the hero awoke, he said, "I had hardly slept when you awoke me." Then Utnapishtim pointed to the loaves, seven of them, and said, "One loaf was baked for each day of your sleep, O mighty king, and look: the first loaf is hard, the second like leather, and the third is soggy. The fourth is mouldy, the fifth is mildewed, the sixth is fresh, and the seventh lies still upon the embers of the oven."

"What then shall I do, O Utnapishtim my father, where shall I go? Already sleep, that painted death, lies hold of my limbs, it crouches in the corner of my chamber. Wherever I put my foot, there I find death."

Then Utnapishtim spoke to Gilgamesh and said, "Go now, and freshen yourself. Cast your pelts aside and bathe. Anoint your hair, renew the fillet upon your forehead, put on fresh clothes. Renew yourself, Gilgamesh, and return to Uruk. The clothes I will give you will show no wear of age while you journey, always they will be fresh upon you."

Down to the water's edge went Gilgamesh and removed his clothes, which Utnapishtim burned upon the shore. And while he bathed, the wife of Utnapishtim said to her husband, "What will you give to Gilgamesh that he can take back with him? For he came here on a long journey. He must not return empty-handed." And Utnapishtim called out to Gilgamesh where he bathed, "Gilgamesh, you have come here on a long journey; you shall not return empty-handed. I will reveal a secret thing, a secret of the gods will I tell you.

"There is a plant that grows deep in the ocean, at the very bottom of the sea. Thorns it has which will wound your hands, but if you pluck it and carry it back, your hands will hold that charm which will return to a man his lost youth."

Then Gilgamesh swam to the deepest part of the ocean. He tied stones to his feet and went to the bottom of the sea. There on the bottom he saw the plant, and the thorns wounded his hand. But he prevailed and cutting loose the stones tied to his feet returned triumphant to the boat of Urshanabi.

"Look, ferryman! Behold this marvelous plant, the means for a man to win back his youth and strength. I will carry it back to Uruk. I will give it to old men to eat. I will call it, 'The Old are Young Again,' and I will eat it myself and have back my lost youth," said Gilgamesh to Urshanabi. Then he put on the clothes which Utnapishtim gave him and set sail for Uruk.

Over the seas they went, the journey of six weeks in three days time. Over the land they went after that, and when they were weary, they made their camp. Then Gilgamesh saw a well of cool water, and he bathed in it and lay down beside it.

But in the pool was a serpent, and the serpent smelled the sweetness of the herb. He came out from the well, he came to the plant even as Gilgamesh slept, and ate it. Immediately, he sloughed his skin and returned to the well.

When Gilgamesh awoke, he looked, and the herb was gone. Then he raised his voice in a loud wail and cried, "O Urshanabi, for this I toiled long and hard. For this I came over the mountain passes and over the sea. For this I was wounded in the hand—that the beasts might benefit from my heart's blood, but not myself. For myself I have nothing."

They returned to Uruk, and Gilgamesh showed Urshanabi the walls of burnt brick, the work of his building. Great is the name of Gilgamesh, lord of Kullab, king in Uruk. He knew secret things, he was wise, he brought us a tale of the days before the Flood. A long journey he went, he was weary and worn out with labor. He returned, and he engraved on a stone the whole story.

Retold by Paul Jordan-Smith

Parabola
Volume: 7.4
Holy War

BEOWULF

In the fiftieth year of Beowulf's reign a great terror fell upon the land: terror of a monstrous fire-dragon, who flew forth by night from his den in the rocks, lighting up the blackness with his blazing breath, and burning houses and homesteads, men and cattle with the flames from his mouth. The glare from his fiery scales was like the dawn-glow in the sky, but his passage left behind it every night a trail of black, charred desolation to confront the rising sun. Yet the dragon's wrath was in some way justified, since he had been robbed, and could not trace the thief. Centuries before Beowulf's lifetime a mighty family of heroes had gathered together, by feats of arms, and by long inheritance, an immense treasure of cups and goblets, of necklaces and rings, of swords and helmets and armor, cunningly wrought by magic spells; they had joyed in their cherished hoard for long years, until all had died but one, and he survived solitary, miserable, brooding over the fate of the dearly loved treasure. At last he caused his servants to make a strong fastness in the rocks, with cunning devised entrances, known only to himself, and thither, with great toil and labor of aged limbs, he carried and hid the precious treasure.

When this solitary survivor of the ancient race died, his hoard remained alone, unknown, untouched, until at length the fiery dragon, seeking a shelter among the rocks, found the hidden way to the cave, and creeping within, discovered the lofty inner chamber and the wondrous hoard. For three hundred winters he brooded over it unchallenged, and then one day a hunted fugitive, fleeing from the fury of an avenging chieftain, in like manner found the cave, and the dragon sleeping on his gold. Terrified almost to death, the fugitive eagerly seized a marvelously wrought chalice and bore it stealthily away, feeling sure that such an offering would appease his lord's wrath and atone for his offence. But when the dragon awoke he discovered that he had been robbed, and his keen scent assured him that some one of mankind was the thief. As he could not at once see the robber, he crept around the outside of the barrow snuffing eagerly to find traces of the spoiler, but it was in vain; then, growing more wrathful, he flew over the inhabited country, shedding fiery death from his glowing scales and flaming breath, while no man dared to face this flying horror of the night.

The news came to Beowulf that his folk were suffering and dying, and that no warrior dared to risk his life in an effort to deliver the land from this deadly devastation; and although he was now an aged man, he decided to attack the fire-drake. Beowulf knew that he would not be able to come to hand-grips with this foe as he had done with Grendel and his mother: the fiery breath of this dragon was far too deadly, and he must trust to armor for protection. He commanded men to make a shield entirely of iron, for he knew that the usual shield of linden-wood would be instantly burnt up in the dragon's flaming breath. He then chose with care eleven warriors, picked men of his own bodyguard, to accompany him in this dangerous quest. They compelled the unhappy fugitive whose theft had begun the trouble to act as their guide, and thus they marched to the lonely spot where the dragon's barrow stood close to the sea-shore. The guide went unwillingly, but was forced thereto by his lord, because he alone knew the way.

When the party reached the place they halted for a time, and Beowulf spoke to his little troop: "Abide ye here, ye warriors, for this is not our expedition, nor the work of any man but me alone; wait till ye know which is triumphant, for I will win the gold and save my people, or death shall take me." So saying he raised his great shield, and, unaccompanied, set his face to the dark entrance, where a stream, boiling with strange heat, flowed forth from the cave; so hot was the air that he stood, unable to advance far for the suffocating steam and smoke. Angered by his impotence, Beowulf raised his voice and shouted a furious defiance to the awesome guardian of the barrow. Thus aroused, the dragon sprang up, roaring hideously and flapping his glowing wings together; out from the recesses of the barrow came his fiery breath, and then followed the terrible beast himself. Coiling and writhing he came, with head raised, and scales of burnished blue and green, glowing with inner heat; from his nostrils rushed two streams of fiery breath, and his flaming eyes shot flashes of consuming fire. He half flew, half sprang at Beowulf. But the hero did not retreat one step. His bright sword flashed in the air as he wounded the beast, but not mortally, striking a mighty blow on his scaly head. The guardian of the hoard writhed and was stunned for a moment, and then sprang at Beowulf, sending forth so dense a cloud of flaming breath that the hero stood in a mist of fire. So terrible was the heat that the iron shield glowed red-hot and the ring-mail on the hero's limbs seared him as a furnace, and his breast swelled with the keen pain: so terrible was the fiery cloud that the Geats, seated some distance away, turned and fled, seeking the cool shelter of the neighboring woods, and left their heroic lord to suffer and die alone.

Among the cowardly Geats, however, there was one who thought it shameful to flee—Wiglaf, the son of Weohstan. He was young, but a brave warrior, to whom Beowulf had shown honor, and on whom he had showered gifts, for he was a kinsman, and had proved himself worthy. Now he showed that Beowulf's favor had been justified, for he seized his shield, of yellow linden-wood, took his ancient sword in hand, and prepared to rush to Beowulf's aid.

Holding on high his shield, he plunged into the fiery cloud and moved towards his king, crying aloud: "Beowulf, my dear lord, let not thy glory be dimmed. Achieve this last deed of valor, as thou didst promise in days of yore, that thy fame should not fall, and I will aid thee."

The sound of another voice roused the dragon to greater fury, and again came the fiery cloud, burning up like straw Wiglaf's linden shield, and torturing both warriors as they stood behind the iron shield with their heated armor. But they fought on manfully, and Beowulf, gathering up his strength, struck the dragon such a blow on the head that his ancient sword was shivered to fragments. The dragon, enraged, now flew at Beowulf and seized him by the neck with his poisonous fangs, so that the blood gushed out in streams, and ran down his corslet. Wiglaf was filled with grief and horror at this dreadful sight, and, leaving the protection of Beowulf's iron shield, dashed forth at the dragon, piercing the scaly body in a vital part. At once the fire began to fade away, and Beowulf, mastering his anguish, drew his broad knife, and with a last effort cut the hideous reptile asunder. Then the agony of the envenomed wound came upon him, and his limbs burnt and ached with intolerable pain. In growing distress he staggered to a rough ancient seat, carved out of the rock, hard by the door of the barrow and said: "Do thou, O dear Wiglaf, bring forth quickly from the cave the treasures for which I lose my life, that I may see them and be glad in my nation's wealth ere I die."

Thereupon Wiglaf entered the barrow, and he flung down the treasures—magic armor, dwarf-wrought swords, carved goblets, flashing gems, and a golden standard—at Beowulf's feet, so that the ancient hero's dying gaze could fall on the hoard he had won for his people. The dying champion roused himself to say, as he grasped his kinsman's hand and looked at the glittering heap before him:

> "I thank God eternal the great King of Glory,
> For the vast treasures which I here gaze upon.
> Wyrd has swept all my kin, all the brave chiefs away!
> Now must I follow them!"

These last words spoken, Beowulf fell back, and his soul passed away, to meet the joy reserved for all true and steadfast spirits. Wiglaf, as he mourned over his dead lord, resolved that no man should joy in the treasures for which so grievous a price had been paid—the cowards who deserted their king should help to lay the treasures in his grave and bury them far from human use and profit.

The Geats, bitterly grieving, fulfilled Wiglaf's commands. They gathered wood for the fire, and piled it on the cliff-head; then eight chosen ones brought thither the treasures, and threw the dragon's body over the cliff into the sea; then a wain, hung with shields, was brought to bear the corpse of Beowulf to Hronesness, where it was solemnly laid on the funeral pile and consumed to ashes.

> There then the Weder Geats wrought for their ruler dead
> A cairn on the ocean cliff widespread and lofty.
> Then in that cairn they placed necklets and rings and gems

Which from the dragon's hoard brave men had taken.
Back to the earth they gave treasures of ancient folk,
Gold to the gloomy mold, where it now lieth
Useless to sons of men as it e'er was of yore.
So all the Geat chiefs, Beowulf's bodyguard,
Wept for their leader's fall: sang in their loud laments
That he of earthly kings mildest to all men was,
Gentlest, most gracious, most keen to win glory.

From *Hero Myths & Legends of the British Race*, by M. I. Ebbutt. Reprinted by permission of George G. Harrap & Company.

Parabola
Volume: 31.1
Coming to
Our Senses

Beyond Rapture

Tim Miller

Circe said it would begin when the wind fell, and we feel that calm all of a sudden, and that silence is here, a silence even in what we see. We know they are near, and the men take down the sail, and the oarsmen begin frothing the water white with the work of their arms, and I slice a wheel of beeswax into small wedges, and after kneading them soft I close everyone's ears but my own.

Eurylochus and Perimedes both come to me as planned, and I hate how they lash me to the mast like some slave, rope on chafing rope around my ankles and wrists, so tight I smell my skin burn in my desire to hear those women sing from the woods. But the river is still so calm, and silent. My men are all at my feet rowing, and with their ears plugged the world is as silent for them as it is for me, but even their silence is different. And with my body bound to this mast I wonder: If I can have a goddess, what can these women do to me? If I can go down to the dead and come back alive, what can these women do to me? If I have so far survived the gods' grudges against me, what can these women do to me?

But it was a goddess who warned me of them, it was Circe who told me what to expect, and there are the first bodies, either rags of skin still clinging to bone or just boneheaps, littering the river's edge. And the bones smell of death and shine so awfully white against the deep green

•

of the Sirens' silent field and forest. My men all see it but they don't turn away—they've seen worse than a few bodies—and some turn and give me foolish looks with foolish plans I hope they won't go through with.

And suddenly those women begin, unseen but with songs of such beauty they aren't only heard, they're felt, they're tasted. My skin reacts in ecstasy, and in my mouth I can taste every woman I've ever had, every draught of wine I've ever drunk, and can feel every loud word I've ever yelled in enjoyment—and can hear them all, too, from my past. And I can smell all of those moments, from the sweat of a woman to the breath of my friends to the rain soon to pour from the sky.

These women are singing of my every rapture, but more, because there is something more to my memories, there is a feeling in my heart and head which the senses cannot reach, a fulfillment they cannot encompass. And what are those women tempting me with but wisdom? When I finally find the words in their songs it's wisdom they offer me, not their bodies, not their breasts or the perfume Circe promised from their spread legs, but a fulfillment I might as well feel with eyes closed, a fulfillment no sound has soiled, no surface has stained, no shape has sullied, no savor has smudged, and no scent has shamed.

I want to wonder if my oarsmen would hear different words if their ears were unplugged, but instead my eyes close and the ropes which bind me fall slack as my body does, and when I come to my men say they never saw me so peaceful.

Adapted from Homer, *The Odyssey*.

Parabola
Volume: 3.4
Androgyny

The Return of Ulysses

Titus Burckhardt

Every path leading toward a spiritual realization requires of man that he strip himself of his ordinary and habitual "I" in order truly to become "himself," a transformation which does not occur without the sacrifice of visible riches and empty pretensions, thus not without humiliation, nor without struggle against the passions of which the "old I" is woven. This is why one repeatedly finds, in the mythology and folklore of almost all peoples, the theme of the royal hero who returns to his own kingdom in the semblance of a poor stranger—even a juggler or a beggar—to recover, after many trials, the property which is legitimately his and of which a usurper has robbed him.

In place of a kingdom to recover, or parallel to this theme, myth often speaks of a wonderfully beautiful woman who will belong to the hero able to deliver her from the physical or magical fetters with which an adverse power keeps her imprisoned. In the case of this woman already being the wife of the hero, the idea that she belongs to him by law is found to be reinforced, as is the spiritual meaning of the myth, according to which the wife delivered from hostile forces is none other than the soul of the hero, boundless in its depth, and feminine because complimentary to the hero's virile nature.[1]

We find all these mythological themes in the last part of the *Odyssey*, the part that describes Ulysses' return to

Ithaca and to his own house, which he finds overrun with young suitors to his wife's hand, who squander his wealth and force him to undergo all kinds of humiliations until the moment when he makes himself known—not only as the master of the house, but as their merciless and quasi-divine judge.

It is also this part of the epic which includes the most direct allusions to the spiritual domain, allusions which prove that Homer was conscious of the deep meaning of the myths that he transmitted or adapted. These openings are nevertheless rare and as if neutralized by a tendency in some way naturalistic—careful to remain within very human bounds. What a contrast with the great Hindu epics like the *Mahabharata*, for example, or even with Germanic mythology, where it is precisely the improbable, the excessive, the discontinuous, and even the monstrous which mark the presence of a transcendental reality!

The last cantos of the *Odyssey* belong, moreover, to the *récit-cadre*, for it is as a guest of the Phaeacians that Ulysses relates his adventures since leaving Troy, so that this entire peregrination is presented retrospectively as a long and painful return toward his homeland, hindered several times by the insubordination or the madness of his companions; it is they who, while Ulysses is sleeping, open the leather flasks in which Aeolus, the god of the winds, had enclosed the hostile winds, entrusting them to the safekeeping of the hero; and the demoniac forces, imprudently freed, fling the little fleet far from its goal. It is these same companions who kill the sun god's sacred cattle, thus incurring his curse. Ulysses is forced to go down to the house of Hades, there to consult the ghost of Tiresias before continuing home; he alone is saved, without his companions; shipwrecked and lacking provisions, he finally reaches the islands of the Phaeacians, who receive him warmly. They transport him to Ithaca and deposit him, sleeping, on the shore. In this way Ulysses reaches his much longed-for home without knowing it; for upon awakening he does not at first recognize the country, veiled in mists, until Athena, his divine protectress, lifts the fog and shows him his homeland.

Here one finds the famous description of the cave of the nymphs, in which Ulysses, following the advice of Athena, hides the precious gifts he received from the Phaeacians. According to Porphyry, the disciple and continuator of Plotinus, this cave is an image of the whole world, and we will see below what this interpretation rests upon.[2] One thing is certain: Ulysses' visit to the cave marks the hero's entry into a sacred space: henceforth the island of Ithaca will no longer be merely the hero's homeland, but will be, as it were, the center of the world. Yet Homer barely touches on this dimension; as always when he speaks of spiritual realities, he expresses himself through allusion:

At the end of the port a long-maned olive
And next to it the dark, welcoming cave,
Consecrated to the nymphs called Naiads.
Inside there are bowls and stone amphoras
   where the bees keep honey.
There also are tall stone looms, on which
The nymphs weave wine-colored cloth, wonderful to see;
There also waters flow ceaselessly. The doors are two,
One which descends toward Boreas is for men,
The other, turned toward the South, is meant for the gods;
Men cross it not, for it is the path of immortals.

According to Porphyry, the stone of which the cavern and the objects found within it are made represents the plastic substance of which the world is a coagulation, for the stone has no form except insofar as form is imposed upon it. It is the same for the waters that gush from the rock: they are also a symbol of this substance in its original purity and fluidity. The cavern is dark because it contains in potential the things of the world. The garments which the nymphs weave on their high stone looms are those of life itself, and their purple color is that of blood. As for the bees that deposit their honey in stone bowls and amphoras, they are, like the Naiads, pure powers in the service of life, for honey is an incorruptible substance.

Like the great cavern of the world, the sacred cave has two doors: one, boreal (northern), is for the souls that go again into the evolutionary process, while the other, meridional (southern), may only be entered by those who, immortal or immortalized, ascend toward the world of the gods.[3] These are the two solsticial doors, *januae coeli*, which are actually two doors in time, or rather outside time, for they correspond to the two turnings of the annual cycle, to the two stopping-moments between the expansive phase and the contractive phase of the sun's movement. In order to understand Homer's allusion, one must be aware of the fact that the "place" of the winter solstice, Capricorn, is located in the meridional hemicycle of the solar orbit, while the "place" of the summer solstice, Cancer, is located in the northern, or boreal, hemicycle.

Porphyry also reminds us that the sacred olive tree which stands near the cave is the tree of Minerva, and that its leaves turn in winter, obeying the yearly cycle of the sun. Let us add that here this tree is the image of the tree of the world, in which the trunk, the branches, and the leaves represent the totality of beings.[4]

There is one thing Porphyry does not tell us, doubtless because in his eyes it went without saying; that is, that the sacred cave is the symbol of the heart. It is in this context, however, that Ulysses' gesture of entrusting all his treasures to the safekeeping of the divine Naiads acquires all its import: henceforth he is like one "poor in spirit," inwardly rich and outwardly indigent.[5] Athena, through her magic, confers on him the countenance of a poor old man.

The fact that Ulysses is the protégé of Pallas Athena, the goddess of wisdom, forces us to believe that guile, which he exhibits on every occasion and which is almost his most salient trait, meant something entirely different in the spiritual cosmos of the ancient Greeks from what it means for a Christian like Dante, who places Ulysses in one of the most terrible regions of hell as a liar and deceiver par excellence. For the Greeks, Ulysses' guile was a positive property of dissimulation, the mark of a sovereign intelligence and almost a magic of the spirit that penetrates and fathoms others' thought. Let us refer to Porphyry, who analyzes the spiritual and moral nature of Ulysses in the following way:

> *It was not possible for him to free himself easily from this life of the senses, and so he set himself to annihilating it at one blow. ...For he who dares to do such things is always persecuted by the wrath of the gods who rule the ocean and the substance of life.[6] Therefore he must first reconcile them with sacrifices, then with the sufferings of a beggar's poverty and other acts of perseverance, at times struggling against passions, and at times using tricks and spells, and from there passing through every possible way of being in order that finally, stripping himself of his own rags, he may become master of all.[7]*

The inhabitants of Ithaca believe Ulysses is dead; Penelope herself, the ever-faithful wife, doubts he will ever return. In fact, he has already returned, stranger to his own house and as if dead to this life. In asking for shelter from the suitors who abuse his property, he puts them to the test, and he undergoes this test himself. Before he came, they were relatively innocent; now, they burden themselves with faults through their outrages toward the stranger, while Ulysses is justified in his intention to destroy them.

According to a more inner aspect of things, the arrogant suitors are the passions which, in the hero's very heart, have taken possession of his birthright, and which seek to ravish his wife, the pure and very faithful depth of his soul. However, stripped of the false dignity of his "I," having become poor and a stranger to himself, he sees these passions for what they are, without illusions, and decides to fight them to the death.

It is the contest that Ulysses himself suggests to his wife that gives him an opportunity to begin the ordeal. It consists in bending the sacred bow and sending an arrow through the holes of twelve hatchets lined up and planted in the ground. The contest takes place at the time of the festival of Apollo, for the bow is the weapon of the sun god. One will recall on this subject the analogous trials undergone, according to Hindu mythology, by certain *avataras* of Vishnu such as Rama and Krishna, and even the young Gautama Buddha: it is always the bow of the sun god which they bend.

The twelve hatchets planted in the ground, through whose holes the arrow had to be sent, represent the twelve months or the twelve abodes of the zodiac which gauge the path of the sun. The hatchet is a symbol of the axis, as is indicated by its Germanic name (*axt* in German and "ax" in English), and the hole of the hatchet, which had to be placed at the end of the handle,[8] corresponds to the "axial" door of the sun at the time of the solstice. There are only two solstices in the year, but each month corresponds, in principle, to a lunar cycle, analogous to the solar cycle and including in its turn an "axial" passage repeating the solstice in some way, whence the row of twelve hatchets. Their number, moreover, made the trial more difficult.

We do not know for certain the form of the hatchets Homer was thinking of: they could have been simple war hatchets; they also could have had the form of Cretan hatchets with double blades. In this last

case, their significance at the same time axial and lunar would be particularly clear, for the two blades of the *bipennis* resemble the two opposing
phases of the moon—waxing and waning—between which is located, in
effect, the celestial axis.

The path of the arrow thus symbolizes the sun's route. One could
object that this route is not a straight line but a circle—however, it occurs
not only in space but also in time, which is compared to a straight line.
From another point of view, the arrow as such symbolizes the beam
which the sun god hurls at the darkness.

The sun's force is at the same time sound and light: when Ulysses
alone succeeds in bending the sacred bow, the string of which he causes
to vibrate "as the path of the swallow," his enemies tremble and foresee
the terrible end he is preparing for them, even before he has revealed to
them his true nature—that of the hero protected by Athena.

The description of the massacre which follows is so horrible that it
would be repugnant to us were it not for the fact that Ulysses incarnates
light and justice, while the suitors represent darkness and injustice.

It is only after having killed the suitors and purified the house from
bottom to top that he makes himself known to his wife. Penelope, we have
said, represents the soul in its original purity, faithful wife of the spirit.
The fact that every day she weaves her nuptial garment and unweaves it
every night to trick her suitors indicates that her nature is related to the
universal substance, a cosmic principle both virginal and maternal: like
her, Nature (*physis* in Hellenism or *māyā* in Hinduism) weaves and dissolves manifestation according to an eternally renewed rhythm.

The much longed-for union of the hero with the faithful wife thus
signifies the return to the primordial perfection of the human state. This
Homer indicates clearly and through Ulysses' own mouth, when the latter names the signs by which his wife will recognize him. No one except
he and she knew the secret of their marriage bed—how Ulysses had built
it and rendered it immobile: with his own hand he had walled in their
nuptial chamber around an old and venerable olive tree, whose trunk
he then cut to the height of a bed, carving in the solidly rooted part the
support of the bedstead made from plaited strips. As in the description
of the nymphs' den, the olive tree is the tree of the world: its oil, which
nourishes, heals, and illuminates, is the principle of life itself; *tejas* in
Hindu terminology. The trunk of the tree corresponds to the axis of the

world, and the bed carved in this trunk is symbolically located in the center of the world, in the "place" where contrasts and complementaries, like active and passive, man and woman, mind and soul, unite. As for the nuptial chamber built around the tree, it represents the "chamber" of the heart, across which passes the spiritual axis of the world, and within which is realized the marriage of intellect and soul.

Translated from the French by Barbara Gutoff, copyright 1978.

Notes:

1. The Hindu myth of Rama and Sita is a special case: Sita, delivered from demons, is repudiated by Rama despite her fidelity.

2. Porphyrius: *De Antro Nympharum.*

3. According to Hellenic eschatology, the only alternatives are deliverance by divinization or the return to evolution; it doesn't conceive of a permanent resting of souls in a paradise, this sojourn being impossible save in the spiritual shadow of a savior or mediator.

4. Note that the olive tree is a sacred tree not only for the "pagan" world, but also for Judaism and Islam.

5. In Islamic esotericism, the initiates call themselves "poor toward God" (*fugara ila-Llah*).

6. Allusion to the anger of Poseidon, god of the ocean, whose son Polyphemus, Ulysses had blinded. According to Porphyry, the ocean represents the universal substance in its terrible aspect.

7. Porphyrius, *op. cit.*

8. Some interpret the text in the sense that the hatchets were handleless and planted in the ground by their blades, the hole by which the arrow had to pass being precisely that where ordinarily the handle fitted in. But that means that the arrow had to be shot two hands above the ground, which is practically impossible. Thus one must believe that the hole in question was located at the far end of the "axis" and ordinarily served to hang the hatchet on the wall.

Parabola
Volume: 27.3
Grace

A Tale of Wonders

Nan Runde

> *On the first night of the year, King Arthur and his court sat at table, a splendid feast laid out before them—untouched. Arthur, ravenous as he was for adventure, would not eat until he had heard a tale of wonders, for it was his custom to whet the one appetite by satisfying the other.*

Though the medieval tale of *Sir Gawain and the Green Knight* begins with a scene of ordinary festivity, Arthur's thirst for the extraordinary sets the tone for what follows. We, too, anticipate a marvel.

> *Suddenly an icy draft swept through the hall. Eyes glanced uneasily beyond the firelight. The laughter trailed into silence at the sound of approaching hooves. In the dark entryway loomed a knight on horseback, a head larger than any natural man. His charger bore him boldly into the firelight, nostrils flaring as his master reined him in. Gasps rose from the company: man and beast were green as grass.*

Whatever Arthur may have had in mind, the size and color of the stranger warn us that we have passed beyond the bounds of what we know. The greenness of the knight is unnatural, but, paradoxically, it is at the same time profoundly natural, in the sense that green is the color we most associate with nature. As bright as lightning, the Green Knight practically crackles with energy and vitality. Though frightening, his appearance in the season of deepest darkness is auspicious.

> *"Which of ye is boldest?" inquired the Green Knight.*
>
> *Arthur frowned. "If it's single combat you want," he said, "any man here will readily stand up to you."*
>
> *"You mistake my purpose," said the other. "I come not in war but in peace, to witness for myself the valiant knights of the Round Table. I have in mind a game. The man bold enough to wrest the axe from my hand may deal me one blow—provided I may return the blow in one year's time."*

The battle-axe he holds gives the stranger an aura of menace, but in the other hand is a sprig of holly, and he is unarmored. The association of holly with Christmas is familiar enough: the holly is green when other trees are bare, yet another sign of vitality in a dead season. But the origins of the Holly Knight are perhaps more telling. In Welsh myth, the Holly Knight and the Oak Knight engage in a beheading match every year, at alternate New Years (i.e. midsummer and midwinter).[1] A similar contest between Curoi and Cuchulainn in the eighth-century Irish story of *Bricriu's Feast* has been interpreted as the annual struggle between the old sun-god and the new.[2] The Middle-English *Sir Gawain*, however, anchored as it is in a Christian milieu, is less concerned with dueling sun-gods than with another aspect of the ancient beheading match: a hero put to the test.

> *They sat in stunned silence. The Green Knight laughed aloud. "Are ye barefaced boys, then, afraid of a man's sport? Where are the fierce knights that the tales celebrate? Are Arthur's brave warriors so easily vanquished—by the mere suggestion of a game?"*
>
> *King Arthur's face flushed red with anger. "Is it cowardice that restrains us?" he demanded, "or prudence? This game of yours is arrant folly."*

That said, Arthur accepts the challenge himself! Sir Gawain promptly asks to take his place, so as to spare him this pointless risk to his life. That Gawain is esteemed the finest of Arthur's knights assures the reader that if anyone can defeat this opponent, he can. The Green Knight bares his neck and waits.

> *Gawain hoisted the axe and, with all his strength, swung it down upon the stranger's neck, severing it. With a thud the green head fell to the floor, where it lay grinning. Gawain watched aghast as the Green Knight bent to retrieve the bloody head and, grasping it by the hair, remounted his horse and held the head high. "Remember," it said, staring at Gawain, "twelve months from this day, as you are a man of honor, you must take from me the same wages that you have dealt me. You will find me at the Green Chapel."*

After the departure of the Green Knight, no one has the heart to speak of what is to come, because no one doubts that Gawain will lose this contest. The opponents are not equally matched: one is impervious to death, the other entirely vulnerable. The story moves to a new level as Gawain begins to look mortality in the eye.

Though Gawain has no way of knowing how far he has to travel, he takes the arrival of All Saints' Day, significantly, as his cue to leave. His shield displays the image of a pentangle, symbol of human perfection and token of *trawthe* (a term encompassing the concepts of fidelity, truth, and one's pledged word or troth). If the writer stops short of declaring Gawain a saint, he nonetheless paints him as a paragon of knightly virtues who places all his trust in God. The inside of his shield bears an image of Mary, from whom Gawain takes courage in times of danger. Clearly, the journey that lies ahead is not just another adventure; it is the journey of a Christian soul.

It is a solitary journey. Gawain has no way of knowing where to go, yet he honors his commitment, the necessity simply to move forward. With no companion but his horse and no one to talk to but God, he must contend with a wilderness that challenges him both physically and spiritually. The farther from home he travels, the more he feels he is headed nowhere.

Realizing that Christmas is almost upon him, Gawain becomes desperate. He prays aloud, beseeching Christ for guidance.

> *Gawain made the sign of the Cross. Mist was gathering, filling the hollow places, veiling the dark trees, as if distance had crept near. The forest lay swathed in a stillness that Gawain could see, a stillness he could breathe. Then, through the mist, he recognized the shape of a castle, and his heart quickened at the sight.*

That moment of recognition is a moment of grace. Though an answer to prayer, it is as sudden and unexpected as a hand reaching from the heavens (or, for that matter, the appearance of the Green Knight in King Arthur's court). It is an emanation from beyond—beyond what he knows, beyond what he can accomplish on his own. Was the castle there all along? He certainly doesn't find it as one would find a fixed location, nor is the discovery a coincidence. It comes as a surprise of the most joyous sort, the kind to which we might respond, "Of course!" without knowing why.

Sir Gawain is welcomed with joy into the castle, and Bertilak, lord of the castle, quickly sets Gawain's mind at rest concerning the whereabouts of the Green Chapel. Bertilak assures him that the place is nearby and encourages him to stay until New Year's, to rest from his harrowing journey and celebrate the Christmas feast in good company.

On December 27, St. John's Day,[3] Bertilak announces his intention to go hunting the next day but urges Gawain to remain behind, since the holiday festivities have left him little time for rest. Then Bertilak proposes a game. Any winnings he brings home he will give Gawain, in return for any gain that comes to Gawain in Bertilak's absence.

The next morning, Gawain awakes to the sound of his door opening. He is dismayed to see Bertilak's beautiful wife entering his room—all the more so when she begins to talk of love. He finds himself having to deflect her advances without offending her. At last she leaves, but only after giving Gawain a kiss. When Bertilak returns from the hunt and presents Gawain with a gift of venison, Gawain turns over his winnings as well: a single kiss.

The next morning passes in a similar fashion. The lady teases and toys with Gawain, and he continues to tread the fine line between courtesy to her and fidelity to his host. When Bertilak and Gawain make their trade that evening, Gawain gives his host what he has received from the lady: two kisses this time. On the third day, the lady succeeds no better in wearing down Gawain's resistance to her charms, beyond bestowing three kisses on him. Knowing that he will leave the next morning, she urges him to accept a token of her love. Politely he refuses.

> *"I have in mind a mere trifle," she said, unwinding from her waist a green belt, "but the one who fashioned it is skilled in the arts of magic. The person who wears this belt cannot be slain." Gawain caught his breath. "You are certain of its power?" She met his gaze evenly. "I am."*
>
> *Seeing that he still hesitated, she pressed the belt into his hand. His fingers closed around it.*

After Mass that morning, Gawain asks the chaplain to hear his confession, so that he will be absolved of sin when he faces the Green Knight. About the belt, however, he says nothing, nor does he give it to Bertilak when they exchange winnings that evening.

The following morning Gawain sets out wearing the green belt concealed beneath his armor. His guide leads him partway, then leaves him to descend by himself into a valley flanked on either side by icy cliffs. There Gawain finds a barrow mound, which looks to him more like a tomb than a chapel. From the crags above comes the unmistakable sound of a blade against a grind-stone. Gathering his courage, Gawain calls out, and the Green Knight comes clambering down the rocks, gripping an enormous axe.

> *There, surrounded entirely by snow and ice, the Green Knight towered as large, it seemed, as the trees standing stiff as guards around him.*
>
> *"Welcome!" he said affably. "Are you ready to collect the wage we agreed on?"*

"With God's help, I will be," said Gawain. Fixing his hopes on the green belt circling his waist, he bent over to receive the blow. The knight raised his axe, swung it down—and stopped short, just nicking Gawain's bare neck.

Gawain, stunned, watched drops of blood fall wine-red onto the snow. Amazed to find himself still alive and whole, he could not speak for joy.

"You are free to go, Sir Gawain."

Gawain leaped to his feet and faced the other. It was the lord Bertilak.

"You kept your bargain with me faithfully for the first two days," Bertilak assured an astonished Gawain. "Had you not broken faith with me the third day, I should not have dealt you so much as a scratch today."

Stricken with remorse, Gawain is shocked to realize that he is not the man he thought he was. Nor is he consoled by the reminder that he has withstood temptations that many could not.

Gawain smiled wanly. "Alas, my lord, my heart is heavy with shame." He sighed, reaching for the silken belt. He pulled it out and tied it around himself crosswise. "Henceforth I shall wear this belt as a reminder to myself and a sign to others that I am a man of frailty no less than strength."

Bertilak laid his hand on Gawain's arm. "Let it remind you rather of Him who causes the grass to spring green from the heavy earth, Him who blesses your frailty with His strength. Remember the frail flower that holds the seed of new life even as it withers." He sighed. "You misconstrue my meaning if you think I sought a champion without flaw. Not so. I sought a champion who knows himself to be flawed, for what man is not?"

The ancient Celtic test of the warrior-hero has become here a test of the Christian hero. On the face of it, Gawain would seem to have failed that test, but the joyous surprise of this story is that his very failure is the key that unlocks his heart, allowing grace to enter. So long as he resists temptation, he feels sufficient unto himself; but pride and self-satisfaction leave no room for God. Gawain wears his virtues the way he wears his armor, convinced that his only recourse against evil is the protection he provides himself. But once he understands that he can fall prey to sin in spite of his best efforts, then he knows in his heart what he already knew in his head: his dependence on a Power beyond his own.

The outcome of Gawain's bargain with the Green Knight sheds new light on the agreement itself. Acting to kill the Green Knight—that is, to remove a threat to his own life—Gawain in fact accomplishes the reverse: he forfeits his life. His subsequent choice to take and conceal the green belt merely repeats the initial decision. The remainder of the story plays out the consequences of that decision. In retrospect, the bargain does not introduce a new peril into Gawain's life, but gives outward shape to a spiritual peril that was there all along but to which he is oblivious. The terms of the bargain articulate the way human beings typically interact: what we do to others is what we predispose them to do to us.

What Tolkien calls the "sudden joyous 'turn'" or *eucatastrophe*[4] in this story is that Bertilak steps outside the terms of the bargain. Rather than deal Gawain the fatal blow that he has, in effect, chosen for himself, Bertilak chooses to be merciful. This unexpected turn is the surprise of grace, which breathes into a human life like a fresh breeze into a dank cavern. With this turn, the author does, in a way, replace an old god with a new one, by offering a new bargain by which to live our lives, according to terms articulated and lived by Jesus Christ. According to this new covenant, we get not what we deserve but the chance to try again, to become more fully human. Knowing ourselves forgiven, we can forgive.

What is perhaps most astonishing about grace is that it works its changes backwards, redeeming the past and imbuing it with new meaning. Before Gawain's adventure reaches its conclusion, he sees evil where hindsight will reveal only good will. Through his distorted perspective, the Green Chapel is *the corsedest kyrk that ever I come inne*, to which the devil has lured him; and the Green Knight is a cold-blooded executioner, if not the devil himself. In that frame of mind, the possibility of mercy doesn't even occur to Gawain. But after his reprieve, he stands before Bertilak as he would stand before God, looking at his own story and seeing it clearly for the first time. The blow that Gawain expected was a death-blow; the blow he receives is the shock of self-awareness—a life-blow.

In *Sir Gawain* the ancient theme of annual renewal in nature has evolved into concern with renewal of the spirit. The power of magic now serves a higher Power. And the sacraments have become a primary agency by which the grace of God works in human lives. On the face of it, a sacrament is just a ritual. But every sacrament invites God to change us, to effect a transition or transformation; and such change is possible only in a receptive heart. To that end, sacramental ritual focuses body, will, consciousness, and spirit all in one direction, enacting outwardly what it effects inwardly, enabling us *in time* to experience with our whole being the presence, the power, and the mystery of God.

Gawain wants a soul free from stain but goes through the motions of the confession ritual without, in any visceral way, recognizing evil in himself. At Bertilak's castle, he makes his confession as casually as he would wash his hands, fully intending to deceive his host afterward in the matter of the green belt. But once he sees how he has deceived himself in the process, he confesses his fault with genuine horror and remorse, his heart now in accord with his words. Though Bertilak is not a priest, when he absolves Gawain[5] we do not doubt that grace works through him. Gawain's life was forfeit, and now is given back to him (*the grace hade geten of his lyve*). He is starting over, freed from the burden of his sins and freed from a false sense of who he is.

While carrying the shield emblazoned with a symbol of perfection (*in bytoknyng of trawthe*), Gawain also carried the burden of living up to it. But displaying the green belt as a sign of fault (*token of untrawthe*) helps him temper pride (the dark side of aspiration) with humility. Together, these symbols proclaim his commitment to his ideals and his recognition that he cannot always attain them. Now he understands the danger of hiding (and hiding from) his sin. Kept in darkness, it would fester and destroy him from within.

The green belt, which is essentially a sacramental sign, brings about another joyous turn. After Gawain returns home and tells his story, the lords and ladies of the Round Table unanimously agree to wear a similar band from that day forward, as a sign of their solidarity with Gawain. Far from disgracing him in their eyes, his frank admission of fault frees them to do the same, heartened by the intuition that the burden of a flawed nature is light when it is shared.

Notes:

1. Robert Graves, *The White Goddess* (New York: Farrar, Straus and Giroux, 1966), p. 180.

2. *Sir Gawain and the Green Knight*, edited by A. C. Cawley (New York: Dutton, 1962), p. xv.

3. According to Graves (p. 180), St. John took over the role of the Oak King in Christian times, with Jesus, as John's successor, assuming the role of Holly King. St. John's Day, which commemorated the day when St. John lost his head, would naturally mark the day of transition.

4. J. R. R. Tolkien, "On Fairy-Stories," in *Tree and Leaf* (London: George Allen & Unwin Ltd., 1964), p. 62.

5. *Thou art confessed so clene, beknowen of thy mysses,*
   And has the penaunce apert of the poynt of myn egge [blade].
   I halde the polysed of that plyght and pured as clene
   As thou hades never forfeted sythen thou was fyrst borne.

•

CHAPTER SEVEN

SEEKERS AND LOVERS

Where is the supreme reality, the sacred, the Center of Life and the source of immortality, where is the Holy Grail?[1]

—Mircea Eliade

Parabola
Volume: 12.1
The Knight
and the Hermit

Le Chevalier Perdu

P. L. Travers

"Is there anybody there?" called the young man as he drew rein at the dilapidated shelter topped with a rusty iron cross.

A weather-beaten shutter creaked open to reveal a greying head almost hidden by a coarse hempen cowl.

"Well," said a voice from within the cowl, "that is never an easy question. Let us put it another way. Is there anybody up there on that horse?"

"It is I, Perceval de Galis!" The youth was ringingly confident. "I thought perchance I could borrow a cup to quench my thirst at the spring yonder."

"You have a cup of your own, young sir." The voice that came from the cowl was kindly. "Merely put your palms together and bend to the water as it flows. It is the way I drink myself, having no other cup."

"Then what is that?" asked Perceval, waving his whip at a roughly carved wooden vessel that stood on a table within the lodge.

"That, as you must be aware, is a chalice, not a mere crock to take to the spring. It is the custom, among knightly men, to partake of the Mass before they set off adventuring. And though I am hidden deep in the forest, an occasional paladin comes my way, and I must be ready to serve him."

"But the wine," said Perceval. "Where does it come from?"

"I make it myself from fruits and berries fermented with a certain herb. And they bring me flour from a nearby steading to bake the unleavened bread. Oh, no more than a crust, but a crust is enough. One day you may need it yourself."

"I well may. Indeed, it is written, I understand, that I am bound for knighthood. But I am the son of a poor widow and all unlearned in knightly things. That is why you find me here, searching through the vales. 'Seek out Sylvanus of the Marshes' my good mother advised me. 'Maybe he would take you as his squire and teach you what you need to know.'"

"Sylvanus? Why he? Why not Lancelot?"

"Have you not heard? It is widely known. Lancelot is away in his wits. He has run mad amid the plantations, naked and raving in his nightshirt. Nobody knows if he will recover. Yet, before he joined the fellowship, it was Sylvanus—surely you know of him—who was thought to be the best knight in the world. No giant was a match for him; he killed the lion of Polgorran, the terror of the countryside, albeit it clawed his face in dying; he brought in chieftains to be the king's vassals and rescued damsels without number. As for dragons, he slew so many that I fear there will not be a dragon left when I receive my sword and spear."

"Such creatures are the ferment of the earth. They are always with us, never fear, and will be till some shriven knight approaches the dragon without enmity, and the dragon lies down to be slain."

"Let that not be soon, I pray the Lord. I envy such encounters."

"You will not be disappointed, I think. They belong to the first degree of knighthood."

"Degrees? I had not heard of those. Are there many that I must pass?"
"There are three. And the first is simply told. It is the degree of Induction. Everyman born into the world is in a sense a knight. A quest is offered him at the outset together with all the great emprises that you so long to meet with. But not everyone, when he comes to manhood, is ready to take up the challenge. Most of them follow the enticements, which, make no doubt, are also offered, and loiter aimlessly at the crossroads or fall asleep by the wayside."

"That would not be for me, I think. Acquaint me with the second."

"Ah, that is the one you dream of now, all high resolve and chivalry— the doughty deeds, the righting of wrongs, the fellowship of knightly men, the jousts, the roisterings, the tourneys (with perchance a lady's sleeve in your helm!); fire-breathing monsters in every glade to be slain at a single stroke; giants sought out and crying 'A-mercy!'; beleaguered castles freed from the fiend; recreant knights brought to court in chains; distressed damsels of every kind rescued and carried home. This is the degree of Action, and if you believe the chronicles the folk tell round their evening fires, most knights are content to go no further than the endless heroic round—the day filled full of deeds of prowess, the night with the telling of them and the feasting, and after that the sleep of the just threaded with dreams of the morrow's adventures, new dragons, new giants, and pastures new.

"But can a man remain young forever? Will he not go grey in these pursuits, ever feebler as to arm and thigh, his courtesy more and more strained as each damsel in distress grows heavier than the last? What will sustain his knighthood in him and lead it to its destined goal when these things come to pass?

"Oh, there is a means, though few men care or dare to use it. It is a matter, if you would know it, of pausing amid the gallimaufry and allowing oneself, committing oneself, to come to the end of the world. And when one comes to the end of the world, there is only one road to take."

"And that is?" Perceval asked intently.

"Inwards. Into the heart of yourself. This is the third degree of knighthood. It is known as Contemplation. This does not mean retreat from the world—though more than one knight has pursued such a course—rather that in undertaking his worldly adventures he encounters them also inwardly. 'Who am I?' he will enquire of himself, 'this man who goes about righting wrongs?' Echo alone will make reply—there is no known word to match that query—but the mere echo may arouse the conviction that within his own essential self there is a wrong to be righted. So it is with the dragons, the ill-famed knights, the distressed damsels, the fiends. They have their reflections in his inner selves that need to be struggled with, exorcised, and, indeed, accepted. The quest from the very beginning has had as its aim the knight's self-transformation. Only one made new by grace or made anew by his own efforts will find what he has sworn to find, a glimpse of the Sangreal."

Perceval's face was eager. "That is my hope. Shall I achieve it?"

"You are young to be asking for oracles. There is, however, a mark on your brow that encourages me to reply. But, I warn you, there will be obstacles and not only in yourself. There is the matter of the Maimed King and the land about him laid waste and from you, Perceval de Galis, the right question to be asked."

"The right question? I shall spend my life thinking about it."

"No amount of thinking will encompass it. If you are to be a Grail hero, what you are, soon or late, will itself ask the question. Now, begone and pursue your adventure."

"Then blessings on your head, Sir Hermit! I will no longer seek for Sylvanus. Any man of true fealty will instruct me in the matter of sword and spear. But if, under God, I achieve my knighthood, it will be to you I owe it."

"No, to yourself. Be blessed and farewell!"

The shutter of the lodge closed as Perceval, full of the morning's encounter, gathered his reins and departed.

The man within took up the chalice and held it high for a moment. And as he did so, the hempen cowl fell away disclosing a face whose left side was striped and scored to the whitened bone as though some animal in its death throes had striven to claw it away.

Parabola
Volume: 31.2
Absence and
Longing

As Far as Longing Can Reach

Peter and Maria Kingsley

What is this longing that drives men and women crazy,
deprives them of sleep, of rest and peace—this longing
that keeps surfacing throughout history in the literature
of people as far apart as ancient Greece, Anatolia, Iran,
and remote places hardly any of us even know? Echoes
reach our ears of those who have been laughed at, perse-
cuted, even killed because they dared to live their longing
in public; but we often choose to make ourselves deaf.
It can be so much easier, so much more convenient, to
pretend they never existed; that their longing can never
be ours; that their timeless teachings are too old and out
of fashion for us now.

And yet, like a heartache that stubbornly persists in
spite of all our best efforts to ignore it, this longing follows us too. It drives us from one place to another, from
one desire to a different one and then another one, as we
go on searching to fulfill ourselves and finally silence the
inner voice that never seems satisfied with anything. But
whatever we do, and however hard each of us tries, we
still sense that something is missing.

Already two and a half thousand years ago a Greek
man from southern Italy called Parmenides spoke about
this longing in a poem he left behind about the journey
he made deep into the underworld to meet the queen of

the dead, Persephone, and be taught by her the secrets of reality. The beginning of his poem starts like this:

> *The mares that carry me as far as longing can reach*
> *rode on, once they had come and fetched me*
> *onto the legendary road*
> *of the divinity*
> *that carries the man who*
> *knows*
> *through the vast and*
> *dark unknown …*[1]

And the clue to the whole poem lies already in the first line. The one crucial factor in this strange affair that for Parmenides influences everything—that determines just how far on this journey toward reality he can actually go—is longing. The Greek word he uses is *thumos*, and thumos means the energy of life itself. It's the raw presence in us that senses and feels, the massed power of our emotional being. Above all it's the energy of passion, appetite, yearning, longing.

Since the time of Parmenides we have learned so well to hedge our thumos in, to dominate our longing, punish and control it. But for Parmenides himself the longing is what comes first, right at the beginning. And there is a profound significance in this, because what he is saying is that—left to itself—longing makes it possible for us to go all the way to where we really need to go.

There is no reasoning with passion and longing, although we like to deceive ourselves by believing there is. All we ever do is reason with ourselves about the form our longing will take. We reason that if we find a better job we will be content, but we never are. We reason that if we go somewhere special we will be happy; but when we get there we start wanting to go somewhere else. We reason that if we were to sleep with the lover of our dreams we would be fulfilled. And yet even if we were to manage that, it would still not be enough.

What we sometimes refer to, so misleadingly, as "human nature" is simply the state of being pulled by the nose in a hundred different directions and ending up going nowhere very fast.

But although there is no reasoning with our passion, it has a tremendous intelligence of its own. The only trouble is that we keep interfering; keep breaking it up into tiny pieces, scattering it everywhere. Our minds always trick us into focusing on the little things we think we want—rather than on the energy of wanting itself.

If we can bear to face our longing instead of finding endless ways to keep satisfying it and trying to escape it, it begins to show us a glimpse of what lies behind the scenes of this world we think we live in. It opens up a devastating perspective where everything is turned on its head: where fulfillment becomes a limitation, accomplishment turns into a trap. And it does this with an intensity that scrambles our thoughts and forces us straight into the present.

Longing is the movement and the calling of our deepest nature. It's the cry of the wolf, the power of the lion, the fluttering of all the birds inside us. And if we can find the courage to face it, it will take us back to where we belong. But just like animals, this longing is dangerous as well as beautiful. Longing is the powerhouse of our being, and on this path of return it breaks everything except what is unbreakable. It shatters all the man-made structures that we try to build up around it and place in its way. It washes away the future and past and leaves us with nothing but eternity. For longing is the creator of time, and time can never contain it.

Time is the sequence of respectable faces and forms that we give to our longing, from moment to moment and day to day. But as soon as we turn away from all these distractions toward the energy of our longing itself, something extraordinary happens. We discover that what we really want is what has been wanting us since before the beginning of time. Longing longs for us. It wants us to wake up, to become conscious. It is divine intelligence longing to become known. All along we thought it was *our* longing: assumed that we could do whatever we wanted with it, even run away from it if we chose. But how can we run away from our own inner nature, our own divine heritage? We were born to know this mystery which, as Gnostics used to say, "has no name but all names refer to it" or which Sufis describe as the nameless mystery that "appears by whatever name you choose to call it." And just like Parmenides, who made the heroic journey into the depths of darkness to find what he called "the unshaken heart of persuasive

Truth," we too can start out on the journey back to reality—guided by the call of our longing.

This journey, "as far as longing can reach," is a journey to end all journeys: way beyond any ordinary human experience. It demands tremendous courage. It changes every cell in our body. Mythologically, it's the journey of the hero. And yet to understand what's involved we have to forget all our concepts of what it means to be a hero. We usually think of a hero as a warrior, a fighter. And yet what will get us where we want to go isn't will power; it isn't struggle or effort. It isn't even a matter of having to do anything ourselves. It's just a question of knowing how to turn and face our own longing without interfering with it or doing anything at all. And that goes against the grain of everything we're used to, because we have been taught in so many ways to escape from ourselves—find a thousand good reasons for avoiding our longing.

Sometimes it appears as depression, calling us away from everything we think we want, pulling us into the darkness of ourselves. The voice is so familiar that we run from it in every way we can; the more powerful the call the further we run. It has the power to make us mad, and yet it's so innocent: the voice of ourselves calling to ourselves. The strange thing is that the negativity isn't in the depression but in running from the depression. And what we imagine we are afraid of isn't what we are really afraid of at all.

It can be so terrifying to face our longing because it makes no allowances for what we think, or what we care for. Like a sharp sword it cuts through all our cares and ambitions and leaves us naked. It wants the whole of us, and we know that in the end this longing is a fire which will consume every part of us. But what in all honesty is the alternative? How long will we go on looking for truth everywhere outside ourselves? How many books do we have to read, how many people do we have to ask?

Always we want to learn from outside, from absorbing other people's knowledge. It's safer that way. The trouble is that it's always other people's knowledge. We already have everything we need to know, deep in the darkness inside ourselves. And our longing, if we dare to follow it all the way, is what turns us inside out until we find the sun and the moon and stars inside.

Note:

1. For more of Parmenides's poetry, and the background to his teachings, see Peter Kingsley's books *Reality* and *In the Dark Places of Wisdom*.

Parabola
Volume: 23.3
Fear

THE MONSTER
OF GRIM PROSPECTS

Trebbe Johnson

Orpheus ascends from the Underworld, step by careful step, as Eurydice follows close behind.

Now that his perilous journey is almost at an end, he considers what he has been through. Standing at the threshold of that dark kingdom from which no one ever returns, he was plagued by fears. What will happen to me? Will she really be there? Will she be changed? Will we escape? Yet on he went, enchanting the ferryman of the dead with his sweet music and making his way through swarms of ghosts. Finally, he presented himself boldly at the throne of Hades to sing his love for Eurydice and plead that she be allowed to live again.

Astonishingly, it worked. Moved by this lover's plea, the lord of the underworld decreed that Eurydice could return with Orpheus. There was but one stipulation: he must lead his beloved out and not turn around until they have reached the bright light of the living world.

Now, so close to home that the birdsong begins to waft down toward him, Orpheus's heart is filled with joy. In moments Eurydice will be in his arms again.

Then something terrible happens, something more insidious than any of the grave dangers that attacked him as he groped along those loathsome walls, something more persistent than the fears that tried to turn him back from those dangers. A little apprehension pinches him. *Maybe she's not really with me after all.*

It grows, this niggling qualm, until it has expanded from a twitch of possibility into a likelihood so huge and vivid that, finally, he is more preoccupied with it than with his urgent mission. And so he does the one thing he absolutely must not do. He glances back over his shoulder. Yes! Eurydice is there! And then, quite suddenly, she's not. She is gone forever.

Why does Orpheus have to look? Why, after everything he has been through, does he ruin it all so close to the end? Is it foolhardiness? A perverse urge to prove that a mortal man can break a covenant with the gods and get away with it unscathed? Did the investiture of his own heroism in the underworld so unnerve him that he now feels compelled to fling himself back to ordinariness—and his wife to death? Suddenly he seems to abandon all sense and heart and destroy what is almost within his grasp simply to ward off the panic that something else might have destroyed it already.

Orpheus is brought down by a different kind of fear from the one that met him at the doorway to Hades. Then, facing real danger, never forgetting his mission, he pushed ahead in spite of his gut-wrenching fear, and he acted with decisive courage, assurance, and grace. No, the subtler, slower-growing, more articulate cousin of that justifiable fear gains power under calmer circumstances, when the hero has leisure to pay heed to it, to follow its erratic movements and bat it around. Orpheus's downfall is the monster of grim prospects that attacks not the belly, but the imagination. Its poison catalyzes in the mind of the man or woman who suffers even a bit of doubt and insecurity, and corrodes whatever faith remains with an endless sequence of detailed pictures showing all the terrible things that will surely happen if she continues on the very course her heart knows is right.

Psyche, too, allows the monster of grim prospects to ravage her happiness bit by lethal bit. Goaded by her jealous sisters, she molds the fact that her husband will not allow her to look upon him into the suspicion that he must therefore be hiding some hideous deformity. When she dares to take a peek at him as he sleeps, her relief has scarcely flared than it is extinguished. Eros, the beautiful god of love, awakens, reproaches her bitterly, and flees.

Whereas Orpheus and Psyche behave impulsively to quell their apprehension, Percival reacts in just the opposite way. The earnest young knight sits in awe as the Holy Grail passes before him, illuminating the melancholy castle of the Fisher King with its holy light. With all his heart Percival longs to ask about the mystery he's witnessing and why his host and all the kingdom ail, but he holds back. "He recalled the admonishment given by the gentleman who had knighted him, who taught and instructed him not to talk too much; he was afraid that if he asked they would consider him uncouth, and therefore did not ask."[1] As self-doubt and longing rage within him, Percival sits mute. He can only console himself with a weak promise that he will ask someone for an explanation the next morning. By then, of course, it's too late; the Grail and all its attending company have vanished and Percival has lost his chance to restore the kingdom to life.

Orpheus's unfortunate act stems from concern that he'll lose what he's almost got. Psyche spins the unknown into the deliberately concealed and cannot rest easy until she's wrested it into the light. Percival keeps silent for fear of what others will think of him. Each is momentarily trapped in an unfamiliar, uncomfortable situation that calls for a new expression of the essential self. Instead of responding with joy, faith, and the willingness to risk a leap into mystery to attain a deeply meaningful reward, each reverts to immature, anxiety-driven behavior. Eros knows well the power this monster has to strike where one is most vulnerable. Long before Psyche has succumbed to her sisters' guile, he discerns the qualms churning within her and pleads: "Do you see what great peril you are in? Fortune as yet but skirmishes at the outposts. Unless you are firm and cautious while she is yet far off, she will close hand to hand."[2] But Eros's warning is futile, for Psyche's destructive imagining now has a life of its own. It will gnaw at her until, finally, she risks everything to assuage it.

We've all done it. Riffled stealthily through a lover's private diary for fear that what we did not know was somehow injurious to us. Kept silent for fear of what others might think, when our hearts pounded and our hands grew moist with the urgency to speak. Tried to talk a loved one out of following some path because of worry about what might happen to him—or to us—along the way. Did nothing when dread of failure superseded the urgency of doing something.

In these circumstances *what if* overrides *what is*, and we either cannot access or refuse to heed our own best judgment of the appropriate action or, as the case may be, deferral of action. Heeding the pictures of doom that plague our imagination, we lurch into conduct that is just the opposite of what we know is right. Marie von Franz has commented on this strange human proclivity to exercise our more ignoble impulses: "Sometimes, right at the bottom of one's own being, one generally does know where one should go and what one should do. But there are times when the clown we call 'I' behaves in such a distracting fashion that the inner voice cannot make its presence felt."[3]

The monster of grim prospects is the beginner's monster. It attacks when we are untried, or when we are tried in a situation unlike any that has ever confronted us before. Into this raw, yet rank environment it worms, convincing us that we are too small and meek to do what must be done, that if we step forth, something terrible will gobble us up.

The two sides of us, one that would leap ahead into its destiny and one compelled to keep things safe and under control, are clearly depicted in tales of parents whose child—as the stories make clear from the outset— has an important destiny to fulfill. Determined to protect their children from adult sorrows and disappointments, these parents try to concoct for them a sheltered paradise where they can dwell in eternal innocence. Briar Rose's parents order every spinning wheel in the kingdom destroyed so none will ever prick her finger. Frigg sets out to exact a promise from each animal, plant, metal, and disease in the Nine Worlds not to harm Balder. Changing Woman and White Shell Woman lie to their boys about their divine parentage and about the monsters ravaging Navajo country. Percival's mother moves her future knight to a home deep in the forest, so the facts of battle, blood, and vengeance will never cross his path and pique his curiosity. Such parents try desperately to oversee the entire universe of their child, personally manipulating every detail so nothing unfamiliar, and therefore potentially dangerous, seeps in. They are like the reluctant heroes Joseph Campbell describes, who refuse to heed the call to adventure. "The future is regarded not in terms of an unremitting series of deaths and births, but as though one's present system of ideals, virtues, goals, and advantages were to be fixed and made secure."[4]

In truth, these parents—and the wary side in each of us—have good reason to fear. To be transformed to a higher state of consciousness, we must, as Coomaraswamy notes, "be negated." All along the hero's path villains lurk in dark woods and dragons breathe fire. The very grasses we pass through turn into knives. Ferocious animals devour us and only later reveal their true identity as our trusted mentors. Grasping souls in the underworld try to bring down the seeker who goes there in search of the treasure that can be found nowhere else. Clearly, the basic drive toward caution is rooted in very good sense.

Yet the monster of grim prospects must be conquered before we can move on to more heroic tasks—and more ferocious monsters. If we are continually brought low by self-doubt we cannot do the sacred tasks that we were born to do. The children in the stories know this. They will go forth to embrace the destiny that calls to them, no matter what the risks. Briar Rose will find the one spinning wheel in the kingdom that has not been burned. Percival will meet a knight on a woodland path and see reflected in that bright armor his own true soul. Each child, each fledgling hero, must walk the path, battle the dragons, and find the grail in his or her own way.

However, like every part of the myth, the monster of grim prospects makes a vital contribution to the tale and to the hero's journey. By forcing us to tilt at possibilities that rarely come to pass, it gives us some practice with emergency scenarios. By neglecting to inform us of the ones that do, it teaches us that no matter how skilled we think we are, we cannot foresee all we will be called upon to undertake. As Frigg learns after her ultimately futile mission, we cannot curry the favor of every possibility in the universe any more than we can battle it under the influence of dread imaginings. We must find a way to live in the mystery of not knowing—including not knowing which of our own responses, moment to moment, crisis by crisis, is the one most likely to get us where we want to go.

Often, moreover, it is only after we have reacted inappropriately to our fear of the unknown, and suffered the consequences, that we can focus more deliberately on the demands that actually confront us. The whole process is part of the hero's journey; the false move is nonetheless a crucial bend along the path. To elaborate on von Franz's metaphor, in life's circus, the bumbling clown often precedes the death-defying high-wire act.

Most of the young heroes in these tales get another chance. Percival is able to ask his urgent question of the Fisher King and hence restore the fertile waters of life to a spiritual wasteland. Psyche undertakes a series of arduous tasks to win back Eros and in the process is transformed from a nervous girl to a woman with a powerful sense of her own strength. The Navajo Twins slay the monsters that ravage the land between sacred mountains. (As for poor Orpheus, that lover whose recklessness lost him his one true passion, he ends his days as a priest in the temple of Apollo, singing praise to the rational god of the sun and inveighing against Dionysus, god of drunken impulsiveness and wild eroticism.)

How do we slay the monster of grim prospects and get on with life? Not by engaging it, but by engaging that part of ourselves that knows so well what we must do. Sometimes it is acknowledgment of the fear itself that spurs the transformation. When the young Navajo boys hear a certain tone in their mothers' hushed voices, some sleeping awareness wakes and whispers to them of their destiny as warriors.

> "Mothers. . . . We recognize fear in your voices," said the boys. "Tell us what you are discussing."
>
> "It is nothing," repeated their mothers. "Go to sleep and do not worry yourselves."
>
> Then the first of the two youths stepped forward. And looking at his mother Asdzáá nádleehé, the Changing Woman, with an intensity he had never before displayed, he had this to ask her:
>
> "Mother," he asked her.
>
> "Who is my father?"[5]

Both mothers continue to evade the question, going so far as to deny that the boys have fathers at all. Nevertheless, the following day, they make bows of juniper wood for their sons, for on a deep level they recognize that the boys must soon make themselves known to their father, the Sun, and receive from him the weapons they'll need to save the land.

Another way of tapping the root of our capabilities is by matching the tactics of the fear that grips us. The *Ramayana* reminds us that, as the monster of grim prospects bombards us with images of how we will fail in the future, we can deliberately evoke a contrary picture of our own most ennobling moments in the past. When the Princess Sita is abducted, Angada, commander of the monkey battalion, asks for a volunteer to cross the great and perilous ocean and rescue her. One by one the monkeys speak up, longing to undertake the task, but certain they will fall short. One insists, "I can only jump so far." "I used to be able to jump vast distances, but now I am too old," sighs another. One monkey remains silent. Hanuman stands on the shore, gazing out at the ocean, sunk in self-doubt and fear of failure.

The wise, elderly monkey general, Jambavan, sees what is happening: Hanuman has quite literally forgotten himself. So Jambavan undertakes to remind him by telling him the story of his life. Hanuman, he recounts, was born of outstanding parentage; his mother was a human woman, his father the Wind. As a newborn, little Hanuman's first conscious act was one of great boldness. Looking up into the skies, he saw the sun and, thinking it a ripe yellow fruit, sprang up in delight to pluck it. Jambavan reminds Hanuman that there is no one equal to him. And Hanuman realizes it is true.

> When his glory was thus sung and he was reminded of his own power, Hanuman grew in stature. ... He grew in size and shook his tail with great delight. He said, "Of course I can cross this ocean! With the strength of my arms I can push this ocean. Always stirred by my legs, the ocean will overflow its bounds. ... I can leap into the sky and sail along."[6]

And so, reunited with his own true magnificence, Hanuman pushes aside the monster of grim prospects that tells him he is not up to this task. He launches himself up and off across the ocean, sailing through the sky like a meteor, with his tail coiled behind him.

To enact the work we believe in, to protect the people and places we love, to follow the path we know is ours demands a constant engagement with scary, unfamiliar demons. Poised and pressured at the threshold, we easily make mistakes, and the monster of grim prospects thrives on our vulnerability. Under its sway, instead of trusting the gods who love us, we pay heed to the mortals who do not. Instead of following the holy light that passes right before our eyes, we make vague promises to ourselves to put off enlightenment till tomorrow. The monster makes us forget that we are anything but ordinary, and convinces us that an insulated fortress of our own making is safer than the mystery that beckons beyond the gates.

We match this monster not with weapons, but with self-knowledge. Standing on the shore of the future's immensity, coiled to spring, we take a moment to look within, to that part of ourselves that knows exactly what we must do to grasp the delicious fruit of the sun.

Notes:

1. Chrétian de Troyes, "The Story of the Grail (Perceval)," *Arthurian Romances* (London: Penguin Books, 1991), p. 420.

2. Erich Neumann, *Amor and Psyche: The Psychic Development of the Feminine* (Princeton: Princeton University Press, 1973), p. 18.

3. Marie-Louise von Franz, "The Process of Individuation," in *Man and His Symbols*, edited by Carl G. Jung (New York: Dell Publishing Co., 1964), pp. 183–5.

4. Joseph Campbell, *The Hero with a Thousand Faces* (Princeton: Princeton University Press, 1972), p. 60.

5. Paul G. Zolbrod, *Diné bahané: The Navajo Creation Story* (Albuquerque: University of New Mexico Press, 1984), pp. 187–8.

6. Swami Venkatesananda, *The Concise Ramayana of Valmiki* (Albany: State University of New York Press, 1988), p. 222.

Parabola
Volume: 19.4
Hidden Treasure

In Search of Hidden Wonder

John Matthews

When the twelfth-century poet Chrétien de Troyes left his poem *The Story of the Grail* unfinished, he created a mystery which has stirred the imagination of countless seekers ever since. Yet the mystery refuses to be codified, identified, or pinned down to a specific time or place. The setting is most often the Middle Ages and the elements of the story follow their own pattern: the Grail itself, variously described as a cup, a dish, a stone, or a jewel; the presence of its guardian, the wounded King who rules over a devastated Wasteland; the Company surrounding the King; and the questing knights who must pose the right question to heal both King and land. Yet despite the millions of words written every year about the Grail, it remains an object of mystery; it is hidden, secret, as the medieval knight and poet Wolfram von Eschenbach wrote in his telling of the myth, where the Grail is:

> *The wondrous thing hidden in the flower-*
> *garden of the king*
> *where the elect of all nations are called.*[1]

The great mythographer Joseph Campbell has a passage in one of his books, which, though in fact referring to Biblical studies, sums up the attitude of many seekers for the Grail.

*It is one of the prime mistakes of many interpreters of mythologi-
cal symbols to read them as references, not to mysteries of the human
spirit, but as earthly or unearthly scenes, and to actual or imaginal
historical events. ... Whereas it is one of the glories of the tradition
that in its handling of religious themes, it retranslates them from the
language of imagined facts into a mythological idiom; so that they
may be experienced, not as time-conditioned, but as timeless; telling
not of miracles long past, but of miracles potential within ourselves,
here, now, and forever.[2]*

It is for this reason that the Grail is hidden—though the hiding is in
plain sight. As Campbell said elsewhere, why should the medieval knights
have needed to look for the Grail—which they saw as a chalice—when
there was a chalice to be found on every altar in Christendom? In the
same way, why do we still seek the Grail when it is in fact everywhere
around us—and within us?

The Grail can be many things: it may be without form, it may appear
in more than one form, or it may not even exist at all in this dimension.
The important thing is that it provides an object for personal search, for
growth, and human development. In fact, those who seek it are often less
concerned with the *object* than with the *actions* of the Grail—the way it
causes changes to happen—in the heart, in the mind, in the soul.

In Western alchemical traditions, this is reflected in the mystery surrounding the transformational quality of the Great Work which lies at the
center of the alchemist's striving for earthly perfection. The transmuta-
tion of base metal into gold is a metaphor for the transformation of the
human spirit, a transformation which takes place within the alembic of
the Grail. Those who encounter the mystery are never the same again.
They are caught up into an entirely new frame of existence, no longer
bounded by time and space: they are transformed by the process of what
they encounter.

We are dealing here with a mystery that is almost too much for us.
But we can learn, and grow, from studying it. Whatever else it may be
the Grail story is first and foremost pure myth, and like all myths, it is
filled with archetypes.

As we follow the Quest Knights of the Arthurian legends we see many turnings which lead to different places in the map of the soul's journey. Nearly all of the characters are in some way archetypal, as are their adventures, their sufferings and their realizations. It would be wrong to regard the stories too literally, but at the same time, they were never intended as parables. This is why we need to go back to the texts as often as possible—to their infinite variety, complexity and subtlety, where we may find ever new meanings.

The thirteenth-century romance of Perlesvaus, for example, seems to say a great deal about the reasons for the quest, now as much as then. The scene is set not long after the Arthurian era. The Grail Castle, where so many strange and wondrous things have taken place, is described as ruinous and empty, a place of ghosts, with its once sacred and mysterious nature already beginning to be forgotten. To this place come two young knights in search of adventure, after the manner of the old heroes of the Table Round:

> They were fair knights indeed, very young and high spirited and they swore they would go, and full of excitement they entered the castle. They stayed there a long while, and when they left they lived as hermits, wearing hair-shirts and wandering through the forests, eating only roots; it was a hard life, but it pleased them greatly, and when people asked them why they were living thus, they would only reply: "Go where we went, and you will know why."[3]

Many people have been "going there" ever since, seeking the mysterious object of which they have heard such marvelous reports—more often than not failing, but sometimes, like the two young knights, discovering things about themselves and their own inner state. The Grail itself remains hidden, elusive, yet most have found that its "secret" is indissolubly linked with the idea of service.

This brings us to the mysterious Grail "Question" which, sooner or later, everyone who seeks the Grail has to ask, and answer: whom does the Grail serve? It may seem an odd thing to ask when you have traveled many hundreds of miles, undergone countless adventures and trials and arrived at last in the presence of the Wounded King and his entourage of Grail maidens and youths.

According to the legend, the Grail is borne through the hall in procession with the spear that drips blood, a large shallow dish, and either a candelabra or a sword. The Wounded King is then fed with a wafer from the chalice. In some versions this is all, in others the entire company is fed with the food they most desire, which can be interpreted as actual or spiritual food. The point is that, in the literal sense, the Grail serves either the Grail King or the Company. Why then, the question?

In part, of course, it is a ritual question, requiring a ritual response which in turn triggers a sequence of events: the healing of King and Kingdom, the restoration of the Wasteland. The texts indicate that the Grail serves the King, the Company, and all who seek it, and it is this last possibility that concerns us.

Here, the Grail is shown to be a gateway, a nexus-point between two states of being—the human and the divine, the worldly and the otherworldly. We can see this in the very shape most often assumed by the Grail, that of a chalice. The upper portion is open to receive the downpouring of blessings of the spiritual realm; the lower half, stem and base, form an upward pointing triangle which represents human aspiration; and the two meet and are fused in the center. The Grail operates its wonderful life-giving properties so that we are each served in the way that the Fisher King is served.

But this only happens in response to the need, urgency, and the drive of the quester—the Grail serves us according to the way we serve it. Like the king who serves the land as the land serves him, we stand in similar relation to the Grail. Our service, love, hope, or desire is offered up to be accepted and transformed into pure energy. If we have behaved in a right manner on our quest, we will reap the rewards, the divine sustenance of the Grail. And, if we open this out still further, our service will help transform the land on which we live and walk and have our being. The Grail does not need to be in view—it is present all around us, in every act of service we do, whether it be, symbolically, for the king or the land.

While the king and the land are suffering the Grail cannot pass openly among us. It is as though a gap had opened between two worlds, leaving us shut out, lost in the twilight looking for the shining power of the Grail … or, as some texts suggest, inhabiting a land where there are no chalices, no means of expressing our own love or hope for the world we inhabit.

Charles Williams sums it up in a passage from a modern Grail story, *War in Heaven*. After many adventures, the moment has come when a celebration of the Eucharist is to be made, using the Grail itself as the chalice. Standing before it, one of the modern questers reflects on its mysterious power:

> *Of all material things still discoverable in the world the Graal had been nearest the Divine and Universal Heart. Sky and sea and land were moving, not towards the vessel but to all it symbolized and had held ... and through that gate ... all creation moved.*[4]

Here, the most important thing is not the Grail itself, but what it symbolizes—"through that gate all creation moved." The object is as mysterious and as "hidden" as ever.

What we have to understand is that the Grail serves us in proportion to our service to the land and to the world about us. It is not some wonderworking artifact but an active principle touched off by the accumulated longing of humankind for what was once ours—for the perfect state of being which can still be ours. It is this which gives the aura of a lost golden age to Arthur's realm and acts.

The Grail is a symbol for our time as much as it is for any time, a contemporary symbol of an utterly current aspiration. The King—call him Arthur or Christ or the World Soul—is wounded *by* as well as *for* us. His wounds impinge upon everyone, and when he is healed, so shall we all be. It is the same story, an utterly simple one: the Grail serves us; we serve the Grail; it will heal us when we use it to heal the wounds of creation.

Each one of us is *already* engaged upon this quest. Each has a chance to redeem the time in which we live, to awaken the Sleeping King, to bring the Wasteland back into flower. We are indeed all "grails" to some degree, and the true object of the quest lies in making ourselves vessels for the light that will bring about these things.

Only then can we ourselves be healed, the Fisher King within us regain his strength, and the land flower. When that moment comes there will no longer be any need for a Grail, it will be everywhere about us, no longer hidden but openly recognized, its presence felt in every particle of our being. As another contemporary writer, Vera Chapman, writes:

> *Like a plant that dies down in winter, and guards its seeds to grow again, so you … must raise the lineage from which all Arthur's true followers are to grow—not by a royal dynasty, but by spreading unknown and unnoticed. … Names and titles will be lost, but the story and the spirit of Arthur [and the Grail] shall not be lost. For Arthur is a spirit and Arthur is the land of Britain. So shall Arthur conquer, not by war, nor by one kingship that soon passes away, but by the carriers of the spirit that does not die.[5]*

We are all carriers of that spirit, and by seeking the inner reality of the Grail *behind* the symbols and stories, we are taking part in an ongoing work without which all we hold most dear would long ago have perished. And if people look at us askance as we wander through the world with a strange look in our eyes, we have only to give the same answer as those knights who visited the ruined Grail Castle: "Go where we went, and you will know why."

Notes:

1. Wolfram von Eschenbach, *Parzival* (Harmondsworth, Middlesex: Penguin, 1980).

2. Joseph Campbell, *The Masks of God* (Creative Mythology) (London: Souvenir Press, 1968).

3. John Matthews, *At the Table of the Grail* (London: Arkana, 1993).

4. Charles Williams, *War in Heaven* (Grand Rapids, MI.: Eerdmans, 1988).

5. Vera Chapman, *The Three Damosels* (London: Methuen, 1978).

Parabola
Volume: 11.1
The Witness

Sir Launcelot's Dream

Retold by Howard Pyle

Sir Launcelot rode for the rest of the day without meeting further adventure, until about evening time, when he came to a bare and naked knoll covered with furze bushes. Here, in the midst of that wild, he beheld an ancient ruined chapel, and he said to himself, "Here will I rest me for the night." So he rode around that chapel, seeking for the door thereof, but he could find no door upon any side of the chapel, but only windows, very high raised from the ground. Then Sir Launcelot said, "This is a very strange chapel that it should have no doors, but only windows so high that I cannot enter by them. Now I will rest here and see what is the meaning of this place."

So saying, he dismounted from his horse, and lay down beneath a thornbush that was not far distant from the chapel.

Now, as Sir Launcelot lay there, a drowsiness began to descend upon him, and though he could not sleep yet it was as though he did sleep, for he could move nor hand nor foot. Yet was he conscious of all that passed about him as though he had been wide awake. For he was conscious of the dark and silent vaults of sky, sprinkled all over with an incredible number of stars, and he was conscious of his horse cropping the herbage beside him in the darkness, and he was conscious of the wind that blew across his face, and that moved the corner of his cloak in the silence

•

of the night time. Of all these things was he conscious, and yet he could not move of his own will so much as a single hair.

Anon, whilst he lay in that wise he was presently aware that some people were approaching the chapel in the darkness, for he heard the sound of voices and of the feet of horses moving upon the road. So, in a little while, there came to that place a knight and an esquire. And the knight was very sorely wounded, for his armor was broken and shattered by battle, and the esquire sustained him in the saddle so that, except for the upholding of the esquire's arm and hand, he would have fallen prostrate down upon the ground.

Then Sir Launcelot, as he lay in that waking sleep, heard the knight say to the esquire, "Floradaine, is the chapel near at hand, for mine eyes are failing and I cannot see." And the esquire wept and he said, "Yea, Lord, it is here. Sustain yourself but for a little and you will be there."

Therewith the esquire drew rein and he dismounted from his horse and he lifted the knight down from his charger, and the knight groaned very dolorously as the esquire lifted him down. Then, breathing very heavily and with great labor, the knight said, "Floradaine, is there a light?" And the esquire said, "Not yet, Messire." Again, after a little, the knight said, "Is there yet a light?" And again the esquire answered, "Not yet, Messire." And again, after awhile, the knight said for the third time, "Floradaine, is there yet a light?" And this time the knight breathed the words, as in a whisper of death. Then of a sudden the esquire called out in a loud and joyful voice, "Yea, Lord, now I behold a light!"

All this Sir Launcelot beheld in that waking dream, and though it was in the darkness of night, yet he beheld it very clearly, as though it were by the sun of noonday. For he beheld the face of the knight that it was white as of pure wax, and that the sweat of death stood in beads upon his forehead. And he beheld that the esquire was young and fair, and that he had long ringlets of yellow hair that curled upon his shoulder. Then when the esquire said that he beheld a light, Sir Launcelot beheld the windows of the chapel that they were illuminated from within with a pale blue lustre, as though the dawn were shining in that chapel. And he heard the sound of chanting voices, at first very faint and far away, but anon ever growing stronger and stronger as the light from the chapel grew stronger. And those voices chanted a melody that was so sweet and ravishing that it caused the heart to melt as with an agony.

Then the walls of that chapel opened like a door and a light shone forth with remarkable lustre so that it illuminated the face of that dying knight, and of the page who upheld him. And at the same time the song burst forth in great volume, as it were a thunder of chanting.

Then forthwith there came out of the chapel a bright shining spear, and two fair hands held the spear by the butt, yet Sir Launcelot could not behold the body to whom those two hands belonged. And after the spear there came forth a chalice, and two fair, white hands held that chalice, but neither could Sir Launcelot behold any body to which those hands belonged. And the chalice seemed to send forth a light of such dazzling radiance that it was as though one looked at the bright and shining sun in his glory.

Then Sir Launcelot was aware that this was the Holy Grail of which he was in search, and he strove with all his might to arouse himself, but he could not do so. Then the tears burst out from his eyes and traced down his cheeks in streams, but still he could not arouse himself, but lay chained in that waking sleep.

So the chalice advanced toward that knight, but the knight had not strength to reach forth and touch it. Then the esquire took the arm of the knight and raised it, and he raised the hand of the knight so that the hand touched the chalice.

Then it was as though Sir Launcelot beheld the virtue of the Grail go forth from it, and that it passed through the hand of the wounded knight, and that it passed through his arm and penetrated into his body. For he beheld that the blood ceased to flow from that wounded knight, and that the color flooded back into his cheeks and that the light came back into his eyes and that the strength returned to his body.

Then the knight arose and he kneeled down before the Grail, and he set his palms together and he prayed before the Grail.

Then, slowly, the light that had been so bright from the Grail began to wane. First the spear disappeared, and then the hands that held it disappeared. Then, for awhile, the Grail glowed with a faint, pallid light, and then it, too, vanished, and all was dark as it had been before.

264 SIR LAUNCELOT'S DREAM

So Sir Launcelot beheld the vision of the Grail, but as in the vision of a dream as I have told it here to you. And still the tears rained from his eyes, for he could not rouse himself to behold it with his waking eyes.

After this the knight and the esquire approached to the place where Sir Launcelot lay asleep, and the esquire said to the knight, "Messire, who is this man, and why sleepeth he here whilst all these wonders pass him by?" And the knight said, "This knight is a very sinful man, and his name is Sir Launcelot of the Lake." Quoth the esquire, "How hath he sinned?" To which the knight replied, "He hath sinned in this way. He had a beautiful and gentle lady, and he deserted that wife for the sake of Queen Guinevere. So his lady went away and left him, and anon she gave birth to Galahad, and in that birth she also gave her life. So Sir Launcelot betrayed his wife, and because of that betrayal he now lieth sleeping, and he cannot waken until after we are gone away from this place."

Then the esquire said to the knight, "Messire, behold; here this knight hath a good, strong horse. Take thou this horse and leave thine own in its stead. For this horse is fresh and full of life, and thine is spent and weary with battle." And the knight said, "I will take that horse."

Then after they had gone, Sir Launcelot bestirred himself and awoke. And he would have thought that all that he had beheld was a dream, but he beheld the worn and weary horse of the knight was there, and that his horse was gone. Then he cried aloud in great agony of soul, "Lord, my sin hath found me out!" And therewith he rushed about like a madman, seeking to find a way into that chapel, and finding no way.

So when the day broke he mounted the worn and weary horse that the knight had left, and he rode away from that place and back into the forest; and his head hung low upon his breast. When he had come into the forest and to the cell of the hermit thereof, he laid aside his armor and he kneeled down before the Hermit of the Forest, and confessed all his sins to him. And the Hermit of the Forest gave him absolution for these sins, and he said, "Take peace, my son. For although thou shalt not behold the Grail in thy flesh, yet shall God forgive thee these sins of thine that lie so heavily upon thy soul."

Then Sir Launcelot arose chastened from his confession. And he left his armor where it lay and assumed the garb of an anchorite. And he went away from that place, into the remoter recesses of the forest. There he dwelt in the caves and in the wilds, living upon berries and the fruits of the forest. And he dwelt there a long time until he felt assured that God had forgiven him. Then he returned to his kind again; but never after that day was he seen to smile.

From *The Story of the Grail and the Passing of Arthur*, by Howard Pyle (New York: Charles Scribner's Sons, 1933).

Parabola
Volume: 13.3
Questions

Quest and Questioning in a Waste Land

James Karman

In the early 1920's, the world seemed to be falling apart. "The war to end all wars" had just been fought. Of the 65,000,000 young men who had answered the call to glory, more than half had been killed, wounded or lost. Those who had survived the trenches, the mustard gas, the artillery fire, the cold, starvation, and disease, returned home through seared fields, on broken roads, to ravaged cities. Europe lay in desolation.

For many artists and intellectuals, the leafless trees and windblown countryside mirrored the condition of the human soul. "We are the hollow men / We are the stuffed men," wrote T. S. Eliot, "Leaning together / Headpiece filled with straw. Alas!"

Having seen a thousand dreams shattered—dreams that glorified a loving God, an orderly world, and a righteous people—and having awakened to a civilization that lay in ruins all around, artists and intellectuals were faced with a grim task. Little could be said or done except to acknowledge the emptiness of human existence.

Eliot himself responded to the crisis by writing *The Waste Land*. In this long poem, published in 1922, he describes a land where "the sun beats, / And the dead tree gives no shelter, the cricket no relief, / And the dry stone no sound of water." Cisterns are empty, wells are exhausted, and though the mountains echo with thunder, there is no rain.

Out of the mountains runs a river, across a flat horizon, through dry, cracked earth, into a city. But the river does not replenish life; it is a "dull canal" that "sweats/Oil and tar." Rats creep along its banks, dragging their slimy bellies through rough and useless vegetation.

The river is the Thames, and the city, London—but the river could be any river and the city any modern city. Eliot uses the Thames to symbolize the flow of human history through Athens, Jerusalem, Alexandria, Carthage, Vienna—all of which he calls "unreal"—and finally through London, a city where everything is falling down.

People in the waste land are in the same condition. "Carious teeth" fill mouths "that cannot spit." One woman, already mad perhaps, draws "her long black hair out tight" and fiddles "whisper music on those strings." Another slowly comes undone. "My nerves are bad tonight. Yes, bad." "Stay with me," she says to a companion, "Speak to me. Why do you never speak? Speak."

Because there is little or no communication, relationships are unproductive and filled with anxiety or boredom. A young woman returns home from a day at the office, heats the contents of various tin cans, clears the breakfast dishes, and, amidst piles of dirty laundry, serves dinner to a friend, then absently submits to his advances and sees him out the door.

For such people, whose personal and cultural experiences are as dry as the landscape in which they live, nothing provides comfort or relief, including religion. There is a church bell in the waste land, but it has a dead sound when it strikes the hours. There is a savior, but he appears only as an hallucination. There is a chapel but, with a broken door and no windows, it serves only as a home for wind.

As a cultured American living abroad, Eliot had witnessed the collapse of European civilization first hand—a collapse that was occasioned not just by World War I, but also by a long series of revolutions in art and thought (beginning, perhaps, with Copernicus and continuing through Darwin, Marx, Freud, and Einstein) that overturned traditional values and beliefs. As a student of the past, Eliot knew that similar crises had occurred many times before. Civilization, he understood, proceeds through fits and starts, creating worlds only to tear them apart. As a poet attempting to come to terms with the time in which he lived, therefore, he knew he was not alone. Other artists and thinkers, facing moments of cultural collapse, had, through the centuries, given voice to their despair.

In recalling the words of other poets, Eliot believed he could illuminate the present situation. Accordingly, *The Waste Land* is composed almost entirely of quotations from and allusions to other works of art. As in a collage, where the whole is created by the sum of disparate parts, insights of Old Testament prophets are present alongside images and ideas drawn from Hindu, Buddhist, Greek, Roman, and northern European texts. The plan of the poem, also fragmented, comes from medieval stories about the quest for the Holy Grail.

Medieval stories about the Grail—such as Chretien de Troyes' *Conte del Graal*, Robert de Borron's *Joseph d'Arimathie*, and Wolfram von Eschenbach's *Parzival*, along with the *Queste del Saint Graal*, *Perlesvaus*, and others—make use of the Grail as a Christian symbol. In these stories, the Grail is described as a chalice, a platter, a jewel, or a stone. When described as a stone, it is imagined to be something like the Philosopher's Stone, an object associated with alchemy. When thought of as a jewel, it is an emerald, perhaps one that fell from the crown of Lucifer (preserving its heavenly virtues) when he was cast down into hell. When seen as a platter, it is the dish on which the paschal lamb was served at Jesus' Last Supper. And finally, when regarded as a chalice, it is the cup from which Jesus drank when he established the ritual of Holy Communion, the same cup that was later used to catch the blood that fell from his wounds while he was hanging on the cross. In whatever way the Grail is imagined, it is always regarded as a sacred object with magical powers, an object well worth pursuing if only to discover what it truly is.

The Grail is hidden: no one ever knows exactly where it is. According to the medieval legends, a knight who embarks upon a search for it has no set path to follow. He can only abandon himself to the quest and hope that he will arrive at the place where he should be.

In many of these legends, the knight who does find the Grail finds it in a castle that is set in the middle of a vast waste land. The castle contains a bedridden, wounded king. The origin and nature of the wound is variously described, but most of the sources say it is an injury to the genitals or to the thigh caused by a lack of faith, the breaking of a vow of chastity, or an accidental stabbing by a stranger. The open wound causes the king to live on, far beyond his span of years, suffering day after day. Though he is attended by a beautiful maiden and a castle full of servants and soldiers, he awaits the arrival of a virtuous knight who will reach out with a comforting hand and ask the right question—perhaps as simple as "What ails you?" When this occurs, the wound will be healed and the king will be restored to health. Natural rhythms will then resume and the old king will eventually be allowed to die. At the same time, waters of life will flow through the countryside, the waste land encircling the castle will blossom forth, and life will be renewed. The Grail will then reveal itself and, by doing so, provide the questing knight with a direct experience of Truth. Thereafter, the knight will be an enlightened initiate, knowing the secret of death and renewal.

Eliot's understanding of the Grail stories was influenced by a study that appeared just before he wrote his poem. As he says in his own footnotes, "not only the title, but the plan and a good deal of the incidental symbolism" of *The Waste Land* came from a reading of Jessie L. Weston's book, *From Ritual to Romance* (first published by Cambridge University Press in 1920, Anchor edition, 1957).

In this provocative study, Weston argues that behind the medieval Grail legends, or embedded deep within them, one can discern the features of a fertility cult that antedates Christianity by thousands of years and has, in fact, endured in one form or another throughout human history. A fertility cult exhibits a set of interrelated rituals and myths that focus on the mystery of life and death. On the one hand, the cult illuminates the meaning of the mystery, and on the other, it seeks to assure that the mystery itself, embodied in the cycles of nature, will continue on.

Though fertility cults are associated with a Great Goddess, they usually involve a husband, son, lover, or brother who personifies reproductive energy. As Weston says, "the ultimate, and what we may in a general sense term the classical, form in which ... the Life principle found expression was that which endowed the vivifying force of Nature with a distinct personality ..." She adds that:

> *The progress of the seasons, the birth of vegetation in spring, or its revival after the autumn rains, its glorious fruition in early summer, its decline and death under the maleficent influence either of the*

scorching sun, or the bitter winter cold, symbolically represented the corresponding stages in the life of this anthropomorphically conceived Being, whose annual progress from birth to death, from death to a renewed life, was celebrated with a solemn ritual of corresponding alternations of rejoicing and lamentation (p. 35).

The life, death, and resurrection of the god, in short, are each respectively associated with and appropriately observed during summer, winter, and spring.

Weston notes that in many ancient cultures (and in some surviving traditional ones), a connection is made between the temporal king who rules his people and the god who controls nature's destiny. Thus, "the king who is without blemish has a flourishing kingdom" while "the king who is maimed has a kingdom diseased like himself" (p. 58). This same conviction, she believes, can be found in stories about the Holy Grail.

I would submit that there is no longer any shadow of a doubt that in the Grail King we have a romantic literary version of that strange mysterious figure whose presence hovers in the shadowy background of the history of our Aryan race; the figure of a divine or semi-divine ruler, at once god and king, upon whose life, and unimpaired vitality, the existence of his land and people directly depend (p. 62).

It is this king, in his autumn aspect (old and wanting to die), that figures in the medieval legends previously recounted. He is called the Maimed King or, in reference to his connection with "the waters of life," the Fisher King. It is also this king who, in medieval imagination, came to be associated with the Holy Grail—that mysterious object sought for but rarely found, that stone that represents, jewel that radiates, platter that serves, or cup that contains Eternal Truth.

Stories about the Grail repose, according to Weston, "upon the ruins of an august and ancient ritual, a ritual which once claimed to be the accredited guardian of the deepest secrets of life" (p. 187). Though the ritual seemed to disappear when new religions replaced the old, when patriarchal myths replaced matriarchal ones, it actually went underground, into memory and imagination, into the repository of human consciousness, where it has never ceased to exist.

Even Christianity, that supreme expression of faith in Father God, could not help but draw its primary symbolism from rituals concerning Mother Earth. Two disparate traditions are fused insofar as faith in the Father and reverence for the Mother can both be expressed through love for the Son. In a Christian culture, therefore, it is no wonder that the ancient story continues to send forth new shoots.

The Waste Land draws on symbolism contained in the Grail legends in order to make a statement concerning personal, cultural, and religious collapse. The epigraph that introduces the poem sets the tone for the poem as a whole. Drawn from Petronius' *Satyricon*, it concerns a statement made by the Cumaean Sibyl, a shriveled up old woman who, according to Greek mythology, had been given immortal life but not eternal youth. When asked "What do you want?" she answers, "I want to die." She cannot die, however; nor, in *The Waste Land*, is there any kind of death that provides relief or offers regeneration. There is only perpetual disintegration.

In earlier versions of the Grail legend, the waste land is something to find and, above all, something to transform. The knight in quest of the Grail has it in his power to heal the wounded king and to dispel the ruin and despair surrounding him. In Eliot's poem, however, the quest is never mentioned, the Grail is never found, and the Fisher King, having long since grown accustomed to his wound, appears to accept life as it is.

There is a way of reading the poem, however, that increases the dramatic tension and admits the possibility of change.

It can be argued that the point of view contained in the poem—the perspective from which the waste land is seen—is that of a questing knight who is near the end of his journey. Having found the waste land, having wandered around within it, having encountered a number of lost and frightened people, and having found the chapel, the castle, and the king, he faces his final test. Will he remember where he is and what he is supposed to do?

The answer to this question can only be found in the reader's imagination. The poem ends with the wounded Fisher King sitting on a river bank mumbling what appears to be nonsense.

I sat upon the shore
Fishing, with the arid plain behind me
Shall I at least set my lands in order?
London Bridge is falling down falling down falling down
Poi s'ascose nel foco che gli affina
Quando fiam uti chelidon—*O swallow swallow*
Le Prince d'Aquitaine à la tour abolie
These fragments I have shored against my ruins
Why then Ile fit you. Hieronymo's mad againe.
Datta. Dayadhvam. Damyata.
Shantih shantih shantih

The questing knight, present by implication, can sit down beside the king, having become a victim of the malaise surrounding him, and not do anything at all. Or, failing to recognize him, he can pass the king by and continue what will thenceforth be a fruitless quest elsewhere. Or he can stop, reach out with a comforting hand, and ask the right question—the question that will heal the king, restore the blighted land, and bring forth the Holy Grail.

The reader faces a similar test. He or she can surrender to Eliot's vision, accept the nihilism and despair that it contains, and stay in the waste land forever (a common fate in this century). Or he can pass through the poem without actually experiencing it and, leaving the abode of the Grail behind, continue a fruitless search for knowledge elsewhere.

Or the reader can take the poem seriously, fully confront its challenges and come through with enough presence of mind to reach out with a heartfelt question—perhaps one as simple as "What does this mean?"—the only response that leads toward regeneration.

Though we are called into question, into questing, by poems like Eliot's, and by the mysteries that stand behind them, most of us fail to respond. We prefer to stay home, metaphorically speaking, and live behind walls—those seemingly permanent structures erected by our forefathers and shored up by every generation since, those myths that stand against and protect us from the wilderness, the waste land and the wounded king beyond. Whether we affirm the values of a traditional faith or look at life through a scientific paradigm, we prefer a landscape that is cut and trimmed, turned into a garden, where only well-worn paths are found.

There is nothing wrong with this. In every area of life—personal, cultural, and religious—we need order and stability.

We need to remember, however, that the place where we live can suddenly dry up, the walls around us can unexpectedly crumble, and the waste land can appear, at any moment, right where we stand.

We also need to remember, when this occurs, that the Grail is near at hand.

Parabola
Volume: 8.3
Words of Power

WHAT AILETH THEE?

P. L. Travers

We know him, the Grail Hero, under many names—
Gawain, Perceval, (Parsifal in Wolfram von Eschenbach's
version), Bors, Galahad. Lancelot is not in the list, for though
he is brought near to it, he is denied the full sight of the
Grail because of his long liaison with Guinevere—though
whether that event ever really occurred needs, I think, in
spite of all the corroborative evidence, to be questioned.

Malory, quite probably, may not have heard of
Tantrism, but he could not have failed to be familiar with
the ordinances of the Courts of Love. It is, therefore,
quite possible that those two doughty combatants may
have taken on a far more poignant and rigorous task—
that of faithfully serving their mutual love while mutually
foregoing the taste of its wine. Otherwise, how account
for Arthur? The High King, *sans peur et sans reproche*, who
with Merlin's help laid down the rules of knighthood—is
it conceivable that he would have allowed his paladin
among knights to cuckold him at his own Round Table
and not reach for Excalibur? Did he look on consenting?
It has always seemed to me that in this matter the myth
is hiding a card up its sleeve.

Galahad, whom we may think of as Lancelot's unspot-
ted part, is par excellence the Grail's true man, but he dies
of his own wish so early in the story that he does not serve
to carry it forward so that he can speak to *our* needs.

So let us settle for Perceval, the widow's son, sealed from the world by his mother's love and arriving tardily at court, a homespun and untutored warrior. He is received with mockery. Churl, clown, clodhopper, they call him. But his enthusiastic habit of bringing defeated vassals to the King and lugging in the bodies of hitherto unbeatable villains, stuffs their mockery back into their mouths. His bumpkin herohood forces them to accept him as a true member of the Round Table.

But, cloudily, in his innocent heart though not yet in his rustic head, he knows there is something more to knight-errantry than demolishing giants and rescuing damsels. He is called to something else—but what?

So he sets out, not choosing, merely letting himself be drawn to whatever adventure lies in wait. Wandering through woods and wildlands, following chimerical roads that cross and wind about each other with no apparent destination, he comes, on a sudden, on a magical tower, the great walled keep of Montsalvesche.

Not knowing it for the Grail Castle and all unlearned in knightly procedure, he enters it as he would any other and stands transfixed by what confronts him. This is nothing less than the ceremonial of the Grail feast. Before him reclines the Grail King, *Roi Pescheur, Roi Mehaigné*, unmanned by his secret wound and about him, in a blaze of moving light, knights and maidens led in procession by the Grail Queen carrying the Grail itself.

Undone at finding himself in such surroundings, he watches the pageantry in silence, partakes in silence of the sacred meal, in silence allows the shining figures to bow him to his bed place. And in silence he awakes at daybreak to find that the Castle has disappeared. He is alone in a vast spreading wasteland where all streams are dry and voiceless, trees naked of their leaves and no bird sings.

Bemused, knowing himself under enchantment, he makes his slow way back to the court to be accosted at the entrance by a boar-tusked female riding a mule. And there, amid his welcoming peers, he is arraigned for unknightliness. Why, the creature demands, having seen the Fisher King sore wounded and because of that wound the land itself wasted and wounded, had he not asked the healing question?

Unknightliness! The sting of it, to one who has valiantly, if belatedly through no fault of his own, set himself to master the courtesies of knighthood, of which to refrain from unasked-for questions is high among the list!

Within himself Perceval rages, even against the God he is seeking, and determines at all costs to find again the place of his misjudgment.

Now, the myth requires that the question be asked even if it means thereby that one of its own rules be broken. It gives him a second chance. After long years of searching he finds himself in the place where he had stood before. The miraculous ceremony is once more performed. And he, gathering all his forces, steps forth and asks the question.

"Sir, what aileth thee?"

We know the rest. The King is healed and therefore the land. Birds sing and the desert blooms. We know the rest, for the myth takes us back to the first syllable of recorded time, to its roots in the pagan vegetation rites of the death and resurrection of such heroes of Tammuz, Adonis, Attis.

The theme of the question is a late addition. It arose because it was required. Myth answers every need. It is not static, once and for all, a phenomenon caught in the web of the past but rather an ever-living process. It speaks to us with ancient voice that is forever new and properly to understand it we will have to live it as it marches with us.

For the question is our own question. In our rational, fragmented, technological world, it is we, seeking deliverance, that need it to be asked; we ourselves must become the Grail Hero who will set the waters free, not only in ourselves but in others. Secretly, we are all sore wounded and need that the wound be noted and the necessary words of power spoken.

What aileth thee, neighbor? Friend? Brother?

Reprinted by permission of the P. L. Travers Will Trust.

Parabola
Volume: 17.2
Labyrinth

SLEEPING BEAUTY

Retold by P. L. Travers

What is time? We live in it but never see it. From here to there it carries us but we neither taste, hear, smell, nor touch it. How, then, can we describe its passage? By watching something grow, perhaps, or watching something fade.

Think of the woodcutter's cypress seed. After a season in the earth it sends up a small white thread. Then the sun gets to work on it and changes the white to green. "Look, it has sprouted!" cries the woodcutter's son. And, since cypress trees are long in the growing, he grows old watching the sprout become a sapling. And watching the sapling become a tree, his son, too, grows old. Generation after generation, the woodcutters watch the tree thicken and stretch its branches upwards. Till at last it attains its full height and shows us the shape of time.

Yearly the tree's shadow lengthened and there came a day when it reached the hedge. And at the same moment the charm that had been set in motion by the Wicked Fairy completed its full circle.

The day was heavy and slow to move. A mottle of clouds hung over the sun. Men in their pointed turned-up slippers dragged one foot after another. "What can be the matter?" they asked each other. "We seem to be waiting for something." And they longed for the day to come to an end so that what was to be might disclose itself.

At length it was over. The water clocks, filling one bowl from another, drop by drop wore the hours away—noon to sunset, sunset to dark.

The woodcutter, grandson many times removed of the one who had planted the cypress seed, settled himself at the edge of the thorn hedge, with his axe across his knees. Here he would wait, as his ancestors had done before him, to guard and watch and warn.

Meanwhile, by road and desert, field and mountain, a young prince from a distant land was marching to that selfsame spot. And if before him through the night there flowed a cloudy indigo shape with head and foot of flashing gold, he had no notion of it. He strode on all unseeing— looking perhaps within himself, as though he were his own compass and was drawn on by his own fate.

The woodcutter stirred at the sound of footsteps.

"Who goes there?" he demanded sharply.

"I am a prince from a far country. I have come to seek the Sleeping Princess."

"Then I beg you, Prince, heed my warning. Turn your steps from this fearful place, lest you suffer the fate of all those who were once the sons of kings."

The woodcutter waved his axe at the hedge where the white bones hung in the branches. Chalky hands, still wearing jewels, gripped at the fronds of briar. Crowned skulls bent, grinning, from the thorns. Tatters of turban, cloak, and slipper, tarnished from their original brightness, waved in the midnight breeze.

"A king of China hangs there," said the woodcutter, "and a prince from the Western Sea; potentates from India; khans from the hills and deserts. Begone while there is time, young lord, lest you, too, leave your bones on the thorn."

"Everyone must die," said the Prince. "I would rather leave my bones here than in any other place."

The woodcutter sighed. "Many a youth has spoken so and yet gone to his death. Besides, Prince, you are unarmed. No knife, no sword, no spear, no sickle. How will you cut a path through the hedge?"

"I am indeed, all unarmed. But all my life, without ceasing, I have bent my thought to this quest."

"Well, it shall not be said that I failed to warn you. Do as you will and must."

The dead twigs crackled under his feet as the Prince strode towards the hedge.

The woodcutter made one last effort. "Prince, beware!" he said, anxiously—and then stood rooted to the earth, mouth open, hand in air.

For as the Prince drew near the hedge the thorny tendrils broke apart like a skein that is unravelled. The spiky branches loosed their hold, the great trunks leaned away from each other, making an open pathway. And as the Prince stepped through the gap every bough and frond and twig burst into buds and flowers.

A great shine lit the woodcutter's eyes as he realized what had happened.

"He is himself his own weapon. The time must be ripe," he said. And he ran as fast as his legs would go to tell the news to his wife.

"The hundred years are gone!" he shouted, swinging his axe round his head.

"Are gone, are gone!" ticked the water clocks. And everywhere in towns and villages, in desert tents and in mountain caves, men stirred a little in their sleep, knowing that something new had happened.

Meanwhile, the Prince marched through the forest and as he went the boughs broke out in fountains of bloom and all that had been knotted and tied was loosened and set free. Every barbed and spreading briar, locked to another in a long embrace, gave up its thorny partner and parted to let him pass. As the last branch fell away he stepped out of the hedge's shadow and beheld the sleeping palace.

Veils of dust hung upon the briars, the dust of years littered the thorn forest, but the palace lay there all untouched by earth mold or the mold of time.

The first dawn for a hundred years was breaking as the Prince picked his way among the sleepers. It shone on colored tents and carpets, on plump cheeks and glossy hair, all fresh and unfaded.

Ducking his head under the jugglers' hoops which were still hanging in the air, the Prince skirted the acrobats, asleep with their legs over their heads; hurried past nodding storytellers and leapt over the snoring camels. In the portico he passed the guards, all sprawling against the pillars. And at last he came to the Council Chamber.

Before the throne the Prince paused, folded his hands together and bowed. For though the Sultan, lolling sideways among his cushions was all unaware of his visitor, nevertheless he was a king. And kings, as the Prince well knew, are entitled to obeisance.

But such courtesies were, for the Prince, merely a matter of form. As he bowed, his eyes swept round the hall, searching its every corner. There lay Bouraba on the Sultan's knees; the Sultana, fine as a fine painting, asleep with her cheek upon the footstool and her maidens all about her. But the Prince's gaze did not linger. Something nearer than his inmost pulse told him that she whom he had so long sought was not within the chamber. He pushed aside an embroidered curtain and continued on his way.

For just as the Princess Rose, a hundred years ago, had been drawn by the magnet of her fate, so she herself became the magnet that drew the Prince to his. Steadfast as the compass needle that ever points to the north he moved through chamber and corridor, noting everything he passed but lingering not a moment.

As he passed through it, the palace, as though it were a single body, seemed to rise and fall with the sleeping breaths. And the courtyards rang with his living footsteps as he passed the moveless fountains.

At last, drawn by an unseen thread, he came to the foot of the tower. He glanced upwards and without a moment's hesitation set his foot upon the winding stair. The blue gleam that heralds sunrise shone through the narrow windows and he moved alternately through light and shadow as he took the stairs three at a stretch and came to the upper landing.

And there, for the first time, he paused, as though to gather in himself an even, easy flow of breath and all his lifelong purpose. Then he gently opened the creaking door and entered the little room.

There lay the Princess, hand to cheek, and at this sight the heart of the Prince lost one beat in its fearful joy. He knew himself to be at the center of the world and that, in him, all men stood there, gazing at their hearts' desire—or perhaps their inmost selves. He trembled—aghast at his own daring. A lesser man would perhaps have fled but not for nothing had he spent his life preparing for this moment. The coward tremor passed away and his courage came flowing back. Silently, he vowed to serve the accomplishment as he had served the quest. Then he took a stride towards the divan and bent to kiss the Princess.

She drew a deep shuddering breath, opened her eyes, and smiled.

"I have been dreaming about you," she said, simply. For indeed, what else had been her preoccupation all these sleeping years? "And now," she yawned behind her hand, "now my dream has come true."

Silently he kissed her again and together they plumbed all height, all depth, and rose up strongly to the surface, back to the shores of time.

At the same moment the sun rose and spread like a fan across the house it had not looked on for a hundred years. An awakening sigh, rising as from a single throat, stirred throughout the palace. Fountains trembled and loosed their waters; pennons flapped on the flagpoles. Down in the courtyard the acrobats suddenly leapt to their feet, the jugglers' hoops fell into their hands. Everyone was refreshed and lively as people who have slept well.

And destiny resumed its course.

From P. L. Travers, *About the Sleeping Beauty* (New York: McGraw-Hill Book Co., 1975). Reprinted by permission of the P. L. Travers Will Trust.

CHAPTER EIGHT

•

Psyche's Tasks

*"Oh, no," he replied, "Sister, it is too hard. To break the spell you
must pluck nettles from the cemetery of a church and spin
them into flax. Then you must make shirts for us from the flax,
and when they are done, cast them over us. And for all that time you must
neither speak nor laugh, for if a sound escapes you, all the
work will be lost. It is too hard, little sister."[1]*

—The Seven Swans

*Our real Self ... appears only when all its disguises have been shed;
the bride is unveiled before her husband; and in the same way,
"across Thy [Love's] threshold naked all must pass," ... Every
"property" (in the theatrical and other senses of the word)
must be dispensed with; and only the thread of our existence,
as Rūmī says, is suitable for the eye of the needle. In the last
analysis even our own bodies (personalities) are disguises,
from which only a (the) Prince Charming can extract us ...[2]*

—Ananda K. Coomaraswamy

*"She is always busy with other men. Then she turns, and sees how beautiful
He is."[3]*

—Michel de Salzmann

What shall Cordelia speak? Love, and be silent.[4]

—William Shakespeare

Parabola
Volume: 21.2
The Soul

THE SOUL'S RELIGION

Thomas Moore

As I talk to people involved in a wide variety of spiritual pursuits, I realize that I have an idiosyncratic idea of what religion is. Many people ask me to speak and write about spirituality but not religion. I've been told, after lecturing, that some have been offended by my use of the word "religion." Spirituality is in vogue, but religion, for many, has negative connotations.

It's understandable that men and women who have had unhappy childhood experiences in religious institutions would be wary of religion defined in an institutional sense. Religious organizations have long abused their moral authority by claiming political, financial, sexist, and moralistic power over their members, and today churches align themselves unabashedly with political parties. Churches have often become so political, and so inexpert in matters of the spiritual life, that it may be difficult to find a church where you can contemplate eternal mysteries.

Today many people are discovering the joys of the individual spiritual adventure, finding their own ways toward meaning and transcendence. Traditional theology has long focused on morality, dogma, the interpretation of scriptures, and the philosophical underpinning of belief—important issues, but not directly relevant to the individual searching for spiritual guidance. So the modern individual tends to listen closely not to the theologian, but to the independent writer who offers experiential lessons in spiritual initiation.

What then happens to the deeper, crasser soul, which needs religious attention as much as the loftier spirit does? Usually the soul is neglected, except when psychology offers mechanical adjustments to everyday life, and spiritual practice proceeds without the necessary grounding in life and depth. Spiritual activities may be rooted in narcissistic, ambitious, cruel, and defensive attitudes. Many current magazines devoted to spirituality appear to me to transfer the modern obsession with personal success to spiritual concerns such as meditation, yoga, vision, and discipleship, and many people take a developmental approach to their spiritual practices.

My purpose here is not to elaborate on the problems of spirituality without soul, although that is a subject worth much conversation and analysis. I'm more concerned with the religion of the deep, earthbound soul. What does religion look like when its aim is not spiritual advancement but rather care of the soul?

Clearing religion of its bias toward the transcendent spirit, we first set aside issues of belief, interpretation, moral purity, spiritual achievement, clarity of understanding, and institutional allegiance. In a sense, religion of the deep soul is beneath and prior to this enculturation of belief. It is a prerequisite and grounding for spiritual practice.

The next step is to hear the word "religion" without the spiritual and institutional associations. When I use the word, I don't think of a religion, a thing, as much as an *attitude*, a sensibility. Religion is an attitude of reverence and piety based on a profound appreciation for mystery, both in the world and in the human being. From this perspective, religious people are not necessarily those who profess a belief or attend church or engage actively in spiritual practices—there may be little soul in all of this—but those whose lives are informed by an imagination of life irreducible to physical and social sciences, leaving room for the infinitely profound. Without this fundamental openness, there can be no appreciation for the sacred in any real sense.

The spirit of secularism, paradoxically but understandably, fosters a spiritual reaction. Indeed, the more secularistic our daily environment becomes, the more we seem to hunger and thirst for spirituality in almost any form. But as long as we sustain the defining mythology of this century, with its trust in science and its feeling of having been liberated from traditional piety, a soul-satisfying spiritual life will remain elusive.

The soul's deep-seated reverence for homes and families, for artifacts of the past and nature in the present, for stories that deepen and arts that serve contemplation, provides a necessary inhibitive caution as we develop our learning and fabricate our world. At present, it seems that we have no inhibition to technological development, the use of nature, and the abuse of human labor. One of the most important gifts of the deep soul is the voice of conscience, which can't be heard when the virtue of piety is absent, and yet conscience plays a central role in human creativity, teaching us where to place limits and how to protect our common humanity. Without this soul, human creativity turns into uninhibited, self-destructive productivity, a sign of an untethered, dissociated spirituality.

The traditions and institutions of religion are fertile sources for a natural religion of the soul, but too often, taking the means for the end, they become preoccupied with their own agendas. They defend their positions and language, forgetting their role in tending the soul's religion. Still, the world's religious literature and iconography are such vast sources of learning and contemplation that anyone seriously interested in developing a soul-centered spirituality would be unwise to neglect them.

Spiritual practice, perhaps because of its burning attention to transcendence, tends toward hyperbole and grandiosity in its expression, while the soul favors simplicity. We may glimpse the soulful aspects of Buddhism in the image of the Buddha sitting at the base of a tree, waiting to be awakened, or in the sermon in which he simply raised a flower in his hand; in the simplicity of Jesus's parables and in his humble birth; in the earthiness of Saint Francis's theology of animals; and in the plainness of Lao Tzu's paradoxical wisdom. Models of the grounded sensibility of religion are not difficult to find in the history of religions, but its practice seems to be less visible today than ever before.

I've long meditated on a line from one of Emily Dickinson's letters: "There is so much that is tenderly profane in even the sacredest Human Life—that perhaps it is instinct and not design, that dissuades us from it." Dickinson is one of the great American poet-theologians of soul, and I suspect that she often called herself "pagan" because she was so sensitive to the difference between the soul's religion and the inhumane spiritual religions around her.

Oddly, perhaps, the religion of the soul gives as much value to the secular life as to spiritual practice. Secularity is the opposite of secularism, the latter a repudiation of the concerns of religion. One can live a fully secular life, devoted passionately and profoundly to the particular time and place of one's own existence, only when one appreciates the mystery and sacredness of the everyday and commonplace. As Dickinson wrote in another letter:

> *Lad of Athens, faithful be*
> *To Thyself,*
> *And Mystery—*
> *All the rest is Perjury—*

We are all lads and lasses of Athens, even those among us who repudiate the European roots of our culture, when we place our trust in reason and mechanics, neglecting the reverencing of mystery—the basic act of piety in the soul's religion. The shift from trying to explain all phenomena to giving an honored place to mystery is the primary characteristic of a postmodern return to soul. The principle applies to our posture toward nature and culture and to our relation to ourselves. Modern psychology wants to understand the human psyche fully and exercise complete control over it. The secularization of the soul results in the reduction of human experience to "human behavior" and the intriguing mystery of personhood to the limited idea of a "self."

Once we allow mystery in nature and in our definition of a person, then we discover that our current technological and therapeutic responses are extraordinarily inadequate. We begin to appreciate the role of the arts, not as entertainment or education, but as servants of deep vision and subtle sensibility. We see the need for piety, an attitude of respect for the vast realm of experience we know little about and can't begin to understand. A natural spirituality, a spirit of reverence, and an appreciation of story and ritual as truly sacred and necessary take the place of the narcissistic and ambitious forms of spiritual activity we find in both religious institutions and programs of spiritual advancement.

A certain kind of simplicity, the kind characteristic of a Gospel parable, a Sufi poem, a Zen story, a Dickinson verse, or a scene from Beckett, accompanies the descent of spiritual attention to the lower, earthier regions of the soul. As that attention lowers, it casts a glow on everything mundane, making sacred and secular not opposites, but inseparable companion qualities in a world not torn into spirit and matter, mind and body, or even soul and spirit.

We may find in that reconciled world that our daily work is a major piece in our spiritual path, the food we eat always some form of communion, a walk in a park true meditation, a conversation with friends the fulfillment of a beatitude, a night with a lover a step toward the mystical, and an hour with a child a lesson in natural spirituality. We may discover that stories and images educate the soul, music tunes it to the varieties of experience, and family life gives it fundamental security and comfort.

When spiritual practice is grounded in the low, earthy religion of the soul's ordinariness, then it can soar as high as it wants without loss of humanity. The great cathedrals and temples of the world teach this reconciliation of soul and spirit with their towering steeples, their stained-glass windows and sculptured friezes teeming with stories and images, their community-gathering naves and welcoming portals, and their mysterious, death-inspired, secret-laden crypts. We could learn from these holy buildings how to make a many-tiered life that gives full honor to body, soul, and spirit.

Parabola
Volume: 5.2
Music, Sound,
Silence

THE SILK DRUM

P. L. Travers

In the ancient days there was a great lord who, feeling himself near to his ending, admonished his only daughter.

"The green of the plum tree has come and gone. Now is the time of blossoming. But still you have not chosen a husband. This and that suitor comes and goes but none is to your liking. Must I die and leave you unaccompanied?"

"Not so, my father," said the Lady Yumiyo. "I shall cause to be fashioned a drum of silk—of silk stretched upon a bamboo frame. He who hears the note when my fingers strike it is the man whom I shall marry."

"This is foolishness," her father said. "A silken drum will make no sound. Alas, I shall never see a grandchild."

But the drum, nevertheless, was made. And many a one came to listen, head stretched forward, urgent to hear— some because of the lady's beauty, some for the readiness of her wit, some because it was widely known that she would be well-provided. And some for all three reasons.

But not a sound did anyone hear when she struck the drum with her hand.

"I told you so," her father said.

But the Lady Yumiyo said nothing. She merely went on striking the drum as the suitors came and went.

And then, one day, in the frame of the doorway, there appeared a well-set-up young man, richly appareled, keen of glance, with the air of one who had come a long way.

He made a deep bow to the old lord and a lesser one to his daughter.

"From where do you come?" the father asked.

"From beyond the mountains and seas and valleys."

"And for what have you come, man from afar?"

"For your daughter, the Lady Yumiyo."

"She is for him who can hear the silk drum. Never tell me that the sound has reached you, across the seas and mountains!"

"No sound of the drum has reached me, sir."

"Then why, stranger, linger here?"

"I have heard its silence," the young man said.

The Lady Yumiyo smiled at her father and put the silken drum aside. She no long had any need of it.

Reprinted by permission of the P. L. Travers Will Trust.

Parabola
Volume: 18.1
Healing

The Seven Swans

Retold by Natalie Baan

In a land by the shore of a restless sea, a king mourned for the loss of his wife. She had been more dear to him than the light of day, and in remembrance of her he poured out his love upon his children: they were the sun and stars of his life, and all that could be wished for was theirs. The seven boys grew in time to be youths both strong and gentle, and as for the youngest child, his daughter, she bloomed as merry and as fair as the wild roses running along the castle walls. Her brothers were devoted to her, and she to them, and there was no shadow upon their lives. But in the king's heart there was still a sadness that their laughter could not heal.

In time, then, he sought a new wife. The bride he brought into their home was clever and beautiful, but she was a jealous woman, and could not bear to share her husband with the children of his first love. Most of all she hated the young girl, who as she grew was becoming the very image of the woman she wished to replace.

"First, though, to be rid of the sons," she thought, "so that they'll not hinder me." She had learned the trick of charms and spell casting from her mother, and used her witch-wit now to make seven shirts for the brother, each one lined with swans' down she begged from the king's huntsmen. Then one day, while the king himself was at the hunt, she found the seven youths amusing themselves in the courtyard, and she flung the shirts over their heads. In an instant they were transformed, and seven wild swans rose crying into the air and flew from sight.

The daughter saw all this from her window and she was afraid, sure that her stepmother meant to do her harm as well. She feared, too, that her father would not listen to her words, for she had seen the looks and smiles and soft whispers that passed between the man and his wife, and was for the first time uncertain of his love. So in that very hour she slipped away from the castle and walked far away along the shore. She knew that in time her father would come seeking her, to return her to the home which now held no safety. Yet the kingdom was hemmed in by mountains, forest, and sea: how could she escape? Late in the afternoon, she came across the long, white feathers of swans strewn on the sand, and she wept for her brothers and herself as she twined the feathers into her tangled hair.

Then as the sun spilled itself out of sight, she heard the cries of birds, and the air around her was filled with wings as the seven wild swans came to rest. In the instant that the light faded from the sky, their swan-shapes fell away, and they stood once more before her, her brothers. With tears of joy, they embraced her. Yet as she told them what had befallen her, their faces became grim.

"But can you not come home with me now?" she begged them.

"No," they replied, "for that is a part of the spell: While the sun is in the sky we are wild swans and have the spirits of swans, and even when the sun is set a part of that wildness remains. We may not enter indoors nor sleep beneath a roof, nor may we ever call a corner of sea or land our home. We cannot go back."

"There is worse," the elder brother added, "for the wind and the seasons are calling us away. In the morning we must fly away across the sea, and you will have no protection at all!"

"I wish I had wings as well!" she cried. "I wish I could go with you over the sea."

"Perhaps there is some hope of that," one of the brothers said. "We could weave a net of sea grasses this night, and the seven of us might be able to carry you that way." In the end, that was what they did. As the sun rose above the mountains, the brothers resumed the forms of swans. Quickly, their sister cast braided ropes of grass about them which bound them to the net, and as one creature they spread their seven pairs of wings and, bearing her with them, rose to meet the sky. It was a long flight for her, and a frightening one as well, as she watched the sea surging far below through the spaces in the net. But the youngest of her brothers flew as close to her as possible, the shadow of his wings sheltering her from the midday sun, and she was somehow comforted by that.

So swiftly did they fly that in mid-afternoon she sighted land, and by evening they were winging above a strange countryside. As the day closed itself up the swans came to rest in a wood, and once again became her brothers. They rejoiced in having made the crossing, but at last the oldest brother said, "You are safe now, and we are happy for you. But we cannot stay. There is no rest for us here; we must fly to the south, where the wild swans winter. And you should not come with us: it is a life for swans, not for maidens; you should seek a home and happiness." Her brothers were all of one mind in this, and at last, with reluctance, she agreed. They spent that night together in the wood, and as dawn approached, awoke to say their farewells.

As she embraced her youngest brother, she entreated him, "Will you be swans forever, then? Is there no way I can break the spell?"

"Oh, no," he replied, "Sister, it is too hard. To break the spell you must pluck nettles from the cemetery of a church and spin them into flax. Then you must make shirts for us from the flax, and when they are done, cast them over us. And for all that time you must neither speak nor laugh, for if a sound escapes you, all the work will be lost. It is too hard, little sister. But do not be sad. Only think of us, sometimes, when you hear the swans flying overhead!" And with that, the first light of the sun came through the trees and, wild once more, her brothers took wing and were gone.

For a while she remained where they had parted, sunk in her grief. But at last she roused herself, and began to make her slow way through the wood. After a while she came upon a little forest chapel, long abandoned, its yard given over to weeds and the shelter of its eaves to swallows. Here she paused and, gazing at the overgrown graves beyond the church, recalled the words of her brother. She sighed once, and then, without another sound, went forward into the churchyard and began to gather the stinging nettles.

As her brother had warned, it was a hard task. Soon her fair, soft hands were blistered from plucking the nettles. The chapel was a cold and comfortless resting place; she was often hungry, and the cries of wild animals frightened her at night with their strangeness. But in her silence she neither wept nor complained, and in time became accustomed to that life. She worked away at her labors, pulling the nettles in their season, and at other times, spinning, weaving, and sewing with her makeshift tools.

One spring, the king of that country chose to hunt in the maiden's wood. His huntsmen came across her in the chapel glade; she did not hear them until too late, as she stood watching the wild flocks passing north, seeking the longed-for shapes of swans. Startled, she fled, but the hounds soon brought her to bay in a tree. The huntsmen called off the dogs, and stood amazed. "Who are you?" they cried. "Come down to us!" She only shook her head and, as they persisted, took off her fine gold necklace and dropped it, praying they would take it and go. Still they shouted up to her, so she threw down to them one by one the last remnants of her finery—ring, girdle, and garter—until she had nothing left but her rags. The huntsmen were not diverted, however, and soon climbed the tree and urged her down. They brought her before the king, who was astonished by her beauty. He asked her in all languages that he knew who she was and where she came from, but she said no word. He wrapped her in his cloak then, and took her to his castle, where he had maids dress her in fine clothes and arrange her hair. When she was brought before him again, he looked on her lovely sad face and knew that he could not rest until she became his bride.

"I wish you to be my wife," he said to her, "Will you not say yes?" But she would not say yes or no, and only sat by her window, gazing out toward the forest. He tried every plea and promise he could think of, every kindness that might woo her, but to all she made no response.

Finally, he led her to a small room in the tower of the castle. He opened the door, and there was all her work from the chapel: spun flax and half-sewn shirts! Even her rustic loom and spinning wheel were there. He said to her, "I have had all your things brought from the forest. Will you smile now? For I only want you to be happy here." And yes, she smiled at last, and it was like the first light of the sun touching a grey sea. She looked at the king and nodded once, and he knew that his long-asked question was answered. In but a few days, they were wed.

Both the king and his new queen were content, but there were others in the castle who were not. Many in the court thought her strange and backward, for she showed little interest in the affairs of the castle, or in the balls and feasts with which the king tried to please her. They whispered about her silence and her unknown past, and her habit of working all the day long on shirts for no one. Others spoke of how she was still fey and wild, springing up from the table and running out of doors at the cries of migrating birds, whether the meal be done or no. The king's elderly mother was especially displeased, and spoke nothing but evil about her, which the queen could not deny.

After a time, she gave birth to a son, and the old mother saw a chance to be rid of her. Soon after the birth, she stole the child away, and smeared her daughter-in-law with blood as she lay asleep. She ran to the king and cried to him, "Did I not warn you against this wife? Come and look, she has murdered your only son!"

The king of course was furious and denied his mother's words, but the evidence seemed quite plain to the people of the court. The young queen was only able to shake her head and weep silent tears in her defense. Her husband would not let any harm her, but in private he begged her to break her long silence. "If they find but one more reason to suspect you a witch," he pleaded, "I will not be able to keep you from them. O beloved, speak to me! Tell me you are innocent." But the queen could say no word to reassure him.

There was another, greater worry on her mind. The end of her task lay almost in sight, but she had no more nettles for the last of the shirts. Finally, despite her husband's vigilance, she slipped away to the town's churchyard and gathered as many as she could find, but she was observed, and accused of graverobbing and witchery. Though he argued, threatened and entreated, the king was not able to sway his people and, grieving, he was forced to deliver her to justice. She was sentenced to die by fire.

She was imprisoned in her tower room, but she cared nothing for that: she had her nettles, and she worked feverishly, racing the day of her sentence. The day came at last and she was almost finished, with only the last of the sewing to be done. When they came for her, she would not let go of the shirts. Even as the cart rolled through the streets, carrying her to the fire, her needle flew. The townspeople yelled and jeered. "See the witch! She is still working her charms!" "Hi! Let us take her evil work away! Let us burn it as well!"

As the cart lurched to a stop, she raised her eyes at last. Before her lay the stake, wood piled high around it, but she looked away from it, up into the sky. It was the fall of the year, and the sky was filled with wings. As the crowd surged forward, shouting, wild cries shook the very air, and down out of the southward flying flocks swept seven great swans in a thunder of white. The crowd fell back, mute with surprise, as the birds winged into the square to surround the condemned woman. In an instant she flung the shirts over their heads, and see! they were swans no more, but seven young men, tall, and as fair as the queen herself. In that same moment, she turned to where her husband stood astonished, and cried out, "Now I may speak! I am innocent!"

There was a great confusion then, but at last the whole story of her labor to restore her brothers was told. The king's mother was brought forward, and forced to admit that it was she who had taken the queen's child; she revealed that he was hidden with a poor huntsman's family, and the king sent for him at once.

The queen and her brothers embraced and kissed each other, yet even in her happiness she still mourned a little, for she had not been able to finish the last of the shirts, and so her beloved youngest brother had a swan's wing in place of his left arm. But he laughed and kissed her face. "O, do not be sad, little sister! A swan's wing is a small price to pay. For we are together again, after all, and all that could be healed, has been. And if your husband is willing, perhaps we shall find our rest here, at last."

And indeed, it was so.

Parabola
Volume: 20.4
Eros

THAT OTHER LOVELINESS

Harriet Eisman

Eros brings beauty, meaning and divinity into our lives. It comes to us through a very particular epiphany, a passionate inspiration present in a particular lover, teacher, melody, or landscape. We long to follow it always. But this is not the whole story. For eros also brings us obsessions, cruelty, abandonment, and betrayal. It may come through anguish over my partner's infidelity, or enter my heart as it breaks for a beloved sibling with cancer. At these times, to love seems dangerous, hopeless, or naive. How, in the midst of sorrow that seems too great to bear, can I see through to the truth that my loving is always right, that love is finally, as the Sufis tell us, "the love of the Creator for the creature in which He creates Himself"?[1] And how can I find a path towards my soul's real nature that begins right here where I am shipwrecked, rather than in pious hopes for a perfect life?

The well-known tale of Eros and Psyche offers profound instruction to those of us who find ourselves on the path of love. The sufferings and tasks of Psyche as she seeks to be reunited with her beloved give precise and penetrating images of the work this path demands. Eros, a *daimon* or celestial spirit according to the ancients, travels between heaven and earth, bringing not only beauty, love, and inspiration, but also chaos and disruption as he ignites unexpected and irresistible passions. The thread that leads from this disruption to a vision of the soul's pure beauty, and the skills and means for becoming, ourselves, capable of being with that vision as our lover, are what we can uncover in looking at the labors of Psyche.

Psyche's first vision of Eros is clandestine and overwhelming. She holds a dagger and a lamp, ready to kill him if he is indeed the monster her sisters say he is. She can no longer wonder; she has to obtain her own knowledge of his good or evil nature. And so she steals a glimpse of him in the light:

> She gazed again and again upon the beauty of that divine face and her soul drew joy and strength. She beheld the glorious hair of his golden head streaming with ambrosia, and curling locks that strayed over his snow-white neck and crimson cheeks ... and before the lightnings of their exceeding splendor even the light of the lamp grew weak and faint. From the shoulders of the winged god sprang dewy pinions, shining like white flowers, and the topmost feathers, so soft and delicate were they, quivered tremulously in a restless dance, though all the rest were still.[2]

Filled with this radiance, Psyche picks up one of Eros' golden arrows, is pricked by it, and falls in love with Love. Passion overwhelms her, and she covers him with kisses; like her desire, the hot oil from her lamp overflows onto his body. He awakens badly burnt, chastises her, and flees.

These few moments reveal many of the painful paradoxes of the mystical path. Psyche is not capable of containing her vision of Eros, and yet this is how it must be. The love comes first, far ahead of our ability to make sense of it or manage it. So Rumi says,

> There is no salvation for the Soul
> But to fall in Love.
> It has to creep and crawl
> Among the Lovers first.[3]

We eagerly desire such a glimpse, bask briefly in its beauty, and then clumsily cause it to flee. Psyche has not the faculties, the subtle senses, to meet and be with this vision. We surely do not know how to look at gods, but instead fall onto their bodies and burn them. Brunton notes, "The moment you seek to keep the glimpse, it is gone."[4] How often have we been in the presence of magic, whether brought on by nature, music, meditation, or another person, and sat dumbly wishing to be able to receive what is truly offered? How many times have we mistaken the literal person or place for the true source of the glimpse, and devoted ourselves to possessing that, rather than following the inspiration itself? Plotinus tells us what love really wants:

> Love, thus, is ever intent upon that other loveliness, and exists to be the medium between desire and the object of desire. It is the eye of the desirer; by its power what loves is enabled to see the loved thing. … Desire attains to vision only through the efficacy of Love, while Love, in its own Act, harvests the spectacle of beauty playing immediately above it.[5]

Most of us, like Psyche, make all the mistakes; her tale helps us to know that, at whatever level we meet Eros, we will be given labors which will make us able finally to recognize it for what it is. But at this moment in the myth, the suffering is great. Psyche is abandoned, sobbing on the ground. At last she knows who her lover is, and he is gone. That she is in love with Love foretells that she will have to penetrate to the essence itself: there is no turning back.

This scene is not so much about what Psyche should have done to avoid losing Eros. Rather, it sets up what she really wants and what she will have to do to accomplish it. She is left in a place of utter hopelessness and despair. The one thing she must have is gone. Now the light, in revealing itself, also shines into her darkest places.

Psyche becomes Aphrodite's hostage, and, in a deeper way, her student. Beaten and spat upon by the Goddess of Love and Beauty, her state resembles Evelyn Underhill's description of the mystic death:

> In the Dark Night the starved and tortured spirit learns through an anguish which is itself an orison to accept lovelessness for the sake of Love, Nothingness for the sake of the All; dies without any sure promise of life, loses when it hardly hopes to find.[6]

This gives us an inkling that the path of love and beauty is not what we might expect it to be. The tasks given by Aphrodite seem to be impossible obstacles placed by a cruel and obstructing mother-in-law. In fact, they are purifications and are precisely aimed at uncovering the soul's truth. The tale moves on the path Psyche must walk between two great goddesses, Aphrodite and Persephone, between she who knows the miracle of how to embody beauty and she who knows the miracle of unembodying it. To know the mystery of being with Eros, Psyche must be capable of learning what these goddesses have to teach, and from the very beginning these lessons render worthless all that she knows.

This is the secret of Psyche's innocence, foolishness, and helplessness, which many find annoying and frustrating. She does not appropriate her strengths or accomplishments as she moves through the tasks given to her by Aphrodite. She does not grow in confidence, but rather approaches every task with panic and suicidal despair. This portrayal of the quest recognizes the complete irrelevance of the ego's skills to a genuine penetration of the mysteries of the soul. The powers that help Psyche are not "hers": it is a simple fact that our true inner guide does not and cannot use our ego's storehouse of knowledge, because it is taking us to places beyond our ego's present functioning. Rumi puts it this way:

> *Be quiet in your confusion, and bewildered*
> *When you're completely empty within*
> *that silence, you'll be saying,*
> Lead me
> *When you become that helpless,*
> *God's kindness will act through you.*[7]

It is important that she is able to *hear* the voices of her inner helpers—ants, a reed, an eagle, a tower. Once a task is accomplished, a new faculty may be added to her: in the second labor she is able to use her hands, in the third, a crystal urn, and in the last, Aphrodite's box. But she is still a helpless girl seeking only her Beloved, or death.

The path that leads back to Eros begins with the first task: sorting a huge mountain of seeds, which is done by hundreds of helpful ants. The skill of the ants expresses the deep wisdom of the body, which at every moment must be sorting out in order to keep us alive and recognizable.

Healing is perhaps the most wonderful example of this kind of intelligence: the busy, microscopic work that goes on so that a cut on the hand will be gone in a week, the tissue rebuilt as if by magic. Even the most powerful medical life-support systems do not heal, but only keep us in life with the hope that the ants will come and do their work.

Appreciation of and reverence for the wisdom of the body are essential parts of the search for the higher self, yet there is a tendency to mistreat the body when we are absorbed passionately in "higher things." We don't sleep, we don't eat, we insist on intensity alone. There is a real danger of burning out the body, of disdaining it as a lump of clay. This worthless mess is how the pile of seeds first appears to Psyche; without the ants, she would be stuck in seeing her body this way. Paul Brunton is clear on the importance of caring for it as a living being:

> *The body is our physical home. Therefore it should be well treated and well cared for, kept healthy as far as we can. This is not only a personal need but also a spiritual duty for its condition may obstruct or assist the inner work.*[8]

By morning, the seeds are sorted, and Psyche has learned that the body listens and responds to her, and that she can hear it as well.

Psyche's second labor, collecting golden fleece from rams under a sweltering sun, contains profound lessons about channeling vitality and harvesting the essence of feeling. The danger increases with this task, as the rams of untamed emotion are destructive and violent. A path that follows the heat of erotic inspiration brings us face to face with our own dangerous wildness. We kill for love, we die for love, we go off the deep end. We want to be alive and open, yet through this open door, more often than not, pass the angry beasts we locked up years ago.

The reed which advises Psyche is called "nurse of sweet music, breathed on by some breath divine." The reed by her very nature shows us how we can be a beautiful vehicle for feeling, as all kinds of music breathe through her, unobstructed. The reed's advice to Psyche—to wait under a tree until the sun sinks and then to harvest the fleece from brambles—begins her instruction in being still. The space that stillness brings is the container that can allow us to hold powerful energies without being destroyed by them. As for the rams, with "sharp horns … foreheads hard as stone … and venomous bites," it is no secret that anger and love often contain each other, and that each holds great danger in its wild, uncontrolled form, but tremendous vitality and beauty when approached mindfully.

The difficulty of sitting quietly should not be underestimated, for the power of the rams in us is very great, built up by long habit. To let the sun of our attention set on them when they are so frightening, brilliant, and fascinating requires great discipline. We want to go out to them, as we want to leap on beautiful Eros. But this task teaches the skill of using the heart to see, of using love's heat to burn out an inner chamber where feeling's essence can be known. James Hillman describes this place where we learn to behold the golden fleece:

> *The heart's characteristic action is not feeling, but sight. Love is of the spirit, quickening the soul to its images in the heart. … One turns to the heart because here is where the essences of reality are presented by the imaginal to the imagination. … Not held; beheld, and we beholden to powers, we in their luminosity, watched by them, guarded, remembered; visible presences, enlightening our darkness by their beauty.[9]*

Psyche must be able to gaze again at Eros' astounding beauty with her intense arousal channeled and contained. Mary Campbell advises that looking at the beloved requires us to know how and when to turn away.

> *Ending the gaze is a rupture:*
> *You look away, you abandon the beloved*
> *You travel inwardly. This is freedom*
> *And the hardest part.[10]*

Psyche brings the golden fleece back to Aphrodite, and is called upon to "travel inwardly" even further.

The next task takes Psyche to the freezing, implacable Styx whose water she is to place in Aphrodite's crystal urn. In a way, the urn is the product of the second task, its glass formed both by the heat of the midday rams and by Psyche's own ability to contain herself until the sun goes down.

Now she is called upon to contain love's coldness and cruelty, which includes the implacability of the traditional marriage vow, since the gods themselves swear on the river Styx. This urn must have the strength to contain something extremely dangerous, poisonous, and powerful. The freezing up of feeling, the cold shoulder, is also love, and we can count on it. Not only do we have to be able to survive this coldness, we also have to take it into ourselves as a strength: the cold truth, the cold eye of reason.

This is the forbidding realm of what Joseph Campbell calls the sublime, of immense forces and powers that determine events without concern for individuals. Now Psyche sees the awesomeness of the divine, not just its accessible beauty and loving warmth. The ego shudders at the vision of vastness of the Real, even as Arjuna begged Krishna to take away the overwhelming cosmic vision he had asked for. Yet, in order to attain to a love that does not change, to a continuous, conscious relation to the Divine in us, we must be able to bear the approach of the immutable. Thomas Taylor describes the Styx as:

> that cause by which divine natures retain an immutable sameness of essence. The immutability therefore of divine energy is signified by the Gods swearing by Styx.[11]

Though the words "eternal" and "unchanging" are often used conventionally to comfort us, the actual effect of sensing their import is chilling. How could we tolerate a complete lack of motion? How could we survive the loss of the everchanging flow of images that fill our waking and dreaming lives? When these experiences approach us in meditation, our first reaction is often fear. The heart pounds, we sweat, we long to flee, and only a fierce concentration can keep us still enough to receive what is being offered.

For Psyche to accomplish her task, she must become as still as a stone, lacking "even the solace of tears." It is Zeus' eagle that comes to Psyche's aid with his penetrating eye, his unfailing concentration, his skillful wings, his claws that never lose their grip. He embodies a kind of thinking that has the ruthlessness to tear apart our alibis and excuses, seeing through to the vow that has been made and must not be broken.

With this reasoning power, a bit of the Styx' unforgiving water is carried into ourselves.

Psyche's last labor, the descent to the underworld in search of Persephone's beauty, takes us to the deep mystery of incorporating our sleep into our wakefulness, and our death into our life. For Psyche, it requires a relentless shedding of many qualities normally associated with being a good and beautiful person. She is called upon to abandon her compassion for a lame man, to ignore the pleas of the corpse floating in the Styx, to refuse help to the weaving women. She would be trapped by these appeals to her virtues. As Sogyal Rinpoche reminds us, "the watchword of the *Tibetan Book of the Dead* ... is 'Do not be distracted.'"[12]

The eagle's focus, the Styx's implacable chill, the clear firmness of the crystal urn—all have to be within Psyche for her to survive her journey to Hades. The way through the underworld of shadow, depression, and decay is difficult for a living being. Its protean depths undermine our habitual perspective. Paradoxically, the greatest danger may come from the ego's craving to assert its usual ways of judging, controlling, and making itself look good. Psyche's journey to the underworld is clearly not a civilizing mission, or an effort to overcome, as Hercules did, the denizens of Hades. She is not bringing light, but seeking the essence of this darkness. She enters receptively and honors the laws of the place.

Her teacher, the far-seeing tower, does not do the task for her but prepares her perfectly. The ego's biggest weapons—the hands and the mouth—are stilled, as Psyche's mouth holds two coins for Charon and her hands honeycakes for Cerberus. Charon's filthy fingers in her mouth relieve her of any attachment she might have to the perfection of her earthly beauty, while the terrifying three-headed Cerberus confronts her with her own darkness.

The labors are ended when Psyche disobeys the tower's last instruction, releases Persephone's beauty, and falls into a "hellish and truly Stygian sleep." Even the cautions of the perfect teacher must finally be disobeyed in the surrender to love. What Persephone puts in the box is not simply the essence of bodily death, for the Hades that Psyche has traversed is already peopled with disembodied souls. It is the much more profound state that Plutarch describes as mind separated from both body and animating soul, a second death we experience at the hands of Persephone after her mother, Demeter, has released us from body. This death is to the shadow world of Hades as sleep is to dream, as deep trance is to meditative vision. Anthony Damiani has described the encounter with this unembodied beauty as

> *An inscrutable abyss, a blinding darkness to the intellect, a radiance and joy that can suffocate the unprepared, but illuminate and permanently enlighten the adept.*[13]

It is, in fact, a most exquisite awakening, a state vast enough and still enough to allow Eros to return at last.

It is not only Psyche who is transformed. Eros, the fiery, flighty spirit who came and went secretly and refused to be seen in the light, has acquired at least the substance of a healed wound. The Eros she knows now is, Plotinus tells us, produced by the Soul's contemplation of the Divine Mind; it is the medium through which she can finally be present to "that other loveliness." He is the carrier of divine beauty which must, to become united with psyche and soma, be touched by the pain of earthly life.

Though they go to live among the immortals, this union does not suggest escape from our human existence. Rather, it shows the widest and deepest portrayal of the kind of human we can become on the path of love. This is real commitment and hints at the full extent of what Rumi meant when he wrote: "The price of kissing is your life."[14]

The men and women who have seen these things are changed. Plotinus describes the effects of beholding "the Source of Life and of Intellection and of Being":

> *And one that shall know this vision—with what passion of love shall he not be seized, with what pang of desire, what longing to be molten into one with This, what wondering delight! If he that has never seen this Being must hunger for it as for all his welfare, he that has known must love and reverence It as the very Beauty; he will be flooded with awe and gladness, stricken by a salutary terror; he loves with a veritable love, with sharp desire. . . .*[15]

In pursuing it, we pursue our greatest desire. Yet, after all, we live in ignorance of how it will approach. We can only listen, and pray, for the sound of Eros' soft, quivering wings.

I would like to acknowledge my friends and fellow students who contributed their gifts of thought, feeling and hard work to the study of Psyche's labors.

Notes:

1. Henry Corbin, *Creative Imagination in the Sufism of Ibn 'Arabi* (Princeton: Princeton University Press, 1969), p. 149.

2. Erich Neumann, *Amor and Psyche: The Psychic Development of the Feminine* (Princeton: Princeton University Press, 1956), p. 26.

3. Mevlana Jalaluddin Rumi, *Magnificent One*, Nevit Orguz Ergin, tr. (Burdett, NY: Larson Publications, 1993), p. 16, No. 8.

4. Paul Brunton, *The Notebooks of Paul Brunton*, vol. 14 (Burdett, NY: Larson Publications, 1988), p. 160.

5. Plotinus, *Enneads*, Stephen MacKenna, tr. (Burdett: Larson Publications, 1992), III.5.2, p. 217.

6. Evelyn Underhill, *Mysticism* (New York: E. P. Dutton, 1961), p. 397.

7. Mevlana Jalaluddin Rumi, *One-handed Basket Weaving*, versions by Coleman Barks (Georgia: Maypop, 1991), p. 78.

8. Brunton *op.cit.* vol. 4, part 2, p. 24.

9. James Hillman, *Thought of the Heart* (*Eranos Lecture 2*) (Dallas: Spring Publications, 1981), pp. 18, 24.

10. Mary Campbell, *The World, the Flesh, and Angels* (Boston: Beacon, 1989).

11. Thomas Taylor, *Theoretic Arithmetic of the Pythagoreans*, (New York: Samual Weiser, 1972), pp. 170–171.

12. Sogyal Rinpoche, *Tibetan Book of Living and Dying* (San Francisco: HarperSanFrancisco, 1992), p. 294.

13. Anthony Damiani, *Astronoesis*, (Burdett, NY: Larson Publications, 2000).

14. Mevlana Jalalludin Rumi, *The Essential Rumi*, Coleman Barks with John Moyne, A.J. Arberry and Reynold Nicholson, trs. (San Francisco: Harper SanFrancisco, 1995).

15. Plotinus, *op.cit.* I.6.7, p. 70.

•

THE MARRIAGE OF HEAVEN AND EARTH

*[The Eleusinian mysteries] are the mysteries of Demeter (not of
Persephone, except insofar as she is an aspect of Demeter), of the
Great Mother, whose experience of loss and finding led her to the* hieros
gamos, *the union of earth with the creator God, which means the birth
of the divine child who is the "whole."*[1]

—Helen M. Luke

*... the archetypal pattern is the mythological theme of the marriage
of the Sun god (Lug) with the Earth (Eriu, Ire-land); Gawain's
(and other solar heroes') ... many loves [are] but "different
manifestations, different names for the same primeval divinity"
who is also "Isis, Europa, Artemis, Rhea, Demeter, Hecate,
Persephone, Diana; one might go on indefinitely." ... The Solar
Spirit, Divine Eros, Amor, is inevitably and necessarily "polygamous,"
both in himself and in all his descents, because all creation is feminine
to God, and every soul is his destined bride.*[2]

—Ananda K. Coomaraswamy

*Just as the Earth-lotus in the Vedic tradition blooms on the surface
of the primordial Ocean in response to the down-shining of the
lights of heaven above, so in the Greek tradition the Sun perceives
a fertile land, Rhodos, the Rose, rising from the depths of the Sea,
"and there it was that Helios mingled with the Rose, and begat
seven sons who inherited from him yet wiser minds than any of
those of the heroes of old" (Pindar, Olympian Odes, vii.54ff.)*[3]

—Ananda K. Coomaraswamy

The theme is infinitely varied, but always the same story of the Liebesgeschichte Himmels [the Divine Love Story], the story of a separation and a reunion, enchantment and disenchantment, fall and redemption.

Hero and Heroine are our two selves—duo sunt in homine—*immanent Spirit ("Soul of the soul," "this self's immortal Self") and individual soul or self: Eros and Psyche. These two, cohabitant Inner and Outer Man, are at war with one another, and there can be no peace between them until the victory has been won and the soul, our self, this "I," submits.*[4]

—Ananda K. Coomaraswamy

Parabola
Volume: 29.1
Marriage

HEAVEN AND EARTH

Mircea Eliade

Marriage rites have a divine model, and human marriage reproduces the hierogamy, more especially the union of heaven and earth. "I am Heaven," says the husband, "thou art Earth" (*dyaur aham, pritivi tvam;* Brhadaranyaka Upanisad, VI, 4, 20). Even in Vedic times, husband and bride are assimilated to heaven and earth (Atharva-Veda, XIV, 2, 71), while in another hymn (Atharva-Veda, XIV, 1) each nuptial gesture is justified by a prototype in mythical times: "Wherewith Agni grasped the right hand of this earth, therefore grasp I thy hand. ... Let god Savitar grasp thy hand. ... Tvashtar disposed the garment for beauty, by direction of Brhaspati, of the poets; therewith let Savitar and Bhaga envelop this woman, like Surya, with progeny (48, 49, 52)." In the procreation ritual transmitted by the Brhadaranyaka Upanisad, the generative act becomes a hierogamy of cosmic proportions, mobilizing a whole group of gods: "Let Vishnu make the womb prepared! Let Tvashtri shape the various forms! Prajapati—let him pour in! Let Dhatri place the germ for thee!" (VI 4, 21). Dido celebrates her marriage with Aeneas in the midst of a violent storm (Virgil, *Aeneid,* VI, 160); their union coincides with that of the elements; heaven embraces its bride, dispensing fertilizing rain. In Greece, marriage rites imitated the example of Zeus secretly uniting himself with Hera (Pausanias, II, 36, 2). Diodorus Siculus tells us that the Cretan hierogamy was imitated by the inhabitants of that island; in other words, the ceremonial union found its justification in a primordial event which occurred *in illo tempore*.

What must be emphasized is the cosmogonic structure of all these matrimonial rites: it is not merely a question of imitating an exemplary model, the hierogamy between heaven and earth; the principal consideration is the result of that hierogamy, i.e., the cosmic Creation. This is why, in Polynesia, when a sterile woman wants to be fecundated, she imitates the exemplary gesture of the Primordial Mother, who, in illo tempore, was laid on the ground by the great god, Io. And the cosmogonic myth is recited on the same occasion. In divorce proceedings, on the contrary, an incantation is chanted in which the "separation of heaven and earth" is invoked. The ritual recitation of the cosmogonic myth on the occasion of marriages is current among numerous peoples. ... The cosmic myth serves as the exemplary model not only in the case of marriages but also in the case of any other ceremony whose end is the restoration of integral wholeness; this is why the myth of the Creation of the World is recited in connection with cures, fecundity, childbirth, agricultural activities, and so on. The cosmogony first of all represents Creation.

Demeter lay with Iasion on the newly sown ground, at the beginning of spring (*Odyssey*, V, 125). The meaning of this union is clear: it contributes to promoting the fertility of the soil, the prodigious surge of the forces of telluric creation. This practice was comparatively frequent, down to the last century, in northern and central Europe—witness the various customs of symbolic union between couples in the fields. In China, young couples went out in spring and united on the grass in order to stimulate "cosmic regeneration" and "universal germination." In fact, every human union has its model and its justification in the hierogamy, the cosmic union of the elements. Book IV of the *Li Chi*, the "Yüeh Ling" (book of monthly regulations), specifies that his wives must first present themselves to the emperor to cohabit with him in the first month of spring, when thunder is heard. Thus the cosmic example is followed by the sovereign and the whole people. Marital union is a rite integrated with the cosmic rhythm and validated by that integration.

The entire Paleo-Oriental symbolism of marriage can be explained through celestial models. The Sumerians celebrated the union of the elements on the day of the New Year; throughout the ancient East, the same day receives its luster not only from the myth of the hierogamy but also from the rites of the king's union with the goddess. It is on New Year's day that Ishtar lies with Tammuz, and the king reproduces this mythical hierogamy by consummating ritual union with the goddess (i.e., with the hierodule who represents her on earth) in a secret chamber of the temple, where the nuptial bed of the goddess stands. The divine union assures terrestrial fecundity; when Ninlin lies with Enlil, rain begins to fall. The same fecundity is assured by the ceremonial union of the king, that of couples on earth, and so on. The world is regenerated each time the hierogamy is imitated, i.e., each time matrimonial union is accomplished. The German *Hochzeit* is derived from Hochgezît, New Year festival. Marriage regenerates the "year" and consequently confers fecundity, wealth, and happiness.

WEDDING NIGHT WITH THE GOD

Trebbe Johnson

It's no secret that a god sometimes develops a passion for a mortal, who, of course, has little choice about whether she or he will consent to the union. Wandering among the villages of India, Krishna summoned the women from their tasks and, enchanted, they followed his call to a flowering grove, where the god made each one feel that he was making love to her alone. Zeus was notorious for the creative shapeshifting (bull, swan, shaft of light) he contrived to claim the women he desired. The legendary Irish warrior Cuchullain fell under the spell of the fairy woman, Fand, who desired him as lover and vanquisher of her enemies and let him know that he would waste away with illness until he came to her. It is hard to refuse a god who has his sights set on you.

But the longing for union between divine and human is not the whim of deities alone. The women who made love with Krishna yearned for him forever after, and that yearning breached their hearts and imbued every gesture with meaning—all became a preparation for the next embrace. Parvati brought both body and spirit to the task of winning the love of Shiva. Making offerings to him, she let him glimpse her lovely breasts, then took herself off to the forest to meditate in ascetic isolation. (Shiva was smitten, and their first embrace lasted twenty-five years.)

The shepherd Endymion fell in love with the moon goddess Selene and lay in eternal sleep in a glade in Latmos, dreaming only of her. Nightly Selene would come to him, and though some say she longed for a more robust passion than his somnolent limbs would allow, and others say it was he who yearned for more than her silken touch, it is longing between human and divine that drives the tale.

Most myths of human-god pairings focus on the desire, the drama of the consummation, or the golden child who is begotten. These are tales of one-night stands, either rape or honeymoon, not marriages between two people who choose to orbit the same sun, lovingly accommodating the differences in their gravitational pulls. The myth of Psyche and Eros, recounted by the Roman author Apuleius in the second century, is one exception, and it, too, has its beginnings in the more familiar theme of the god who takes what he wants and the mortal who passively accepts her fate.

Bound to a high crag by the order of the jealous goddess Venus, beautiful Psyche was mutely awaiting her demise when she was spotted by Venus's son, Eros, god of love. He no sooner saw her than he fell in love, and as she fainted into his arms he spirited her away to a remote, unmappable place. Here, in the ultimate honeymoon cottage, bride and bridegroom were blissfully happy. Eros had but one stipulation: his wife could not look upon him.

For a while Psyche was satisfied. Then, egged on by her envious sisters, who convinced her that any man who didn't want to be seen had to be a monster, she realized she needed more. She was determined to have her husband and know him too.

One night, therefore, while Eros slept, she lit a lamp and shone its light upon him. The man in her bed was beautiful, but he was not what she had expected. How can one look upon a god and report what she sees in everyday words? Some say he looked like a young boy, others that a great pair of wings sprouted from his shoulders. Certainly he was no monster. But it is a rule in the mythic domain that no mortal may challenge the will of a god. Eros awoke and departed, and Psyche was left with an abyss of longing that only her divine beloved could fill.

It was longing that compelled the gods to create people in the first place. They had gotten lonely sitting by themselves with their power and their infinite dreams. The world they had made was splendid but dull. And so, with spittle, sweat, mud, clots of blood, and other primal goo, they shaped the beings who, they expected, would honor and obey them and enjoy the bounty of their land. Things didn't always work out as planned. The people grew careless and neglected their responsibilities to their creators, or else they became impatient to flex the muscles they'd been given, to use their marvelous brains, and so they rebelled. The gods retaliated by giving them the ultimate independence: banishment. Along with the favor of the divine, human beings lost much more: our ability to speak the language of the animals, our home in the paradisal garden, the authoritative voice that could always be relied upon to steer us where we needed to go. Ever since, we have been trying to find the path back. We seek intimacy with that immense Power that is greater than we and yet seems to know us utterly.

Goethe called this search for the divine embrace the "holy longing," the desire to be swept up into "a higher lovemaking" that no human partner can satisfy. It is a longing that religious mystics of many faiths have expressed in poetry aflame with erotic language. "There is some kiss we want with our whole lives," wrote the Sufi poet Rumi.[1] "O infinite goodness of my God!" cried Saint Teresa of Avila in the sixteenth century, "O Joy of the angels, how I long … to be wholly consumed in love for Thee!"[2] "My love, you are beautiful," the male lover in the *Song of Songs* exults to the woman, said to be God's beloved female half, the Shekinah. "Your breasts are like two fawns … browsing among the lilies." We seek the eternal and wondrous on earth, and cannot wait for an afterlife. We need a tryst with the Mystery to know the divine in ourselves and bring it to fruition.

And even today, as in mythic times, a wondrous and inexplicable force occasionally sweeps us up and bears us off. A person is miraculously healed from cancer. Someone receives a visitation from the presence of a loved one who has died. A person shares a moment of communication with an animal that ends forever any doubts he may have harbored that all of life is intelligent and aware. William James called this kind of induction into the unknown "a mystical experience" and noted that, although it is by nature transient, it often has lasting consequences. In fact, James said, one of the most significant aspects of such an experience is its noetic quality: "Mystical states seem to those who experience them to be also states of knowledge. They are states of insight into depths of truth unplumbed by the discursive intellect … as a rule they carry with them a curious sense of authority for after-time."[3]

These ecstatic moments—rare, unbidden, and intensely personal—are like an embrace with the god. But, as the holy longing felt by Krishna's followers and expressed in the poems of the religious mystics attests, human devotion to the divine cannot rely only on those precious moments of union. Indeed, it is the constant longing for oneness, the pervasive desire to "be consumed in love for Thee" that bridges the gulf from human to god, not the rare moments of miracle. So, from holy communication in a great cathedral to the Sun Dance on the Great Plains, from an initiation rite in an East African forest to the celebration of Ramadan in New York City, from the carving of plump fertility goddesses in the twelfth millennium BCE to contemporary summer solstice ceremonies, people have created ways to honor the wondrousness of the divine and, just perhaps, to tap it themselves. The gifts and grace the gods may bestow on us are independent of all the work we do to keep the bonds strong.

That was the lesson Psyche learned when she made up her mind to win back Eros. Submitting to the will of Venus, she willingly—if not always graciously—undertook a series of daunting tasks, the kind of mythic onus that the assigner is confident will be the death of her victim, but which the hero, of course, brings stunningly to completion. During this trial, Psyche underwent a metamorphosis. She stopped acting like a victim and settled down to do what had to be done. She grew into a mature human woman, taking the steps necessary to be reunited with her beloved, and by the end of the tale she is a far different soul from that passive girl who never questioned her fate, whether it meant being bound to a crag or bedded by a god.

The process is the point, writes Erich Neumann in his classic study of the tale, *Amor and Psyche*. "With Psyche's love that burst forth when she 'sees Eros,' there comes into being within her an Eros who is no longer identical with the sleeping Eros outside her. … It is in the light of knowledge, her knowledge of Eros, that she begins to love."[4] The human, in other words, can not truly love the god until she becomes conscious of herself as a partner actively engaged in that love. She cannot love the god until she knows that they are two and that she is the initiator of the acts she takes in relation to him.

This consciousness of our separation from what we love and of our responsibility to act in ways that will foster love's shared delight is a hard-won treasure. As there are a thousand names for god, there are infinite ways to embrace that god—through soulful work, service to a cause that tugs the heart, meditation, art that transforms the inexpressible into something that can be expressed only by the artist, taking vows as a Bride of Christ, and losing oneself in the wonders of wilderness, to name but a few. The point is that when we say yes to falling in love with the god, with what calls the soul to its highest joy, then we find ourselves in the arms of the divine. We realize, moreover, that even when those rare moments of spiritual ravishment have ended, we can move on, not as a troubled exile, but as a lover eager to get back on the path that will bring us close to the Beloved yet again. Seeking the divine Beloved, we find ourselves.

What Psyche learned through her journey is that once you devote yourself to courting your soul companion, you step on hallowed ground. Daring to position yourself on the playing field of the gods, you declare your worthiness to join the match and make a match. Psyche had almost finished performing the tasks that Venus had assigned her when, at the very end, she fumbled, peeking once again where she had been warned not to look. This time, though, Eros himself came to her aid, as if to say, "Enough is enough. You love me and I love you, and now I shall go to meet you." He picked her up and flew her off, and this time she was conscious all the way.

Jung called the psychological equivalent of the culmination of Psyche's difficult journey the "*coniunctio.*" This is the inner marriage, in which all the diffuse, fragmented parts of the self (or psyche) are united and one discovers a new sense of passion, wholeness, and joy. When the sacred marriage occurs, writes Nancy Qualls-Corbett,

long-standing attachments to collective beliefs and assumptions are loosened. One becomes open to new approaches to old problems. ... One is more able to empathize with other people, respecting differences. ...

On a transpersonal level, the sacred marriage extends beyond the boundaries of understanding. One is united with the divine, the source and power of love. Through the mystical union a portion of divine love is received and contained within oneself. [One is able] to love on a plane which surpasses human understanding.[5]

Back on Olympus, Jupiter implored Venus to accept this courageous, passionate woman as her daughter-in-law, and Eros and Psyche were wed. Before long, they had a daughter, who was called Pleasure, but whose name Neumann equates with the experience of mystical joy.[6]

Mystical joy, child of the union between the divine mystery that calls us forth and the human determination to answer that call, is the quality that suffuses our being as we move toward the Beloved of the soul. Like Krishna's brides, confident that every act is a sacred preparation for a rendezvous with that which evokes the highest self, we bring our own god-eager presence to every aspect of our lives. And since all the world occupies that numinous space between us and the Beloved, we come to see every bit of it as blessed.

Unlike Psyche, we won't gain a home among the immortals. All our lives we must continue to woo the god, the holy passion that enflames us. A mortal who falls in love with a god must accept that the occasional spell of ecstatic union bears no promise of tomorrow. With the god, it is eternally the wedding night and rarely a domestic partnership. But that's what makes this courtship imperative. If it were possible to remain in the embrace of the god, we would simply curl there, as Psyche did at first, in an undifferentiated tangle of bedding and empyreal demands, and we would never strike out into the world on a sacred path of our own creation. We have to be separate from the god in order to keep striving, time and again, with a heart full of joy, into our holy longing. When we do, we walk into the world as into the arms of a waiting lover.

Notes:

1. Rumi, "Some Kiss We Want," in *The Soul of Rumi: A New Collection of Ecstatic Poems*, translated by Coleman Barks (New York: HarperCollins, 2001), p. 127.

2. St. Teresa of Avila, *The Life of Teresa of Jesus: The Autobiography of St. Teresa of Avila* (Garden City, NY: Image Books, 1960), p. 111.

3. William James, *The Varieties of Religious Experience* (New York: New American Library, 1958), p. 293.

4. Erich Neumann, *Amor and Psyche* (New York: Bollingen Foundation, 1956), pp. 80–81.

5. Nancy Qualls-Corbett, *The Sacred Prostitute: Eternal Aspects of the Feminine* (Toronto: Inner City Books, 1988), pp. 85–86.

6. Neumann, p. 140.

Parabola
Volume: 29.1
Marriage

Of the "Chemical Marriage"

Titus Burckhardt

The marriage of Sulphur and Quicksilver, Sun and Moon, King and Queen, is the central symbol of alchemy. It is only on the basis of the interpretation of this symbol that a distinction can be made between, on the one hand, alchemy and mysticism, and, on the other, between alchemy and psychology.

Speaking in general terms, mysticism's point of departure is that the soul has become alienated from God and turned towards the world. Consequently the soul must be reunited with God, and this it does by discovering in itself His immediate and all-illuminating presence. Alchemy, on the other hand, is based on the view that man, as a result of the loss of his original "Adamic" state, is divided within himself. He regains his integral nature only when the two powers, whose discord has rendered him impotent, are again reconciled with one another. This inward, and now "congenital," duality in human nature is moreover a consequence of its fall from God, just as Adam and Eve only became aware of their opposition after the Fall and were expelled into the current of generation and death. Inversely, the regaining of the integral nature of man (which alchemy expresses by the symbol of the masculine-feminine androgyne) is the prerequisite—or, from another point of view, the fruit—of union with God.

●

If the distance—and the relationship—between man and God is represented by a vertical line, then the distance between man and woman, or between the two corresponding powers of the soul, is represented by a horizontal line—which results in a figure like an inverted T. At the point where the two opposed forces are balanced, that is to say, at the center of the horizontal line, the latter is touched by the vertical axis, descending from God, or rising up to God. This corresponds to the supra-formal spirit, which unites the soul with God. ...

As all active knowledge belongs to the masculine side of the soul, and all passive being to its feminine side, thought-dominated (and therefore clearly delimited) consciousness can in a certain sense be ascribed to the masculine pole, while all involuntary powers and capacities connected with life as such, appear as an expression of the feminine pole. This would seem to resemble the distinction made in modern psychology between the conscious and the unconscious. There is therefore a temptation to interpret the "chemical marriage" (the expression is that of Valentin Andreae) simply as an "integration" of unconscious powers of the soul into the ego-consciousness, as is claimed by so-called "depth psychology."

In order to judge how far this interpretation is right, and to what extent it requires correction, it is necessary to recall the three-sided relationship that was represented above by an inverted T. True union of the two powers of the soul can only take place at that point where the supra-formal spirit, the Divine Ray, touches their common level. This means however, that what man regards as his own "I" can never become the axis of a real "integration," for, according to all spiritual traditions, the "I" which modern psychology regards as the real kernel of "personality," is precisely the barrier which prevents consciousness from being flooded by the light of Pure Spirit, or, in other words, which hides the Spirit from our consciousness. Thus the "chemical marriage" is not an "individuation," at any rate not in the sense of an inward process by means of which the ego imprints on a wave of collective instincts its own particular form—a form necessarily limited, both temporally and qualitatively. It may well be that the influx of hitherto unconscious influences may widen the ego-consciousness, for this lies within the range of an ordinary sublimation in the psychological sense of the word. Nevertheless this has quite definite limitations, which are in fact those of ordinary ego-consciousness. ...

In a sense, therefore, ego-consciousness lies between two unconscious realms, one below, which in its latent and as yet un-formed nature can never become completely conscious, and one above, which only appears as unconscious "from below." To the extent that the supraconceptual light acts on the realm of the soul, the "natural" power of the "lower" consciousness is tamed and assimilated.

The alchemical process has thus a dual and ambiguous aspect, since the development of the two fundamental powers of the soul (masculine Sulphur and feminine Quicksilver), brought about by spiritual concentration, is able to reflect the non-conceptual Spirit to the extent that it includes the involuntary, and in this sense natural, realms. The reason for this is that Nature, in her non-conceptual and more or less unconscious or involuntary aspect, is the inverse image of the creative spirit, in accordance with the words of the "Emerald Tablet," that whatever is above is like that which is below, and vice versa. Thus the fundamental masculine and feminine powers are anchored in the unconscious and instinctive nature of man. The two powers experience their full development on the plane of the soul, but realize their fulfillment only in the spirit, for only here does feminine receptivity attain its broadest breadth and its purest purity, and is wholly united to the victorious masculine. ...

The marriage of the masculine and feminine forces finally merges into the marriage of Spirit and soul, and as the spirit is the "Divine in the human"—as is written in the *Corpus Hermeticum*—this last union is related also to mystical marriage. Thus one state merges into another. The realization of the fullness of the soul leads to the abandonment of soul to spirit, and thus the alchemical symbols have a multiplicity of interpretations. Sun and Moon can represent the two powers in the soul (Sulphur and Quicksilver); at the same time they are the symbols of Spirit and soul.

Closely related to the symbolism of marriage is that of death. According to some representations of the "chemical marriage" the king and queen, on marriage, are killed and buried together, only to rise again rejuvenated. That this connection between marriage and death is in the nature of things, is indicated by the fact that, according to ancient experience, a marriage in a dream means a death, and a death in a dream means a marriage. This correspondence is explained by the fact that any given union presupposes an extinction of the earlier, still differentiated, state. In the marriage of man and woman, each gives up part of his or her independence, whereas, the other way round, death (which in the first instance is a separation) is followed by the union of the body with the earth and of the soul with its original essence.

On "chemical marriage" Quicksilver takes unto itself Sulphur, and Sulphur, Quicksilver. Both forces "die," as foes and lovers. Then the changing and receptive moon of the soul unites with the immutable sun of the spirit so that it is extinguished, and yet illumined, at one and the same time.

From Titus Burckhardt, *Alchemy: Science of the Cosmos, Science of the Soul*, translated from the German by William Stoddart (Louisville, KY: Fons Vitae, Quinta Essentia Series, 1997), pp. 149–156. Reprinted by permission of Fons Vitae, www.fonsvitae.com.

Parabola
Volume: 29.1
Marriage

THE TALE OF BAUCIS
AND PHILEMON

Jane L. Mickelson

What is marriage?" muses Joseph Campbell. "The myth
tells you what it is. It's the reunion of the separated duad.
Originally you were one. You are now two in the world,
but the recognition of the spiritual identity is what marriage is."[1] And of course, in the rich language of metaphor
this is the case. But for every folk and fairy tale that concludes "and they lived happily ever after," there is another
that speaks of the betrayal and bitterness, the hostility
and disappointment of marriage.

It would be difficult to find a human relationship that
embodies a greater complexity than marriage—with its
blend of the civil, social, spiritual, and physical—and
stories reflect this. An examination of Greco-Roman
mythology, so profound an influence on the symbolic
systems of Western society, provides models of marriage
that few mortals would wish to emulate. There is the tale
of poor cuckolded Hephaestus, trapping Aphrodite and
Ares in the act of adultery, then calling all the other gods
and goddesses to witness their shame; or the kidnapping
and rape of Persephone by Hades, who has arranged the
marriage with the young woman's father, Zeus. And of
course, there are Zeus and Hera, the very archetypes of
marriage, who seem to spend eternity in battle over his
philandering and her reprisals against his countless con-

quests and their offspring. The deities don't seem to fare much better than characters in folktales when it comes to a long-lasting marriage.

How ironic, then, that it is in the work of Ovid, the brilliant, cynical, and gifted poet and author of the manipulative *Art of Love*, that we find one of the most touching and beautiful stories of marriage ever written, and that it involves both Zeus and Hermes, whom Ovid calls by their Roman names of Jupiter and Mercury. Ovid's masterwork, *Metamorphoses*, focuses on myths and stories of transformation, most of which occur under duress. One of the few with a truly happy ending is the tale of Baucis and Philemon, and it presents us with a model of an ideal marriage. This story, of two elderly people whose one remaining wish is to be united in death as they have been in life, represents not only the final days of a fulfilling relationship between two people who love and care for one another—a recognition of that unity which Campbell celebrates—but also provides a metaphor for the ultimately enviable state of a human soul, just before death, when it has found final wholeness and integrated all its disparate parts.

In the opening lines of Ovid's tale, the poet brings the old story to life by placing the narrator on site, in the everyday world rather than the otherworld of the gods, though of course they must play a major role. We know immediately that his recounting will be on a human scale. He tells us,

> *An oak-tree stands*
> *Beside a linden, in the Phrygian hills.*
> *There's a low wall around them. I have seen*
> *The place myself.[2]*

Ovid then speaks of a time when Zeus and Hermes descend to earth, disguised as wanderers. They go from house to house asking for food and shelter, but are turned from the door at each one. At last they come to a tiny cottage on the very edge of the town, higher in the foothills of the mountain. At their knock, an elderly man bids them enter, and his equally elderly wife prepares a meal for them. They have little, but they share all. Ovid's loving description of the meal preparation is enchanting, rather like reading an M. F. K. Fisher essay on a memorable dinner savored in Provence decades ago. The utensils are those of a peasant household: beechwood cups and earthenware bowls. The ingredients are simple, but gathered ripe from their garden, freshly made from the milk of their own goats, provided by the labor of their own bees, or plucked from their own fruit trees and arbors. ("Remember how apples smell?" Ovid asks the reader with poignant nostalgia.) At this meal there was "nothing mean or poor or skimpy in good will."[3]

Mysteriously, the earthenware bowl of wine never empties, no matter how much is drawn out, and the old couple become fearful. At this point, the gods reveal their true identity. Zeus tells Baucis and Philemon that he is going to punish their neighbors, but that they will be spared for their devotion to his dictum that a traveler and a guest must be welcomed as a god. The old couple weep when their neighbors are destroyed as punishment for flouting the god's command. But as they stand on the mountainside, watching the flood that has swept away the town below, their tiny cottage gradually, magically, becomes an exquisite temple. Zeus tells them that they are "good people, worthy of each other"[4] and that he will grant them any favor.

Unlike countless couples in folk and fairy tales, Baucis and Philemon do not demand a mansion, great riches, youth, or beauty. Instead, they respond to Zeus's offer by asking for a few moments of privacy to talk it over. And upon their return Baucis voices their humble request:

> *"What we would like to be*
> *Is to be priests of yours, and guard the temple,*
> *And since we have spent our happy years*
> *   together,*
> *May one hour take us both away; let neither*
> *Outlive the other, that I may never see*
> *The burial of my wife, nor she perform*
> *That office for me." And the prayer was granted.* [5]

The old couple lives on until one day when

> *talking the old days over, each saw the other put forth leaves, Philemon watched Baucis changing, Baucis watched Philemon, and as the foliage spread, they still had time to say "Farewell, my dear!" and the bark closed over sealing their mouths.*[6]

One becomes an oak, the other a linden tree, and the two grow on together, side-by-side, branches entwined.

More than any other myth from the Greco-Roman canon, this one speaks to the longing all couples have that their love can outlast death, that neither should have to bury the other. It also dwells intimately on the beauty of lives well lived: the warmth of a harmonious household; the awareness that the most important things in life are not wealth and power over others, but rather love for one another; the delight of welcoming others into one's home; and the joy of preparing the fruits of the earth for one's guests. These are the years when the volatile flames of early passion have burned off, leaving mature coals on Hestia's hearth: still capable of a sudden flare, but primarily the radiant heart of home, providing warmth and light.

In the myth of Baucis and Philemon, we see a marriage that glows with a patina of authenticity and integration. As Ovid tells us, "It would do you little good to ask for servants or masters in that household, for the couple were all the house; both gave and followed orders."[7] This couple has found a balance in their lives together. Their simplicity has honed them down to the precious essentials, and in their generosity toward the gods they reveal a sharing of tasks developed over years of interacting in the maintenance of their home. The external transformation of the house into a temple is echoed in their own transformation into priest and priestess. Baucis and Philemon's is a household of harmony, love, and such generosity of spirit that even those extremely cynical gods Zeus and Hermes, inured to the vices of humanity and so familiar with the underbelly of human behavior, are moved to grant these two mortals their final rest together. For Zeus especially, with his eternal search for union with the feminine, this relationship must touch that unfulfilled longing, must show him something that humans could achieve even if it is beyond his godly capacity. The Baucis and Philemon story demonstrates a purity of mortal love that moves the gods by its beauty.

Both Hermes and Zeus are superb at disguise and come to the door of the humble cottage dressed as poor human wanderers. This motif assumes the doubleness of a pun: in ancient Greece the guest in one's home was to be considered as a god, but these guests are already gods. The act of grace that Baucis and Philemon commit is that they are treating the gods as gods while in ignorance of their true identity.

Finally, there is the emotional satisfaction of witnessing Hermes himself shift roles: from god of instability and duplicity, who makes light of adultery, to one who honors the value and the beauty of a deep, loving, and lasting relationship.

In Baucis and Philemon's final request, that of asking these particular gods to grant them union in death as in life, there is an irony. Neither of these restless deities will ever experience Joseph Campbell's definition of marriage: "the two that are one, the two become one flesh."[8] I think here, as well, of mythologist Wendy Doniger's statement concerning the attraction mortals have for the gods: that the precious fleeting life of constant change is more alive than static immortality.[9]

When we view the integration of Baucis and Philemon as a metaphor for the fortunate person who has reached the end of life and knows that body and soul are in harmony, that the events of a lifetime have joined them, we see yet another gift of mortality that is denied to the gods. The tale of Baucis and Philemon shows a marriage that has aged to perfection. This union has weathered the storms of life, honored the beloved other and the divine, and as a result is blessed with the gift of complete integration. On both a marital and a personal level, it is "happily ever after" most profoundly expressed.

Notes:

1. Joseph Campbell and Bill Moyers, *The Power of Myth* (New York: Doubleday, 1988), p. 6.

2. Ovid, *Metamorphoses*, translated by Rolfe Humphries (Bloomington, IN: Indiana University Press, 1955), lines 617–620.

3. *Ibid.*, lines 682–683.

4. *Ibid.*, line 705.

5. *Ibid.*, lines 710–716.

6. *Ibid.*, lines 719–794.

7. *Ibid.*, lines 637–639.

8. Campbell, p. 6.

9. Wendy Doniger, *Splitting the Difference: Gender and Myth in Ancient Greece and India* (Chicago: University of Chicago Press, 1999), p. 198

Contributor Profiles

Natalie Baan was formerly Managing Editor of *Parabola* and had a number of epicycles and other pieces published in the magazine.

Titus Burckhardt (1908 -1984) was a German-Swiss author of the traditionalist school. His writings include *Fez, City of Islam* (Islamic Texts); *Sacred Art in East and West* (Sophia Perennis et Universalis); and *Alchemy* (Fons Vitae).

Joseph Campbell (1904-1987) was the best-known writer, editor, and lecturer of his time in the field of mythology. He taught at Sarah Lawrence College for almost forty years. His work can be found in his many books, including *The Hero with a Thousand Faces* (Princeton, 1973), *The Masks of God* (Arkana, 1991), and *The Inner Reaches of Outer Space* (Alfred van der Marck Editions, 1986); as well as audio and video recordings (*The Joy of Myth; The Hero's Journey; Inward Journey: East and West; The Myths and Masks of God*, etc.)

Ananda K. Coomaraswamy (1877-1947) was "both art historian and pilgrim ... among the great religious and metaphysical ideas" (Roger Lipsey). Born in Ceylon (Sri Lanka) of a Ceylonese father and English mother, he moved at ease through the intellectual worlds of both East and West and brought to his writings on myth and traditional symbolism a greater range in breadth, depth, and altitude than any other explorer in these fields.

Ann Danowitz (formerly Himler) has been afloat on the ocean of story since her grandfather began telling her Polish folktales many years ago. Studies in literature, language, religion and folklore provided tools with which to navigate, but searching for the secret to illuminate the spirit always steers the raft.

Edward F. Edinger (d. 1998) was a Jungian analyst who practiced in New York and Los Angeles. His many books include *Ego and Archetype: Individuation and the Religious Function of the Psyche;*

Melville's Moby Dick: An American Nekyia; and *Eternal Drama: The Inner Meaning of Greek Mythology*.

Harriet Eisman holds Master's Degrees from Cornell University and Syracuse University, and works as a public library director. She has studied Embodied Dreamwork with Jungian analyst Robert Bosnak, philosophy and myth at Wisdom's Goldenrod Center for Philosophic studies, and mind/body healing at the IM School of Healing Arts. She lives near Ithaca, NY with her husband and two dogs.

Mircea Eliade (1907-1986), world-renowned scholar of the history of religions who taught in Europe and the United States, was the editor of *The Encyclopedia of Religion*. His many books include *Shamanism* and *A History of Religious Ideas*.

Everett Gendler was one of the first rabbis to engage issues of ecology and their relation to Judaism. He has served congregations in Mexico, Brazil, Princeton, N. J., and Lowell, Mass., and was a Chaplain and Instructor at Phillips Academy, Andover, Mass. He lives in Massachusetts, and also travels annually with his wife, Mary, to India, where they devote two months each year to community education work among the Tibetan exiles.

René Guénon (1886-1951) wrote extensively on Hinduism, Taoism, and Islam. His books include *The Crisis of the Modern World* and *Man and His Becoming According to the Vedanta* (Luzac).

Martha Heyneman is the author of *The Breathing Cathedral: Feeling Our Way into a Living Cosmos*, and *The Productions of Time: Collected Essays*. Many of her essays have appeared in *Parabola* over the years.

Trebbe Johnson is the author of *The World is a Waiting Lover: Desire and the Quest for the Beloved*, published in 2005. As the director of Vision Arrow, she leads journeys and workshops worldwide that combine adventure travel, the mythic imagination, and the quest for meaning. See www.VisionArrow.com.

Paul Jordan-Smith is a storyteller who lives in Seattle, where he works as an independent folklore scholar and writer. He served as an editor of *Parabola* and with its founder, D. M. Dooling, edited *I Become Part of It: Sacred Dimensions of Native American Life.*

James Karman, Professor Emeritus of English and Religious Studies at California State University, Chico, is the author of *Robinson Jeffers: Poet of California,* and the editor of *Critical Essays on Robinson Jeffers; Of Una Jeffers;* and *Stones of the Sur: Poetry by Robinson Jeffers, Photographs by Morley Baer.*

Maria Kingsley holds degrees in European Languages and Traditional Chinese Medicine, and has taught and practiced shiatsu for several years. Since 2003 her focus has been on bringing back the awareness of the sacredness of Western culture and, in particular, the presence of the divine feminine at the roots of our Western world.

Peter Kingsley is internationally recognized as the author of three books: *Reality; In the Dark Places of Wisdom;* and *Ancient Philosophy, Mystery and Magic;* as well as numerous articles about ancient philosophy and the sacred origins of Western culture. Together with his wife he works to bring back to life the forgotten mystical tradition which lies at the roots of the Western world. For further details, visit www.peterkingsley.org.

Denise Levertov (1923-1997) was one of the foremost poets of her generation. Born in England, she moved to the United States in 1948. Her inner journey can be traced through her many books, from *With Eyes in the Back of Our Heads* and *O Taste and See,* to *Evening Train* and the posthumous *This Great Unknown.*

Helen M. Luke (1907-1995) was a student of C. G. Jung and one of the founders of the Apple Farm Community. Her books include *Old Age, Kaleidoscope,* and *Such Stuff as Dreams Are Made On.*

John Matthews has written over eighty books on the Arthurian Legends, Grail Studies, and Celtic spirituality. He was the historical advisor to the Jerry Bruckheimer movie *King Arthur*, and has made appearances on both History Channel and Discovery Channel specials on Arthur and the Holy Grail. He lives in Oxford, England.

Jane L. Mickelson is a cultural mythologist. She lives in Northern California with her husband, Don Smith, where she lectures, writes, teaches, and co-hosts the program "Questing: Where is the Path?" on radio station KWMR.

Tim Miller's second novel, *Language of the Living*, was published by Six Gallery Press. He is currently working on *To the House of the Sun*, a long poem based around Ancient, Irish, and American history and mythology.

Thomas Moore is a psychotherapist and spiritual commentator who lectures widely. His books include *The Care of the Soul, The Re-Enchantment of Everyday Life*, and *Dark Nights of the Soul*.

Seyyed Hossein Nasr is author of over twenty books and over two hundred articles. His works concern not only aspects of Islamic studies but also comparative philosophy and religion, philosophy of art, and the environmental crisis.

Howard Pyle (1853-1911) was a renowned artist, writer, and teacher. Known as one of America's best loved illustrators and founder of the Brandywine school of painting, Pyle had an enormous impact on the world of American illustration.

Nan Runde is a free-lance writer with a background in medieval language and literature. She lives with her husband in Hartford, Connecticut, where she runs her own photo-restoration business and continues to write.

Lawrence Russ has published poems and prose in numerous magazines and books, including *Parabola; Image: A Journal of the Arts and*

Religion; The Nation; The Iowa Review; Atlanta Review; The Virginia Quarterly Review; and *Art at the Edge of the Law* (the catalogue for the acclaimed exhibition of that name at the Aldrich Contemporary Art Museum). A sampling of his poetry may be found at Tarlton.law.utexas.edu/lpop/etext/lsf/28/russ.html.

Laura Simms is a storyteller, author, teacher, recording artist, and humanitarian. Her most recent works include *Moments of Mercy, Reconciled in the Book of Secrets*, and *The Robe of Love: Secret Instructions for the Heart* (Codhill Press). She cofounded the Life Force Project, an international initiative using storytelling, creativity, mediation, and reconciliation for individuals and communities in crisis. Laura is a fellow at the Arthur Mauro Peace and Justice Center at the University of Manitoba, and an Associate with Columbia University's International School for Conflict Resolution. She is a long time student of Shambhala Buddhism.

William Sullivan is the author of *The Secret of the Incas: Myth, Astronomy, and the War Against Time* (Crown Publishers 1996). From 2001 to 2004 he was co-director of excavations at an Inca site in Ollantaytambo, Peru, and between 2002 and 2007 he worked as a consultant developing content for a proposed museum of world mythology. At present he is working on several projects involving North American Native American astronomy and myth.

P. L. Travers (1899-1996) was a consulting editor to *Parabola* from its inception. Best known as author of the six *Mary Poppins* books, she also wrote *Friend Monkey* and *The Fox at the Manger*. She wrote and lectured extensively on the subject of Myth and Story, contributing more than forty pieces to *Parabola* on such themes as The Hero, Creation, Death, The Hunter, Androgyny, and Exile. Her essays are collected in *What the Bee Knows*.

Laurens van der Post (1906-1996), born in the interior of southern Africa, lived among the people who created the first blueprint for life on earth, and became the principal chronicler of the Stone Age Kalahari Bushmen. He was also one of C. G. Jung's closest friends for sixteen years. He dedicated his life to teaching the meaning and value of indigenous cultures in the modern world. Author of many books including *Venture into the Interior, Heart of the Hunter*, and *Mantis Carol*, he was knighted by Queen Elizabeth in 1981.

Diane Wolkstein travels throughout the world performing myths and folktales and giving workshops on storytelling. She is the author of twenty-three books of folklore, including *Treasures of the Heart* and *The Magic Orange Tree and Other Haitian Folktales*. Her most recent DVD, *A Storyteller's Story*, features her 40 years of storytelling. She continues to direct the storytelling program in Central Park and is the co-founder of the New York City Storytelling Center.

For Further Reading

Studies of Myth and Meaning

Burckhardt, Titus. *Alchemy: Science of the Cosmos, Science of the Soul*, translated by William Stoddart. London: Stuart & Watkins, 1967.

Calasso, Roberto. *The Marriage of Cadmus and Harmony,* translated by Tim Parks. New York: Vintage Books, a division of Random House, Inc., 1994.

Campbell, Joseph. *The Flight of the Wild Gander: Explorations in the Mythological Dimensions of Fairy Tales, Legends and Symbols.* New York: Harper Perennial, A Division of HarperCollins Publishers, 1990.

_____. *The Hero with a Thousand Faces.* Princeton: Princeton University Press, 1972.

_____. *The Inner Reaches of Outer Space: Metaphor as Myth and as Religion.* New York: Alfred van der Marck Editions, 1986.

_____, assisted by M. J. Abadie. *The Mythic Image.* Princeton: Princeton University Press, 1975.

_____. *The Masks of God: Primitive Mythology.* New York: Penguin Books, 1976.

_____. *The Masks of God: Oriental Mythology.* New York: Penguin Books, 1976.

_____. *The Masks of God: Occidental Mythology.* New York: Penguin Books, 1964.

_____. *The Masks of God: Creative Mythology.* New York: Penguin Books, 1976.

Coomaraswamy, Ananda K. *Coomaraswamy: Selected Papers. Vol. 1: Traditional Art and Symbolism.* Ed. Roger Lipsey. Princeton: Princeton University Press, 1977.

_____. *Time and Eternity.* Ascona, Switzerland: Artibus Asiae Publishers, 1947.

_____. *The Transformation of Nature in Art.* New York: Dover Publications, 1956.

Eliade, Mircea. *The Myth of the Eternal Return; or, Cosmos and History*, translated by Willard R. Trask. Princeton: Princeton University Press, 1971.

335

_____. *Patterns in Comparative Religion*, translated by Rosemary Sheed. Cleveland: The World Publishing Company, 1963.

Eliot, Alexander. *The Global Myths: Exploring Primitive, Pagan, Sacred, and Scientific Mythologies*. New York: Continuum, 1993.

von Franz, Marie-Louise. *The Interpretation of Fairy Tales*, Revised edition. Boston: Shambhala, 1996.

Graves, Robert. *The White Goddess: A Historical Grammar of Poetic Myth*. Amended and enlarged Edition. New York: Farrar, Straus and Giroux, 1948.

Guénon, René. *Symbolism of the Cross*. Translated by Angus Macnab. London: Luzac & Company, Ltd., 1958.

Harrison, Jane. *Prolegomena to the Study of Greek Religion*. New York: Meridian Books, Inc., 1955.

Heyneman, Martha. *The Breathing Cathedral: Feeling Our Way into a Living Cosmos*. San Francisco: Sierra Club Books, 1993.

_____. *The Productions of Time: Collected Essays*. Philadelphia: Xlibris, 2002.

Luke, Helen M. *Old Age: Journey into Simplicity*. New York: Parabola Books,. 1987.

_____. *The Way of Woman: Awakening the Perennial Feminine*. Foreword by Marion Woodman. Introduction by Barbara Mowat. New York: Doubleday, 1994.

Rahner, Hugo, *Greek Myths and Christian Mysteries*. Translated from the German by Brian Battershaw. New York: Harper & Row, Publishers, 1963.

de Santillana, Giorgio, and Hertha von Dechend. *Hamlet's Mill: An Essay on Myth and the Frame of Time*. Boston: Gambit Incorporated, 1969.

Sullivan, William. *The Secret of the Incas: Myth, Astronomy, and the War against Time*. New York: Three Rivers Press, 1996.

Travers, P. L. *About the Sleeping Beauty*. New York: McGraw-Hill Book Company, 1975.

_____. *What the Bee Knows: Reflections on Myth, Symbol, and Story*. New York: Penguin/Arkana, 1994.

Weston, Jessie L. *From Ritual to Romance*. Garden City, NY: Doubleday & Company, Inc., 1957.

Zimmer, Heinrich. *The King and the Corpse: Tales of the Soul's Conquest of Evil*. Edited by Joseph Campbell. New York: Pantheon Books, 1956.

Some Collections of Myths and Fairy Tales

The Book of the Thousand Nights and One Night. Rendered into English from the literal and complete French translation of Dr. J.C. Mardrus by Powys Mathers. In Four Volumes. New York: St. Martin's Press, 1972.

Bulfinch, Thomas. *Mythology*. A Modern Abridgement by Edmund Fuller. New York: Dell Publishing Co., Inc., 1959.

English Fairy Tales. Retold by Flora Annie Steel. Illustrated by Arthur Rackham. New York: The Macmillan Company, 1919.

Fairy and Folk Tales of Ireland. Edited by W. B. Yeats. Foreword by Benedict Kiely. New York: Macmillan Publishing Company, 1986.

Favorite Folktales from around the World. Edited by Jane Yolen. New York: Pantheon Books, 1986.

Gayley, Charles Mills. *The Classic Myths in English Literature*. Boston: Gill & Company, 1903.

Grimm's Fairy Tales. Complete Edition. Introduction by Padraic Colum. Folkloristic commentary by Joseph Campbell. New York: Pantheon, 1944.

Hamilton, Edith. *Mythology: Timeless Tales of Gods and Heroes*. A Mentor Book. New York: The New American Library, 1942.

Italian Folktales. Selected and retold by Italo Calvino. Translated by George Martin. New York: Pantheon Books, 1956.

Lang, Andrew, ed. *The Pink Fairy Book*. London: Longmans, Green and Co., 1907. This, as well as the *Blue, Red, Green, Orange, Brown*, etc. *Fairy Books* have been reissued by Dover Publication, Inc., New York, unabridged and unaltered, with original illustrations.

Malory, Sir Thomas. *Le Morte d'Arthur: The Book of King Arthur and His Knights of the*

Round Table. In Two Volumes, Bound as One. New Hyde Park, NY: University Books, Inc., 1961.

Ovid. *Metamorphoses*, in two volumes, translated by Frank Justus Miller, with Latin facing. Third edition, revised by G. P. Goold. Loeb Classical Library. Cambridge, MA: Harvard University Press, 1977.

Perrault, Charles. *Perrault's Complete Fairy Tales*. Translated from the French by A. E. Johnson and Others. New York: Dodd, Mead & Company, 1961.

The Poetic Edda: The Mythological Poems. Translated and with an Introduction by Henry Adams Bellows. New York: Dover Publications, Inc., 2004.

Russian Fairy Tales. Collected by Aleksander Afana'ev. Translated by Norbert Guterman. Folkloristic commentary by Roman Jacobson. New York: Pantheon Books, 1945.

Sturlusson, Snorri. *The Prose Edda: Tales from the Norse*. Translated by Arthur Gilchrist Brodeur. New York: Dover Publications, Inc., 2006.

Warner, Rex. *Men and Gods*. New York: Random House, Inc., 1959.

Individual Stories

Apuleius, Lucius. *The Golden Ass*. Translated by William Adlington (1566). Edited, with an Introduction, by Harry C. Shnur. New York: Crowell-Collier Publishing Company, 1962.

von Eschenbach, Wolfram. *Parzival*. Translated by A.T. Hatto. New York: Penguin, 1980.

Ferry, David. *Gilgamesh*. A New Rendering in English Verse. New York: Farrar, Straus and Giroux, 1993.

Heaney, Seamus. *Beowulf*. A New Verse Translation. New York: Farrar, Straus and Giroux, 2000.

Homer. *The Iliad*. Translated by Robert Fitzgerald. Garden City, New York: Anchor Press/Doubleday, 1975.

_____. *The Odyssey*. Translated by Robert Fitzgerald. Garden City, New York: Doubleday & Company, Inc., 1963.

Kalevala: The Land of the Heroes. Translated by W. F. Kirby. Introduced by M. A. Branch. London and Dover, NH: The Athlone Press, 1907.

Mitchell, Stephen. *Gilgamesh.* A New English Version. New York: Simon & Schuster, Inc., 2004.

The Quest of the Holy Grail. Translated with an Introduction by P. M. Matarasso. Harmondsworth, Middlesex, England: 1969.

The Romance of Tristan and Iseult. As retold by Joseph Bédier. Translated by Hilaire Belloc and Paul Rosenfield. Garden City, NY: Doubleday & Company, Inc., 1953.

de Troyes, Chrétien. *Perceval, or The Story of the Grail.* Translated by Ruth Harwood Cline. Athens: The University of Georgia Press, 1985.

Virgil. *The Aeneid.* Translated by Robert Fitzgerald. New York: Random House, 1984.

Chapter Citations

The Call of Myth

1. P. L. Travers, "On Unknowing," *Parabola* 10:3, "The Body," p. 78.
2. Ananda K. Coomaraswamy, "Symplegades," *Coomaraswamy: Selected Papers I. Traditional Art and Symbolism* (Princeton, NJ: Princeton University Press, 1977), p. 521.
3. *Ibid.*, p. 369n., quoting N. Berdyaev, *Freedom and the Spirit* (New York, 1935).
4. *Ibid.*, p. 354n.
5. William Sullivan, "Night Windows," *Parabola* 21:1, "Prophets and Prophecy," p. 66.
6. Barre Toelken, "Fieldwork Enlightenment," *Parabola* 20:2, "The Stranger," p. 29.
7. Richard Temple, "The Mountain of God," *Parabola* 13:4, "The Mountain," p. 34.
8. Lama Anagarika Govinda, "The Way of the White Clouds," *Ibid.*, p. 51.
9. Helen M. Luke, "The Threshold of the Mountain in Dante's Divine Comedy," *Ibid.*, pp. 53-54.
10. Edward F. Edinger, "The Tragic Hero: An Image of Individuation," *Parabola* 1:1, "The Hero," p. 67.
11. Laura Simms, "Through the Story's Terror," *Parabola* 23:3, "Fear," p. 46.
12. Thomas Moore, "The Soul's Religion," *Parabola* 21:2, "The Soul," p. 22.

Chapter 1

1. Joseph Campbell, *The Hero with a Thousand Faces* (Princeton: Princeton University Press, 1972), p. 3.
2. Laurens van der Post, *Parabola* 7:2, "Dreams & Seeing," p. 38.

Chapter 2

1. Mircea Eliade, *The Myth of the Eternal Return; or, Cosmos and History*, tr. Willard R. Trask (Princeton: Princeton University Press, 1954), p. 12.
2. Martha Heyneman, *The Breathing Cathedral: Feeling Our Way into a Living Cosmos* (San Francisco: Sierra Club Books, 1993), p. 60.
3. Coomaraswamy, Ananda K., *Coomaraswamy: Selected Papers,* © 1977 Princeton University Press, 2005 renewed PUP. Reprinted by permission of Princeton University Press.
4. C. S. Lewis, *The Last Battle*, Book 7 in T*he Chronicles of Narnia* (New York: The Macmillan Company, 1970), p. 176.

Chapter 3

1. Giorgia de Santillana and Hertha von Dechend, *Hamlet's Mill: An Essay on Myth and the Frame of Time* (Boston: Gambit Incorporated, 1969), p. 2.
2. William Butler Yeats, "The Second Coming," *The Collected Poems of W. B. Yeats*, edited by Richard J. Finneran (New York: Simon & Schuster Inc., 1996), p. 187.
3. *Hamlet's Mill*, pp. 163-164. *Makalii* is the Polynesian name for the Pleiades.
4. Martha Heyneman, "After the Flood," *A Journal of Our Time* No. 3 (Toronto: Traditional Studies Press, 1982), p. 27.
5. Mircea Eliade, "Observing Sacred Time," *Parabola* 15:1, "Time and Presence," p. 21.
6. T. S. Eliot, "Burnt Norton," *Four Quartets* (New York: Harcourt, Brace and Company; Faber and Faber Ltd., 1943), p. 5.

Chapter 4

1. Joseph Campbell, *The Inner Reaches of Outer Space* (New York: Alfred van der Mark Editions, 1986), p. 17.

2. *The Sacred Pipe: Black Elk's Account of the Seven Rites of the Oglala Sioux,* recorded & edited by Joseph Epes Brown. (Norman and London: University of Oklahoma Press, 1953), pp. 5-7.
3. William Sullivan, *The Secret of the Incas: Myth, Astronomy, and the War Against Time* (New York: Three Rivers Press, 1996), p. 29.

Chapter 5
1. Lucius Apuleius, *The Golden Ass* (New York: Crowell-Collier Publishing Company, 1962), pp. 263-4.
2. T. S. Eliot, "The Dry Salvages," *Four Quartets* (New York: Harcourt, Brace and Company; Faber and Faber Ltd., 1943), p. 26.

Chapter 6
1. "The Man of Lore," Irish, retold by Tom White. *Parabola* 17:3, "The Oral Tradition," p. 39.
2. Joseph Campbell, *The Power of Myth*, with Bill Moyers. Edited by Betty Flowers (New York: Doubleday, 1988), p. 123.

Chapter 7
1. Mircea Eliade, "Nostalgia for the Present," *Parabola* I:1, "The Hero," p. 15.

Chapter 8
1. "The Seven Swans" (European), retold by Natalie Baan, *Parabola* 18:1, "Healing," p. 57.
2. Coomaraswamy, Ananda K., *Coomaraswamy: Selected Papers* © 1977 Princeton University Press, 2005 renewed PUP. Reprinted by permission of Princeton University Press.
3. Dr. Michel de Salzmann (informally).

4. William Shakespeare, *King Lear*, Act One, Scene One.

Chapter 9
1. Helen M. Luke, "The Perennial Feminine," *Parabola* 5:4, "Woman," p. 21.
2. Coomaraswamy, Ananda K., *Coomaraswamy: Selected Papers* © 1977 Princeton University Press, 2005 renewed PUP. Reprinted by permission of Princeton University Press.
3. *Ibid.*, p. 361n.
4. *Ibid.*, p. 366.

Photography Credits